Praise for

HONOR THY MOTHER

"Father wounds have often been the centerpiece in conversations around parental traumas. Usually, out of a natural honor for the matriarchs in our lives, we ignore, deflect, or sanitize the particular pain we carry. And not surprisingly, it's that peculiar silence that may result in us living out the dishonor we're trying to avoid. What Dr. Sarita has given us is not just a book or even a resource but a lamp. As only she can, Dr. Sarita offers words that counsel, comfort, and confront, so those who have been broken can be healed—discovering how to love God and our neighbor, which includes our mothers."

—Jackie Hill Perry, bestselling author and speaker

"*Honor Thy Mother* is a deeply honest and healing invitation to confront the complexities of the mother wound with courage and compassion."

—Nona Jones, author of
The Gift of Rejection and *The Power of Petty Prayers*

"*Honor Thy Mother* is the definitive book on healing a mother wound. Dr. Sarita Lyons approaches this topic with a pastoral heart for those who feel angry, lost, lonely, and like they've been left longing."

—Sheila Wise Rowe, MEd, author of
Healing Racial Trauma; Young, Gifted, and Black; Healing Leadership Trauma; and *Seeds of Racial Healing*

"With grace, biblical wisdom, and vulnerability, Dr. Sarita Lyons not only helps you navigate complex feelings but also equips you with practical tools for true healing."

—Jada Edwards, speaker, Bible teacher, and author of *A New Way to Love Your Neighbor*

"This wise and compassionate book invites us to consider the sacred call to honor our mothers with both grace and honesty."

—Jen Wilkin, author and Bible teacher

"Each page is infused with profound theological insights, clinical expertise, and a deep well of compassion that speaks directly to the heart. Dr. Lyons illuminates the path to healing, reminding us that there is indeed profound freedom waiting on the other side of our journey."

—Christine Caine, founder of A21 and Propel Women

"Sarita Lyons holds authentic grief and honor in the same hand. She tells the truth about the pain we carry and the truth of God's healing love both at once. She does not minimize harm, rush forgiveness, or confuse honor with denial. She shows what it looks like to bring our grief and need for healing to God, extend the love Jesus extended to us, and walk in wise truth and justice all at the same time. Honest, faithful, and rare . . . This is a needed guide for anyone learning that surrender is not collapse but consent: an opening of the hands to the healing work God is doing in us as we learn to love and honor our mothers with wisdom."

—Matthias J. Barker, LMHC, founder of Estrangement.com

"In *Honor Thy Mother*, Dr. Sarita Lyons takes readers on a journey from grief to healing with surgical precision. Whether one has a great relationship with their mom or a strained relationship with their mom, she helps them embrace their parental experiences with hope and healing. This book is not simply a must-read but also an instrument of healing. Readers will feel seen, engaged, enlightened, and strengthened."

—Jerome Gay, Jr., pastor and author of *How to Speak Man: Discovering the Respect Languages Men Need*

"Dr. Sarita T. Lyons brings wisdom, compassion, and truth to one of the most complex relationships in our lives. In *Honor Thy Mother*, she helps us face our wounds honestly while guiding us toward healing and peace. This is a timely and necessary book that leads readers out of pain and into freedom."

—Lecrae, Grammy-award-winning artist, author, and speaker

"I had the best mother in the world . . . maybe that's because she did not have the best mother. History is full of surprise witnesses who testify that cycles of momma trauma can be broken. Dr. Sarita Lyons has bequeathed to you an accessible and accurate road map of where to turn to heal from what your momma got wrong—and where to park in what your mother got right."

—Dr. Charlie Dates, senior pastor of Progressive Baptist Church of Chicago and senior pastor of Salem Baptist Church of Chicago

"This is more than a book—it's a necessary journey. With spiritual depth and practical insight, Dr. Sarita Lyons courageously addresses the often unspoken reality of mother wounds. Her voice is honest, healing, and empowering. *Honor Thy Mother* is rooted in more than feelings; it's where faith and facts collide. If you're ready to stop surviving and start healing, this book will meet you right where you are—and lead you forward."

—Erica Campbell, gospel singer and songwriter in the duo group, Mary Mary

ALSO BY DR. SARITA T. LYONS

Church Girl

HONOR
THY
MOTHER

HONOR THY MOTHER

HOW TO GRIEVE, HEAL, AND MAKE PEACE WITH YOUR MOTHER WOUNDS

DR. SARITA T. LYONS

WATERBROOK

WaterBrook

An imprint of the Penguin Random House Christian Publishing Group,
a division of Penguin Random House LLC

1745 Broadway, New York, NY 10019

waterbrookmultnomah.com
penguinrandomhouse.com

Some names have been changed to protect the privacy of the individuals involved.

LIBRARY OF CONGRESS CATALOGING-IN-PUBLICATION DATA

NAMES: Lyons, Sarita T. author
TITLE: Honor thy mother / Sarita T. Lyons.
DESCRIPTION: First edition. | New York, NY : WaterBrook, [2026] | Includes bibliographical references.
IDENTIFIERS: LCCN 2026015985 (print) | LCCN 2026015986 (ebook) | ISBN 9798217152452 hardcover | ISBN 9798217152469 ebook
SUBJECTS: LCSH: Motherhood—Religious aspects—Christianity | Motherhood—Biblical teaching | Parenting—Religious aspects—Christianity | Parenting—Biblical teaching | Interpersonal relations—Religious aspects—Christianity | Interpersonal relations—Biblical teaching | Reconciliation—Religious aspects—Christianity | Reconciliation—Biblical teaching
CLASSIFICATION: LCC BV4529.18 .L96 2026 (print) | LCC BV4529.18 (ebook)
LC record available at https://lccn.loc.gov/2026015985
LC ebook record available at https://lccn.loc.gov/2026015986

PRINTED IN THE UNITED STATES OF AMERICA

1st Printing

First Edition

The authorized representative in the EU for product safety and compliance is Penguin Random House Ireland, Morrison Chambers, 32 Nassau Street, Dublin D02 YH68, Ireland. https://eu-contact.penguin.ie

Book design by Kim Henze Walker

Hydrangea photograph by Maksim Shebeko/Adobe Stock

For details on special quantity discounts for bulk purchases,
contact specialmarketscms@penguinrandomhouse.com.

This book is dedicated to the
cycle breakers and the peacemakers.

CONTENTS

START YOUR JOURNEY HERE

Honor your father and your mother so that you may have a long life in the land that the LORD your God is giving you.

—EXODUS 20:12

When we think of the role of mothers, most of us conjure images of them cooking, cleaning, and nursing us back to health when we are sick. We picture mothers cheering for us at our games even if we play terribly or ride the bench. Mothers ask us about our day and help us with our homework. Many mothers work hard to check off our Christmas and birthday lists even if they don't have the money, and they loan us money when we are adults because we will always be their babies. Mothers teach us to stand up to bullies, they take our sides when we have enemies, and they believe in us when we don't believe in ourselves. Mothers are our first counselors and confidants. They worry about us, pray for us, and cry with us. Mothers sacrifice their own comfort and dreams so we can have our own.

Observe any championship sporting event, music awards show, or graduation speech and you'll see that some of the people involved—from husky football players to rappers and nerdy valedictorians—may thank God, but almost all of them thank their mothers. Mother's Day is one of the top three most packed church services of the year, sharing that honor with only Christmas and Easter.[1] Mother's Day is the one day a mother can usher all her children from far and wide, saved and unsaved, into the church. On that day, you can barely get a dinner reservation at a restaurant. Street corners and intersections are lined with people selling roses, teddy bears, and "I love Mom" balloons, and entire sections of greeting-card stores are dedicated to honoring mothers. There's no doubt that mothers are special. They carry us in their wombs, in their arms, and in their hearts. That's the kind of mother we all experienced, right?

The truth is that for many people, just reading those arbitrary descriptions of a mother is so painfully unfamiliar that it causes their chests to burn and their eyes to fill with tears. Some children didn't just miss out on having *amazing* mothers; they didn't even have healthy mothers, kind mothers, or present mothers. Too many of us have navigated life feeling like we had no mother at all—just a woman, a womb, a birther, a human who gave us DNA but never L-O-V-E. Or, if our mothers were present and, at times, helpful, loving, and supportive, their presence was so inconsistent or intertwined with traces of their own insecurities, trauma, and self-hatred that it left us feeling unsafe, forced to parent our parents, and walking on eggshells.

If you're someone who has had extremely hostile and hurtful interactions with your mother, simply wants to pursue a better relationship with her, or desires to grow into the kind of mom who is easy to honor, I invite you to dive deep into these pages. We're taking a bold step together; we're entering into precarious territory by talking about mothers. We have read books and articles, watched talk shows and podcasts, and seen a plethora of statistics about the impact of the wounds of fathers, but we don't often talk about the pain caused by our

---

1 Aaron Earls, "Easter Remains a High Attendance Day for Most Churches," *Baptist Standard,* March 26, 2024, https://baptiststandard.com/news/faith-culture/easter-remains-a-high-attendance-day-for-most-churches/.

mothers. Certainly, there is research on the effect mothers have on their children, but because we typically don't like to talk about our difficult relationships with our mothers, it's a serious topic that largely goes unaddressed, especially in the church.

Mothers, though imperfect like all humans, have been granted an invisible pass and have generally been off-limits for being talked about honestly. Depending on your cultural background, it may be unheard of, even sacrilegious, to speak a negative word about your mother. Wars have been fought on playgrounds around the world because some kid crossed the line and dared to yell out a "yo mama" joke. "Yo mama is so fat . . . ," "Yo mama is so ugly . . . ," and "Yo mama is so dumb . . ." have caused many fights and school suspensions because everybody knows, "You can talk about me, but you better not say nothing about my mama."

Mothers, though imperfect like all humans, have been granted an invisible pass and have generally been off-limits for being talked about honestly.

But how do we honor someone who has caused us harm and hurt? Exodus 20:12 may be one of the most confusing and distressing scriptures in the entire Bible. Sure, you may think my argument is an exaggeration, but you're likely to agree with me if you've had a difficult relationship with your mother. This command ("Honor your father and mother")—a command given with a promise ("so that you may have a long life")—can feel like an unfair demand if your mother has not lived honorably. Isn't it hard enough to just try to live a good life and get past the trauma of being raised by a hurtful parent?

While it may seem absurd or unfair to have to give honor where it seems undue, the motivation for honoring can never be based on the character of the parent exclusively. All honor toward others, even difficult parents, must first flow from our desire to honor God. Obedience to him is how he says we show we love him, and obedience is the key to having a blessed life, having success, and being a "treasured possession" to him.[2]

However, we know obedience to God is not always easy. I want you to anchor your soul to this truth: The Lord loves you and knows that doing hard things, loving difficult people, and honoring the dishonorable is challenging. In fact, Jesus struggled with obedience, though he perfectly obeyed (see Matthew 26:36–39). He sees, cares, and is grieved that you have been hurt. But he also sympathizes with you and wants to help you. The Bible tells us in Hebrews 4:15–16 that "we do not have a high priest who is unable to sympathize with our weaknesses, but one who has been tempted in every way as we are, yet without sin. Therefore, let us approach the throne of grace with boldness, so that we may receive mercy and find grace to help us in time of need."

What I'm presenting to you here isn't just a call to honor your mother; it's first a call to heal and place your hope in God. I am inviting you on a journey where we leave denial and avoidance behind so you can reach a place of healing and peace. This journey requires courage, confrontation, and a willingness to face and sit with unpleasant memories and feelings. The process of healing is worth it, but it takes honesty, trust, and the desire to experience the abundant life God has promised you. If you don't want to stay bound, broken, and beat-up by your past or present pain, there is freedom and blessing on the other side.

My aim in writing this book is not to make injured children feel guilty for struggling to freely offer honor, nor is it to give wounding parents the right to beat back the cries and critiques of their children. Rather, I have four specific goals. The first is to offer biblical wisdom, perspectives, and interventions to help you grieve, heal, and make

---

2 See John 14:15; Deuteronomy 28:1–14; Joshua 1:8; Exodus 19:5 (ESV).

peace with your mother wounds. Second, I want to provide insight to how the effects of your mother wounds may be subtly showing up in other areas of your life and to offer hope in the gospel for pursuing restoration and reconciliation. Third, I want to answer the nagging question of how to honor God by honoring your mother even when she has not lived honorably. And last, I want this book to help you draw closer to God, the perfect parent, where through his parenting, you will experience freely and abundantly what all children want and need.

Through exploring the deep and dark, *Honor Thy Mother* is an invitation to take a healing path with twists and turns and tears and fears, but I promise, there is light for our journey, and the destination is rewarding. It's uncomfortable to think about the pain you carry from one of the two people on the planet who should love you the most. Whether your mother wound is "We struggle to get along" or "She's so critical of me" or something more serious like "She left me," "She abused me," or "She didn't believe I was being abused," it matters and deserves care. All mother wounds need to be grieved and healed, and you deserve to find peace. If mother wounds are minimized, stuffed, projected, or deflected, they can cause grave consequences for your sanity and your soul. If your mother wounds are not grieved and do not heal, they will fester and your closest relationships will be altered, your dreams may be deferred, and one day you may wake up and realize you became the very person who hurt you.

I also want to take a quick moment to recognize a reality that all moms face: There is a mythological image of mothers in our society that leads to children feeling severely judged for speaking honestly about their wounds while also allowing unhealthy mothers to fly under the radar. But on the other end, we can also see all wounding mothers as unredeemable because of their bad behavior. As shocking and debilitating as what you may have experienced may be, I want you to lean in and hear this truth: As a society, we put pressure on mothers to never fail. That doesn't mean abuse, neglect, and immature parenting should be brushed aside and minimized, but we do have to reckon with the myth of "the perfect mother."

We expect to not always get along with our siblings, friends, bosses, fellow church members, and—dare I say—fathers, but mothers are expected to get it right and make us feel good all the time. They're expected to always know what to do, be available, say the right thing, sacrificially nurture, ignore their own wants, and be pristine in their functioning as if they never experience deep physical and psychological pain. If you bristled at these statements, please don't hear me making excuses for your mother's hurtful behavior, inability to nurture, or lack of desire to love you well. What I invite you to hear is this: Don't think it strange when mothers utterly fail. June Cleaver and Clair Huxtable were characters on television, but your mother and you (if you are a mother) are real, and real people utterly fail, which is why Jesus had to come and die. Living in a fallen world with sinners, even those saved by grace, means we all have been hurt by our mothers. Every mother will hurt, and every mother has been hurt. In fact, one reason for reading this book is so you can heal and not carry on the legacy of trauma and wounding that was passed on to you from your mother.

Whether or not you ever have a child of your own, your mother wounds, if ignored and allowed to live unhealed in you, will eventually migrate beyond the walls of your psyche and heart and affect someone else in the world. We will talk later in the book about the importance of embracing our mothers' humanity, but for now, as we traverse through the pain toward healthy grieving, healing, and finding peace, I'm making these potentially uncomfortable declarations because I want to begin to chip away at the shock and confusion you might feel over your mother causing you pain. Whether the meddling mother or the murdering mother, what all mothers have in common is they are sinners who had children and they need Jesus. All of us reading these words need him whether we realize it or not. Your mother needed Jesus to come and die to pay the debt for her sins and offer her a new life and a new way of living, and the good news is he did just that. Whatever you feel at this stage is okay; we are just getting started. Be sad, be angry, be exhausted, be on edge, be cautious, be unsure, be curious, but also be willing to loosen your grip on being shocked. That "all have sinned and fall short of the glory of God" (Romans 3:23) is not an excuse; rather, it's an explanation.

Though our situations may be dark, Scripture reminds us that God is with us in the darkness: "Though I sit in darkness, the Lord will be my light" (Micah 7:8). We do not have to be afraid to face pain or do the work of healing, because God will help us. He says in Isaiah 41:10,

> Do not fear, for I am with you;
> do not be afraid, for I am your God.
> I will strengthen you; I will help you;
> I will hold on to you with my righteous right hand.

God sees, God cares, and God wants to heal you and your mother (if she is alive and willing to be helped).

Have you ever prayed for things to get better? Have you ever cried about your relationship with your mother? Have you desired to be healed? Look at this beautiful promise from God: "I have heard your prayer; I have seen your tears. Look, I will heal you" (2 Kings 20:5). Whatever your situation—if you want to be whole, if you want to be free of the heaviness and instability your mother has caused—there is hope for you, healing is available, and change in a relationship that feels impossible is possible with God.

> There is hope for you, healing is available, and change in a relationship that feels impossible is possible with God.

If you're reading this book and have a tough relationship with your mom and would describe yourself as having a distant relationship or no relationship with God, I want to encourage you to keep reading. The truth, healing, and hope that lie in the pages ahead have the power to not only help you with your mother but also introduce you to a new way of experiencing God.

REFLECTION QUESTIONS

1. *Why might it be difficult for you to face the truth about your difficult relationship with your mother?*
2. *What is your reaction to the "mythical mother," and how has that influenced your view of how mothers are seen and treated?*
3. *As you begin this journey, take a moment to name your thoughts and emotions after having read this chapter.*

PRAYER

Lord, help me be open to what you have planned for me as I embark on this journey. Help me sense your nearness and voice. Amen.

HONOR
THY
MOTHER

CHAPTER 1

SOMETIMES I FEEL LIKE A MOTHERLESS CHILD

Even if my father and mother abandon me,
the LORD cares for me.

—PSALM 27:10

Children were herded like young calves, forced to climb atop a small stump of an auction block as if it were a mountain, inspections of babies' black bodies—their nails, hair, teeth, muscle tone—can they be stripped even more of their dignity and humanity to become like an ox in a cotton field? There the mother, trying to calm her children who are about to lose the woman who bore and nursed them, is trying to plead with the sellers and buyers to give her clues so she can find them one day. She contemplates; is this the moment she fights though she will surely be severely maimed or put to death on the spot for resisting the inevitable? A price is yelled out, one by one they are sold, scattered in different directions like seeds blown by a ruthless wind. The children are confused as they are brutally ripped from the care of their mother, going to a land that feels as far away as Africa. Carried away as if a tsunami mercilessly swallowed their young lives. They strain to see their

> mother, who is fading from view as the enslaver's carriage disappears into the horizon. They are alone, worse than orphaned—motherless until perhaps they reunite in heaven.[1]

"Sometimes I Feel like a Motherless Child" is a powerful African American spiritual that tells the horrors of slaves being forced to separate from their families and homeland, Mother Africa. This song "first came to wide public prominence when it was performed by the Fisk Jubilee Singers in the 1870s."[2] Once they heard it, audiences could not forget its haunting and soul-stirring sound. "It has since been performed and recorded by countless singers and instrumentalists, from many different genres."[3]

The title and lyrics captivate listeners because of the painful thoughts about a child who must live in a motherless state. I was seven years old when I first heard this song performed by the Celestial Choir at my Philadelphia home church, Bright Hope Baptist, at a Christmas concert with a dark moody organ accompanying. The audience members seemed to be holding their breath as the soloist sang with such uncomfortable and painful vibrato, gripping her robe around her chest as tears escaped from her closed eyes. She sang as if she herself had been motherless for many years. I remember sitting next to my mom, who had just turned forty, and thinking, *I never want to be motherless. I couldn't imagine a life without my mother's love and care.* I grabbed her hand tightly, as if my little hand could stop her from leaving me. I never could have imagined at seven years old that my mom's hand, then smooth and supple from her ritual application of Avon's Skin So

---

1 Adapted from Henry Louis Gates, Jr., *The Classic Slave Narratives* (Berkley, 2012). See also Debra Lew Harder, "The Story Behind the African-American Spiritual That Evokes the Cry of the 'Motherless Child,'" WRTI Arts Desk, January 15, 2019, www.wrti.org/arts-desk/2019-01-15/the-story-behind-the-african-american-spiritual-that-evokes-the-cry-of-the-motherless-child.

2 Harder, "Story Behind the African-American Spiritual."

3 Harder, "Story Behind the African-American Spiritual."

Soft products, would be the same soft hand I would hold almost forty years later, when she would take her last breath, forcing me to release my grip as she slipped into the arms of Jesus. In the physical sense, I became a motherless child on January 13, 2024, and ever since then, that song has been lodged in my throat, threatening to strangle me if I for one second forget the sovereignty and nearness of God.

So much is lost when a child loses their mother, no matter the reason. Whether it's to slavery or enslavement to drugs, to abandonment or emotional unavailability, to mental disorder or death, a loss is a loss. To be motherless is a cruel, disorienting, and brutal reality for children. The physical death of a good mother is hard, but I believe it is more devasting if one becomes motherless when they still have a living mother who has resigned herself to playing dead in her child's life. It is like being pushed out of the nest before learning to fly: How could a chick or child survive that fall?

Let's go back to the title of the song for a moment: "Sometimes I Feel like a Motherless Child." I want to draw your attention to the word *sometimes.* If there is any hope in this sad song, it is found in that easily dismissed adverb. *Sometimes* implies there are moments, even if brief, when the child doesn't feel motherless at all. Could those "sometimes" moments of security, closeness, connection, and care be when the child remembers that though their mother is not present, God is there and that is enough? Is that the message for us?

You don't need to be connected to the history of slavery to take this gut-wrenching song that reminds us of the horror of slavery—where children were ripped from their mothers' arms never to experience their love and nurturing again—and compare it to your distant, divided, daunting, and maybe even dark relationship with your own mother. The painful wound wants you to focus on the word *motherless,* but I implore you to not miss the word *sometimes.* Perhaps you will feel the grace that's available if you shift where you place your attention.

That is why the psalmist tells us, "Even if my father and mother abandon me, the Lord cares for me" (Psalm 27:10). God knows that "it is not good for the man to be alone" (Genesis 2:18), nor is it good for a child to become motherless, so the psalmist assures us that God steps in and does what the mother cannot do or refuses to do. If you've been wounded by your mother, think what would happen if you focused your attention not just on the woman who left, the woman who physically or emotionally is in and out of your life with no rhyme or reason, or the woman who has hurt you with her hands, her words, and her silence, but instead on a fact: The Lord *will* take care of you. Whatever you missed from your mother, God provides. That truth does not take away the pain of the mother wound (and in later chapters, we'll talk about practical ways to move toward healing), but sometimes, many times, all the time if you are willing to notice, the pain of feeling motherless is not without a balm named Jesus. If he is a balm in Gilead,[4] surely he can be a balm in the middle of your motherlessness and offer you healing, comfort, and a way forward with him.

I remember clearly a client's (Kim's) words to me in her first therapy session: "I'm starting to think my mom ruined my chance at having a normal life." She went on to explain, "She used to tell me that she is just direct—that she tells it like it is—and she would proudly remind me how I should be happy she was honest, saying, 'At least you know I'll never lie to you, because I'm a straight shooter.'" But her mother's words were as sharp as a knife; they always cut and wounded. Kim continued, "She told me she loved me, but her words never felt like love. In fact, I always felt like she hated me, so I worked as hard as I

4 The interpretation of Jesus being the balm of Gilead is based on Jeremiah 8:22, which symbolizes him as the ultimate healer and source of spiritual comfort: "Is there no balm in Gilead? Is there no physician there? So why has the healing of my dear people not come about?" That verse was made popular by Karen Clark Sheard's version of the song "Balm in Gilead"; "Balm in Gilead," track 9 on Karen Clark Sheard, *Finally Karen,* Island Black Records, 1997.

could in school, always hoping that would draw kindness from her lips. I waited patiently for years for the love to show up. It never did."

What eventually did show up were slaps across the face when her mother's cruel words didn't appease her anger. There were constant threats of violence if Kim ever dared protest or act upset about her mother's behavior: "You think you can beat me? You want to fight me, little girl? I wish you would." Her mom worked two jobs, cooked, kept the house clean, made sure Kim had nice clothing, even faithfully took her to dance class, but also repeatedly called her a whore, dirty, dumb, and too skinny. Every time Kim did something her mother didn't like, her mother would remind her that Kim got that behavior from her father. Her mother's voice played in Kim's head over and over until it became Kim's own voice. Over time, Kim had internalized the verbal punches as truth. She felt worthless, ugly, weak, unlovable, and guilty because she was now screaming at her own daughter, whom she'd vowed to love better than she was loved. On her counseling intake form, when asked what had brought her to therapy, she wrote, "To be stopped." She later explained further, "I need to be stopped before I become my mother."

Your story may not be the same as Kim's, but I'm sure you have one that is worth telling and processing. Over my years as a psychotherapist and church leader, I have counseled and consoled men and women as they shared their pain regarding their mothers. Here are some of their reflections on the topic:

> "I can't even think straight. I just got a text from my mom, and she is mad and cussed me out for not inviting her to my birthday party, which was just a girlfriends' night out. She told me I don't love her or appreciate her and that when she dies, I'll regret how I've treated her."

> "I told my mom her boyfriend made me uncomfortable and I didn't like him spending the night at our house. She said,

'He puts food on the table and is taking care of us. He's not thinking about you.' When he started coming in my room at night, I told her and I was glad that she cried so hard, cried with such anger. For a moment, I was happy and relieved. I felt like she was going to stand up to him and call the police, but she never said a word to me about it again and never put him out until he decided to leave her, and I watched her cry so hard and be so angry again."

"My mom hates my wife, and it doesn't make sense. My wife hasn't done anything but be kind to her. I think she resents her for us having a healthy marriage when she never had one. I thought my mom would be proud that I found a good woman, but she's so angry. It's weird to see your mom be jealous of your wife."

"I knew when my mom was mad because she would shut down and stop talking. I don't mean for a few days; my mom has gone months without speaking to me, and we lived in the same house."

"People think it's normal to hear your mom tell you she loves you. I can't remember the last time I heard mine say she loves me. I know she does, but there is some kind of block; she just doesn't hug or kiss me or say she loves me. My friend's mom told me she loved me as we were leaving her house. It was so jarring, but I hadn't known how much I needed to hear those words. Why can't my mom say it?"

"My mom was mad at me about something. I don't even remember what it was, but she didn't come to my middle school graduation. I walked home alone with my cap and gown, and when I walked in the house, she was still not speaking to me."

"Is it possible for a mother to be jealous of her child? It's embarrassing to admit, but it always feels like she hates me for my success. My mom sacrificed a lot for her children, and I appreciate that, but I thought she would be proud of how I turned out. Instead, she seems angry at me for accomplishing what she didn't get a chance to accomplish. She even said once, 'Y'all ruined my life.' I have empathy for her, but her jealousy gets in the way of me feeling safe and opening up to her."

"My mom will say anything but 'I'm sorry.'"

"Nothing physical or inappropriate ever happened, but I've basically been my mom's husband since I was in high school. I thought I was being a good son until I realized I was filling a void that a son should not be responsible to fill. It wasn't clear until I got engaged."

"My mom was never there for me, but she's jealous and threatened by the other women who have mothered me when she didn't. Those women can't take her place, but they stepped in when she was not there. Now that she's back in my life, she wants me to kick them out."

"I am a nervous wreck when my mom comes to visit me and my family. No matter how beautiful my home is, she will find dust to turn her nose up at. No matter how well I cook, it's never as good as how she makes it. She makes snarky comments about me gaining weight. She stresses me out. She puts me down in front of my kids and competes with me for my children's affection. I would love to hear her say, 'I'm proud of you.' I know I'm not perfect, but I want to at least be enough."

"She's amazing when she's clean and sober, but she always chooses the alcohol and drugs over her children."

"I would say my mom loves me, but when it comes to me and my siblings, I'm at the bottom. I don't know how I got there, but kids can feel when they aren't as important as the other siblings. I got the worst punishments, there was no grace for me, and my siblings were allowed to think as bad about me as she did. I believe I was the child who reminded her that she wasn't perfect, but I always tried to show her how much I love her."

"I know my mother did the best she could. It wasn't enough, but it was her best. She didn't have a good mother or upbringing. When I look at her, I see a woman struggling to give me something she never received. I also see she is ashamed that she failed, but she covers her shame with anger toward her own child."

"It's been painful to realize that I was never parented well and that the role I've always had with my mother is to act as her parent. I think my mom has been mentally ill my entire life, but she was never diagnosed or treated. Instead of being cared for, I've always had to treat her like she was my child. Even when she's hurt me, I've had to absorb it like a parent instead of an injured child."

> "If I hear one more person tell me how great my mom is, I'm going to scream! The person everyone loves at church never comes home."

> "I never got to have a childhood. When my mom was running the streets, I was doing her job in the house. I cooked, cleaned, and took care of my siblings like I was their parent."

> "I have never said it out loud, but I did write in my journal once, 'I hate my mother.' I can never forgive her for what she allowed to happen to me. I'm ashamed to admit that, but it's true."

Okay, take a deep breath. I know that probably was a lot for you to read, as it was a lot for me to hear and record. Can you relate to any of those stories? How many of the experiences sound familiar? Take a moment to check in with yourself. What are the emotions you're feeling right now?

Let's pause and pray this prayer:

Lord God, you know how I feel reading these words and remembering the unique ways I've been injured. Father, touch my heart as the trauma, disappointment, anger, and sadness surface. Remind me that I am safe and free to feel whatever is real. Please be with me and bring comfort and care. For the injured and injurer, be a present help in a time of trouble. Be a guiding light through the darkness, be medicine for the ache of the soul, and fill my heart and mind with love and the hope that is only truly found in you. Help me keep pressing through the process so I can get the healing and peace that you want to provide. In Jesus's name. Amen.

The stories and experiences are diverse, and for some people, they are also deeply buried. If you need a moment, come back to this exercise later, but if you can do it now, grab a journal or use your phone to summarize your mother wound or a defining experience.

More on Mother Wounds

Have you noticed that many people are beginning to talk about the complexity of their relationships with their mothers and the impact they've had on their lives? From people being on talk shows to content creators taking to YouTube to share their stories to help others, more and more people are raising their hands and owning the dysfunctional and strained relationships they have with their mothers. That's a good thing when done in a healthy way. What I've found very encouraging is that many women aren't just complaining about their mothers; rather, they want help. In our advanced technological age, social media has helped people start having these difficult conversations, with some becoming vocal about a topic that previously seemed completely off-limits. Going to therapy has also helped awaken individuals to their families of origin and their effect on present life functioning.

Many social scientists, researchers, coaches, writers, and clinicians have given thought to the mother wound and have offered definitions and explanations to help us understand this phenomenon:

> The mother wound occurs when a mother offers their child physical but not emotional support.[5]

---

5 "Understanding and Healing the Mother Wound: A Comprehensive Guide," The Attachment Project, www.attachmentproject.com/psychology/mother-wound/.

> The concept of the "Mother Wound" refers to the psychological impact that arises from an individual's relationship with their mother.[6]

> The best way to think of the mother wound is a loss or a lack of mothering. This is typically a deficit in the mother-daughter or mother-son relationships that is passed down through generations, and it is a reflection on how we have experienced parenting and how we parent.[7]

> [The] personal mother wound [is] a set of internalized limiting beliefs and patterns that originates from early dynamics with our mothers that causes problems in many areas of our adult lives, impacting how we see ourselves, one another, and our potential.[8]

> The mother wound refers to all the pain or trauma "immature, absent[, or] abusive" mothers inflict upon their children.[9]

You need to view your pain as yours alone to explore and work through rather than as something to be disqualified through comparison with others' pain. No matter where the severity of your wound falls on the spectrum of mother-derived pain, it's important that all rela-

---

6 Becky Spelman, "Mother Wound: Understanding Its Impact on Men and Wom[e]n," Private Therapy Clinic, October 16, 2023, https://theprivatetherapyclinic.co.uk/blog/mother-wound-understanding-its-impact/.

7 Sherry Gaba, "The Mother Wound: How Our Relationships with Our Mothers Effect Our Codependency," *Psychology Today,* October 25, 2019, www.psychologytoday.com/us/blog/addiction-and-recovery/201910/the-mother-wound/amp.

8 Bethany Webster, *Discovering the Inner Mother: A Guide to Healing the Mother Wound and Claiming Your Personal Power* (William Morrow, 2021), 6.

9 Stephi Wagner, "What Is the Mother Wound?," Mother Wound Project, November 16, 2025, www.motherwoundproject.com/post/whatisthemotherwound.

tional difficulties with our mothers be taken seriously and attended to, especially if the goal is to be personally healthy, have relationships with our mothers that reflect God's expectation and love for human families, and honor our mothers as he commands.

> [A mother wound is] the psychological, physical, and spiritual injury a child sustains from their wounded mother that affects the child's functioning and beliefs about themselves, others, the world, and God.

In addition to those common definitions and descriptions of the mother wound, I would like to offer this one: the psychological, physical, and spiritual injury a child sustains from their wounded mother that affects the child's functioning and beliefs about themselves, others, the world, and God.

My definition, like others, highlights the wide reach of the consequences of the mother wound, but it also asserts a spiritual implication because everything is spiritual. You will never be injured by a human, especially a mother, where that injury avoids causing a spiritual impact. In fact, the injury itself is spiritual because "our struggle is not against flesh and blood, but against the rulers, against the authorities, against the cosmic powers of this darkness, against evil, spiritual forces in the heavens" (Ephesians 6:12). We will talk more about this in the chapter on healing our mother wounds, but for now I'll just say that the wounds from your mother, your dysfunctional relationship, your volatile arguments, and your maladaptive ways to soothe or project the pain, the abuse, or just the pervasive tension and lack of closeness are all spiritual warfare. And so is the healing.

We've heard before that "hurt people hurt people,"[10] and in that context, unhealed wounded daughters are wounding their children.

---

10 Sandra D. Wilson, *Hurt People Hurt People: Hope and Healing for Yourself and Your Relationships* (Our Daily Bread, 2015).

Others have said something similar: that the mother wound "starts with the idea that every wounding mother is a wounded child inside—and an outsize cultural expectation of selflessness that's too large for any woman to bear."[11] As we continue on this journey, you will see my intentionality in exposing the real enemy in your relationship with your mother. The enemy is not drugs, bipolar depression, controlling behavior, anger, selfishness, victimhood, or poor impulse control. The real threat, the real culprit behind motherless children and the struggle to honor dishonorable mothers, is not one's mother at all. What you are experiencing today, or in years past, are the reverberations of an ancient war between God and evil. Every poor choice, whether abdication of responsibility or refusal to protect and provide, was either your mother's uncontrollable disordered thinking due to brain chemistry or her willful decision to be a co-conspirator in the plan of the devil to lie, deceive, kill, steal, and destroy everything in his wake at the expense of God's glory and your peace.

That is evidence that we live in a broken and fallen world, and Jesus will one day permanently restore it. Every wound is part of a cosmic breach, which is why the solutions and strategies for healing cannot be *only* psychological and earthly. There are many helpful and healing therapeutic interventions, and we need those things for sure. I've used them in my own counseling practice with clients and have personally been helped by them. However, since we do not wage war according to the flesh, we also need non-fleshly weapons: weapons that are not carnal but are powerful through God

> Every wound is part of a cosmic breach, which is why the solutions and strategies for healing cannot be *only* psychological and earthly.

11 Elise Loehnen, "What Is the Mother Wound?," *Oprah Daily,* April 10, 2024, www.oprahdaily.com/life/relationships-love/a60297924/what-is-the-mother-wound/.

for demolishing strongholds (see 2 Corinthians 10:3–5). Also, we need to get dressed in the full armor of God (see Ephesians 6:11–17).

Although God has allowed, in his permissive will, terrible things to happen and does not always prevent them, he does have a plan to one day completely restore all brokenness,[12] heal all pain,[13] execute vengeance against all evil,[14] and give us victory over sin and death.[15] Those assurances of a life to come without pain and suffering are real and can be trusted, but for the here and now as we navigate this broken world, God offers his us his grace, which is sufficient,[16] and the Helper, the Holy Spirit,[17] to lead, guide, teach, convict, intercede for, and comfort us. He offers us his Word to instruct us on how to live in a way that pleases him and represents what it means to be not of this world but of his kingdom and under his lordship.[18] He also offered us Jesus to be our substitutionary atonement for our sins,[19] the propitiation satisfying the wrath of God that our sin caused[20] and also through his sacrifice reconciling us back to a holy God.[21]

Although we have the future hope of everything being made right, he has not left us without hope, healing, and help now, and most of all, he has not left us without himself.[22] In fact, no matter how abusive, abdicating, aloof, or absent your mother was or is, no matter how

12 See 1 Corinthians 15:49–53; Revelation 21:4–7.

13 See 1 Peter 5:10; Revelation 22:1–4.

14 See Romans 12:19; Revelation 20:11–15; 21:8; 22:12.

15 See 1 Corinthians 15:57.

16 See 2 Corinthians 12:9. That God's "grace is sufficient" means that the Lord gives us undeserved and unearned favor and help that is enough to bring us through any difficult situation, even when we feel weak, inadequate, and overwhelmed in our own strength. God provides us the strength, heavenly resources, and divine power to face any challenges and live victoriously.

17 See John 14:16–17, 26.

18 See 2 Timothy 3:16–17.

19 See 2 Corinthians 5:21; 1 John 2:2.

20 See Romans 1:18; 2:5.

21 See Romans 3:24–25; Hebrews 2:17.

22 See Hebrews 13:5.

much you *sometimes* feel like a motherless child, one thing is for sure: God has not left you parentless. God himself is your parent, and not just any kind of parent; he is a perfect parent!

That truth does not dismiss or minimize the struggle of your relationship with your mother; rather, it is a reminder that you have not lost everything, nor have you been left by everyone. Your journey of grieving, healing, and making peace with your mother wound is not a solo journey, and sometimes anchoring yourself in the reality of the parental presence and care of God is just what you'll need to keep going.

REFLECTION QUESTIONS

1. *In what ways have you felt like a motherless child?*
2. *Which of the statements from others who experienced a mother wound resonated with you the most, and what reflection would you add that wasn't mentioned?*
3. *Does the idea that your struggles with your mother are rooted in an ancient spiritual battle help you understand your relationship with her better?*
4. *Write out Psalm 27:10 three times in your journal. What hope can be found in understanding that God will never abandon you?*

PRAYER

Lord, thank you for your Word and the reminder that you have never left my side. Please give me courage and peace as I move forward to learn, grow, and heal.

CHAPTER 2

THE PERFECT PARENT

You therefore must be perfect, as your heavenly Father is perfect.

—MATTHEW 5:48 (ESV)

Parenting is hard because the consequences for compromised parenting are grave. Even if you want to do a good job as a parent, there are so many things that you have to overcome that seem to fight against your best efforts, such as socioeconomic disparity; inequality in access to resources like health care, educational opportunities, childcare, and food; systemic bias toward racial and ethnic minorities; gender inequality in the workplace; unequal pay; and barriers to support for disabilities (ableism) and mental health care. And if you survive those obstacles, you still have to manage the toll of constant responsibility, vigilance, emotional strain, sleep deprivation, fatigue, financial pressure, balancing multiple roles and wearing multiple hats, behavioral challenges, lack of support, societal judgment, navigating the developmental stages, and the overwhelming self-doubt and guilt that most mothers find difficult to talk about.

As a mother, I can't tell you how many times I have been gripped by guilt as my husband, Mark, and I have parented our children. With every childhood sickness we couldn't cure, every young adult sin we couldn't stop, every sadness we caused by our heavy-handed correction or an outburst of anger we didn't control, I have felt like a failure. But I remember the day the Lord lifted that guilt from my heart and helped me see him more clearly. I was praying about a situation concerning one of our children. I felt completely powerless to change, counsel, and protect that child. To be frank, I felt embarrassed that the wisdom, counsel, and support that so many spiritual children desire to receive from me was being outright rejected from my actual child, whom I wanted to be a great parent to. "What am I doing wrong?" I would ask God. He answered, but he did not say, "Sarita, it's okay. You're doing everything right." Rather, what he gently spoke to my heart revolutionized how I understand parenting and how I see him as a parent. God whispered to my aching heart, "Sarita, I am a perfect parent, and even I have wayward children. My children don't always listen to me." *What?* That's so true. I'm a child of God and I don't always follow his voice, respect his words, or obey his commands. I am a child of God and I have deliberately rejected his counsel and lived in opposition to his will. Those things are all so true, but what stuck with me the most is this description of him as a perfect parent. There is absolutely no parent on the earth who can make that claim, but he can. I believe embracing that truth will not only deeply affect weary, guilt-ridden parents but also provide healing and a shift in perspective for children who've been wounded by imperfect parents. No matter what kind of earthly parents you've had, you have access to a perfect parent in God. Spending time understanding how he is our perfect parent and how he mothers us will set up the needed foundation for the rest of this book and your healing. Welcoming that truth will help balance your expectations, shift your dependency for love and acceptance from a flawed human to a perfect God, and bring you healing and freedom from the lie that you are forever limited by the emotional health of your mother. Let's dive into how God's perfection can help you heal and move forward in life.

God Is Perfect

We all have been hurt, and we all have caused hurt. You did not have a perfect father or mother, and as wonderful as you may be, they didn't have a perfect child. You may have a great spouse, wonderful children, and amazing friends, yet none of them are perfect. But if you have a relationship with God, you have a relationship with the only being in the entire universe who is perfect. *Perfect,* or *perfection,* "describes something that is complete, whole, or without blemish. It can also refer to someone who is blameless and has integrity."[1]

In the Bible, God is the standard of perfection. You find that in the Old Testament, "it does describe His work (Deut 32:4), way (2 Sam 22:31; Pss 18:30), and knowledge (Job 36:4) as perfect (תָּמִים, *tamim*). The New Testament explicitly describes God as perfect. For example, in Matt 5:48, Jesus calls His followers to 'be perfect, as your heavenly Father is perfect' (ESV). Romans 12:2 also describes God's will as perfect (τέλειος, *teleios*). Hebrews describes Jesus as being made perfect (τελειόω, *teleioō*) through suffering (Heb 2:10; 5:8–9)."[2]

Perfect can also mean "without blemish."[3] Take that in for a minute. God is perfect in every way. He is flawless. In our cultural vernacular, we have come to appraise a lot of lesser things as flawless. After we beat our faces, put on the right fits, and have our hair dyed, fried, and laid to the side, we love to tilt our heads in the mirror with Beyoncé's song as the soundtrack of our minds and tell ourselves that we woke up like this: flawless. But none is flawless but God!

Why should any of this matter to you, a woman working through her mother wounds? It matters for several reasons. First, as professor and author Michael F. Bird explains, "If God is perfect in his nature,

---

1 Dale A. Brueggemann, "Perfect," *The Lexham Bible Dictionary,* ed. John D. Barry et al. (Lexham, 2016), https://biblia.com/books/esv/Jn3.16.

2 Brueggemann, "Perfect."

3 Brueggemann, "Perfect."

purpose, promises, and person, then change is strictly impossible for him."[4] You can rest in knowing that he won't be kind and available one day and mean and ghost you the next day. God doesn't need to self-reflect, go to therapy, work on his tone, or read a self-help book. He won't get any better, because he's already perfect, and he won't get worse, because he can't change. That's good news for you if you've been injured by the whims and instability of your mother. If you never knew which version of her you were going to talk to or see from day to day, that is not a concern with God—he's consistent. His having attributes of immutability and perfection means you will always have access to a consistently perfect God and are not waiting for the other shoe to drop.

Second, if God is perfect, then he can never fail you, because he doesn't make mistakes. He plans and executes perfectly,[5] he never lies and he keeps every promise perfectly,[6] his law is perfect,[7] he judges perfectly,[8] he perfectly counts the number of hairs on your head,[9] and even as hair falls from your scalp or gets collected in your brush, he adjusts the count with perfection. God doesn't miss, and he cannot mess up; he does everything perfectly. You can completely trust him with your life. He is so perfect that he can take the mess your mother may have made of her life and yours and turn it into a masterpiece for your good, because no mess or wound is too big for a perfect God. "We know that all things [including the mess and wounds] work together for the good of those who love God, who are called according to his purpose" (Romans 8:28).

Third, because he is perfect, he is the standard by which everything else will be measured and judged. "God's standard is set by his own

---

4 Michael F. Bird, *Evangelical Theology: A Biblical and Systematic Introduction,* 2nd ed. (Zondervan, 2020), 187.

5 See Isaiah 46:10–11.

6 See Numbers 23:19.

7 See Psalm 19:7.

8 See Romans 2:1–16.

9 See Matthew 10:29–30.

perfection."[10] If that is true, there is no authority or standard higher than him, meaning no one's opinion of you, including your mother's, is the final authority of your life. Even if you have elevated her critical voice in your head, it must bow to what God has already declared about you. His word, opinion, and vision for your life are just as flawless as he is. In Ephesians 1:19–23, Paul prays that we would understand the power and authority of God and that his power is at work in us through Jesus:

> What is the immeasurable greatness of his power toward us who believe, according to the working of his great might that he worked in Christ when he raised him from the dead and seated him at his right hand in the heavenly places, far above all rule and authority and power and dominion, and above every name that is named, not only in this age but also in the one to come. And he put all things under his feet and gave him as head over all things to the church, which is his body, the fullness of him who fills all in all. (ESV)

Last, because God is perfect, he parents you perfectly. As a perfect parent, he is safe and dependable, understands you, provides all your needs, loves you without limits or conditions, and will never leave you. "What great love the Father has lavished on us, that we should be called children of God!" (1 John 3:1, NIV). Let that truth wash over you and begin to clean and heal the wounds of your soul. Bathe in this pool of Bethesda and say out loud, "I have a perfect parent in God." Receive it, in Jesus's name!

> Because God is perfect, he parents you perfectly.

10 William Klock, "The Sermon on the Mount: A Kingdom Manifesto: God's Perfect Standard," Living Word, October 5, 2008, https://livingwordrec.ca/archive/gods-perfect-standard/.

God Is a Parent

ANTHROPOMORPHISM AND ANTHROPOPATHISM

Knowing and experiencing God as our parent has an important influence on how we function as disciples and can heal from the wounds of our imperfect mothers. "God is spirit" (John 4:24), which means he is invisible, immeasurable, infinite, eternal, and unchangeable; he is self-existing and not bound by human limitations. Yet he represents himself in Scripture in a human form and function among his people. He describes himself as a parent, specifically a father. This triune God is made up of three distinct persons: God the Father; God the Son (Jesus), who is both fully God and fully man and is the image of the invisible God (see Colossians 1:15); and God the Holy Spirit.

The first time he refers to himself in Scripture as a father is in Exodus 4:22–23, where he tells Moses that Israel is his firstborn son and demands that Pharaoh let his people go from Egyptian oppression so they can worship him. Though we cannot see God or experience him in the way we see and experience other humans, he graciously condescends to human context, relationship, and language to reveal himself in ways we can better understand him. This is an example of anthropomorphism and anthropopathism, defined as "the assigning of human forms, actions, and emotions to God."[11] Anthropomorphism and anthropopathism are similar in their ability to help people communicate about and conceptualize God, but they have different meanings:

---

11 Timothy T. N. Lim, "Anthropomorphism and Anthropopathism," *The Lexham Bible Dictionary*, ed. John D. Barry et al. (Lexham, 2016), https://biblia.com/books/esv/Jn1.16.

Anthropomorphism refers to portrayals of God having human forms and performing human actions. For example, the biblical writings describe God as:

- having hands (Isa 59:1);
- seeing with His eyes (2 Chr 16:9; Isa 63:15; 1 Pet 3:12);
- hearing with His ears (Psa 34:15; Isa 59:1);
- having a face that "the upright shall behold" (Psa 11:7);
- planting a garden (Gen 2:8);
- walking "in the cool of the day" (Gen 3:8);
- standing (Amos 9:1);
- laughing (Psa 2:4);
- smelling the pleasant aroma of offerings (Gen 8:21);
- whistling (Zech 10:8–12);
- whispering (1 Kgs 19:12);
- presiding over the divine council (Psa 82:1);
- judging (Psa 75:7);
- rebuking (Rev 3:19);
- holding (Isa 41:10); and
- lifting up (Psa 145:14; Jas 4:10).

The term anthropopathism, on the other hand, refers to ascriptions of human emotions, feelings, and passions to God, such as:

- anger (2 Sam 24:1);
- regret (Gen 6:6–7; 1 Sam 15:11);
- grief (1 Sam 15:35; Eph 4:29–32); and
- hatred (Prov 6:16).[12]

---

12 Lim, "Anthropomorphism and Anthropopathism."

One important relationship God established between himself and his people is that of a father and children. An interesting point is that "while the Jews of Jesus's day were hesitant to call God their Father (and angry at Jesus for doing so) [see John 5:18], Jesus claimed God as his Father and taught his followers to do the same."[13]

THE GIFT OF ADOPTION

There are many images of salvation in Scripture,[14] and one important image is that of adoption. "The word for 'adoption' (*hyiothesia*) means 'sonship,' and it refers to the process in the Roman world by which a child was brought into a new family, receiving all the rights of a natural child and taking the name of the new family."[15] The metaphor of adoption is unique to the Pauline Epistles and adapted from Roman law. "In Roman society *adoptio* was the process whereby an adoptee shifted from being under the authority of his family to being under the authority of his adopted father. The adoptee would then become a member of the new household and sometimes the sole heir to the father's estate. . . . For Paul, adoption and sonship meant becoming part of God's people. . . . The exodus was the great act of redemption and adoption, and the same is no doubt true of the new exodus."[16] Adoption is a major doctrine of Christianity through which God shows his great love and commitment to those who put their faith in Jesus Christ:

> He chose us in him, before the foundation of the world, to be holy and blameless in love before him. He predestined us to be

---

13 Gerald Bray, "God as Father," The Gospel Coalition, 2025, www.thegospelcoalition.org/essay/god-as-father/.

14 See John 1:12–13; 3:3–6, 16–18, 36; 14:6; Acts 2:39; 4:2; 16:30–33; Romans 1:16; 5:1; 6:23; 10:9–10; Ephesians 1:7, 13–14; 1 Thessalonians 5:9–10; Titus 2:11–14; 3:5.

15 Grant R. Osborne, *Ephesians: Verse by Verse,* Osborne New Testament Commentaries (Lexham, 2017), 20.

16 Bird, *Evangelical Theology,* 626.

adopted as sons through Jesus Christ for himself, according to the good pleasure of his will. (Ephesians 1:4–5)

The language of adoption that Paul uses is specific and intentional. God is not just saying we are the children of God because of Jesus Christ; rather, he is saying we are the adopted sons and daughters of God. The word *adopted* carries both legal and spiritual significance. In Roman culture, the birth parent was legally able to disown their birth children. If a child grew up and became a disgrace to the family, the father could legally disinherit the child. However, if someone adopted a child, that child was chosen specifically, with all their strengths and weaknesses, and a father could never say he didn't know what he was getting into. According to Roman culture, it was illegal to disown an adopted child.[17] God uses this picture of adoption to show us how secure and permanent our relationship with him is. Once we are the adopted sons and daughters of God, we can't lose our position no matter our performance or flaws.[18] You may feel like you have been disowned by your mother, but because you are a child of God, he wants you to know that it would be as though he were breaking his own law if he were to do that to you. Once you belong to him, you are sealed and have in him a perfect parent who will love, protect, provide, and care for you forever. Amen.

God Is a Metaphorical Mother

God chose to reveal himself as a father, the Father of Israel (see Deuteronomy 32:6; Psalm 103:13), the Father of Jesus (see John 3:16), and the Father of all believers he adopts into his family. With that, it is

---

17 Kathy Collard Miller, "A Roman Father Couldn't Disinherit an Adopted Son," Heart Change, April 6, 2018, https://kathycollardmiller.com/a-roman-father-couldnt-disinherit-an-adopted-son/.

18 Miller, "Roman Father Couldn't Disinherit an Adopted Son."

imperative to remember that all scriptural and theological language is analogical, meaning our finite human language can never fully capture the infinite character and nature of God. Because he desires to be close to us and known by us, he has graciously chosen to reveal aspects of his nature in ways our finite minds can comprehend. That means of self-disclosure is an act of love to help us peer behind the veil of the mystery of God. While he has called and revealed himself as Father, he has not limited the revelation of himself to only masculine characteristics.

In Scripture, God has shown us parts of himself that cannot be understood with the Father analogy alone; rather, he tells us much about his love, care, protection, faithfulness, and provision by using maternal language. That doesn't mean we should begin to call God "Mother God" or "our heavenly Mother." Adding the word *Mother* to God's name does not reflect how Jesus referred to his heavenly Father (see Mark 14:36; John 5:18; 17:11) and instructed us to refer to God in Scripture (Matthew 6:9). To make God a mother (identity) versus "like" a mother (characteristic) is a rejection of God's own self-disclosure.

God is neither male nor female; he is a spirit. As one writer stated, "The united witness of the church through the ages is unquestionably that God is beyond gender, and that speaking of God as male, or even as promoting a masculine account of Himself, is a grave error."[19] My thought is to name God as he has chosen to name himself in Scripture, even though he is so much more than those human categories and names can contain. Instead of replacing *Father* with *Mother*, a more helpful option is to "appreciate and appropriate biblical presentation of God's maternity."[20]

Have you ever thought of God in maternal terms? We so often hear about "Father God" or "our heavenly Father" that we might

19 Steve Holmes, "If God Is Male . . . ," Shored Fragments, February 5, 2012, https://shoredfragments.wordpress.com/2012/02/05/if-god-is-male/.

20 Bird, *Evangelical Theology*, 200.

miss how he sees so much value and beauty in motherhood that he describes himself as acting like a mother for his people. Let's make this more personal. Have you ever seen and experienced God being a mother to you? If not, can you imagine how impactful it would be for you—a person who wants to healthily grieve and heal their mother wounds—to experience him in the very ways you wish you could experience your earthly mother? Remember that God is perfect, is a parent, and wants you to experience the perfection of motherhood through him. Let's look at this maternal imagery of him together and discover how each truth about his maternal nature brings healing.

A COMFORTING MOTHER

As a mother comforts her child,
so will I comfort you.
—ISAIAH 66:13 (NIV)

Understanding the context of this verse highlights just how important God's comfort was to his people. The sixty-sixth chapter of Isaiah closes the book, which speaks of both judgment and restoration of God's people. This verse, written more than seven hundred years before the birth of Christ, points to the promise of a coming savior who will bring complete restoration and comfort to God's children struggling with the pains of life because of sin. The scripture is a promise of hope and comfort in times of hardship and despair. God is portrayed as a loving, tender, compassionate mother. He could have said, "As a *father* comforts, I will comfort you"—surely fathers bring comfort to their children—but this verse suggests that God knows there is no human comfort greater than that of a mother. Theologian Charles Spurgeon said, "A Father can comfort, but . . . he is not much at home in the work. When God speaks about his pity, he compares himself to their father.... But when he speaks about comfort, he selects the mother."[21]

How This Truth Heals

In Isaiah 66:13, God demonstrates that he expects mothers to comfort better than anyone else, so much so that he wants to describe his comfort like that of a mother. There is a distinct difference in the quality of comfort that healthy, caring mothers reflecting his love should offer their children. If you have not felt the comfort of that type of mother, just know God believes you should have.

Mothers comfort their children not just when something bad happens to them but also when they are the cause of their own suffering. The Israelites were known for their disobedience to God and were punished by being exiled, but he did not leave them in that state. He promised to deliver them and return them to their land. Good mothers comfort even when their children are wrong, and if you haven't experienced that with your mother, you can experience it with God.

You don't have to be perfect to receive his comfort. You can be in despair and be responsible in part for the consequences experienced and he doesn't harshly tell you, "You should have listened; you made your bed, so lie in it," but he disciplines with deliverance in mind. Oh, what a motherly comfort God brings!

He says, "I'll comfort you," or as other translations put it, "I will comfort you." He promises to comfort you. It's a simple truth, but if you are hungry for motherly comfort, it's a healing promise to cling to. If comfort with your own mother was elusive because she was not able

---

21 Charles Spurgeon, quoted in Candice Lucey, "Why Is God's Comfort Compared to a Mother Who Comforts Her Child?," Christianity.com, October 3, 2023, www.christianity.com/wiki/god/why-is-gods-comfort-compared-to-a-mother-who-comforts-her-child.html.

to be emotionally present or had a way of demanding that she be the only recipient of comfort in your relationship; if she offered only hurt but never a comforting apology, hug, listening ear, or "Baby, it's going to be all right," please know that you do not have to live without the comfort of a mother. God's loving arms, tender embrace, and sweet promises of a better day are on the way to comfort and keep you until the day of Jesus Christ.

A REMEMBERING MOTHER

> Can a woman forget her nursing child,
> or lack compassion for the child of her womb?
> Even if these forget,
> yet I will not forget you.
> —ISAIAH 49:15

Using a persuasive rhetorical question, we see that God answers the concerning question of whether he will ever forget his children. That demonstrates how he views the love mothers have for their children. Professor and author Gary Smith explained that point:

> Is it possible that a nursing mother would forget (*šākaḥ*) her infant child? The obvious answer would be no, this could never happen. A second example asks if a mother could live without having any loving compassion for one of the children from her own womb? Most people who hear this question would say that it is almost unimaginable that such a thing could even happen. Having created a vivid picture of the ideal mother who does not forget her children, the second half of the verse compares God's lack of forgetfulness with a mother's lack of forgetfulness. "Even though" "these" two mothers might possibly forget (*šākaḥ*) their children for a brief time (2 Kgs 6:24–30; Ps 27:10; Lam 4:10), God emphatically promises that "I myself" will never forget

> (*šākaḥ*) you, meaning Zion. This is a strong affirmation of his love and care for his people. It is unconditioned by any "if" clauses and absolute in its commitment.[22]

How This Truth Heals

God will never forget you, because he hears your cries. He paints a vivid picture of how loving mothers are attentive and responsive to their children. A nursing mother knows she is the only source of her child's nourishment that sustains their physical life. God is like this nursing mother in that he remembers to care for his children. When you cry out like a child to him for what you need, he does not forget you. He hears, he cares, and he responds. If you have felt forgotten by your mother; if your cries as a child for your basic needs were forgotten and unattended to; if your cries of hunger for affection, respect, independence, support, and love were ignored; or if your mother was so busy with other things that seemed to be more of a priority than you, remember that God is not like your mother. The God who remembers you will also respond to you.

He will never forget you, because he made you. The second part of this verse is a tender picture of him as a loving mother who remembers the child she created and carried in her womb. Despite going through the morning sickness and other struggles of pregnancy, a mother has fond memories of feeling the baby kick in the womb, talking to her baby, rubbing her belly, and having dreams for her child and great excitement about the future. God is like that kind of mother. He made you, he carried you, he knew you, and he had plans and purposes for you before there was a physical you. He wants you to know that even if your mother has forgotten those stages of your life; even if she behaves as if she has amnesia of how special it was for her to conceive,

---

22 Gary V. Smith, *The New American Commentary: An Exegetical and Theological Exposition of Holy Scripture,* vol. 15B, *Isaiah 40–66* (Broadman and Holman, 2009), 364–65.

carry, and care for you; and even if she has treated you like she has no maternal bone in her body and no affection for the child of her womb, God has fond memories of you and love for you, the child he made and carried through the stages of embryonic development. He will never forget you.

A TEACHING MOTHER

It was I who taught Ephraim to walk,
taking them by the hand.

—HOSEA 11:3

Some scholars feel this verse refers to God as a loving father teaching his child to walk,[23] while others believe it displays him in a loving teaching moment as a mother. Attributing this activity to a maternal characteristic of God is a fair conclusion, especially in the context of the culture of this text and even today. Mothers often spend the most time with their children in the early stages of their development and are more likely to be the parent teaching the child to walk. This scripture refers to Israel as *Ephraim* and visually represents God like a mother teaching her children to walk. The metaphor appears to relate to Israel's walking out of Egypt.[24] God taught his people, who'd spent so much time in slavery and had never taken steps of freedom, how to trust him with their deliverance and walk in the wilderness as he led and supported them. That is a picture of his tenderness, patience, and support of his children when they are in a vulnerable state but learning a new and important skill. He is there, holding his children and guiding them as they strengthen their own legs to walk. He doesn't always

---

23 Richard D. Patterson and Andrew E. Hill, *Minor Prophets: Hosea–Malachi,* Cornerstone Biblical Commentary 10, ed. Philip W. Comfort (Tyndale, 2008), 67.

24 Duane A. Garrett, *The New American Commentary: An Exegetical and Theological Exposition of Holy Scripture,* vol. 19A, *Hosea, Joel* (Broadman and Holman, 1997), 223.

grab us up and carry us, but as a loving parent, he builds our confidence and helps to build up our own muscles so we will be able to stand and walk on our own two feet.

How This Truth Heals

God is patient as he instructs you. Patience may not be the first thing that comes to mind when you think of your mother; instead, you may think of words and actions far from patient, gentle, and affirming. Some of us have heard our mothers say things like, "How many times do I have to repeat myself?" or "I showed you how to do this a thousand times. Are you stupid?" or "Figure it out for yourself. I have better things to do" or "You can't get it. You'll never get it." After experiencing frustrated sighs, exhales, profanity, or discouragement from our mothers, some of us wish we had patient and committed mothers who wanted to teach us what we needed to learn from them, no matter how long it took.

You may not have had that from your mother, but you have that in God. God and healthy mothers know that there are some things only they can teach and that it takes time for children to learn. God knows how to encourage you to move forward and take a step of faith, and he knows when to say, "Slow down. You don't want to hurt yourself." Walking in Scripture is a metaphor for life. God taught Ephraim how to live free in him and under his care, and he teaches you everything you need to know through his Word so that you can live well and have a happy life:

> How happy are those whose way is blameless,
> who walk according to the LORD's instruction!
> Happy are those who keep his decrees
> and seek him with all their heart.
> They do nothing wrong;
> they walk in his ways. (Psalm 119:1–3)

Take a moment to think back on what life lesson you depended on your mother to teach you that she never tried or finished. Throughout my career, I've had people share a variety of ways that came out in their lives, whether it was something as basic as their mother not having the patience to teach them to read, help them with homework, show them how to navigate menstrual cycles or handle a bully in school, assist with college applications, teach them how to cook, or help them manage friends or a romantic interest. Because some of us weren't taught how to walk through life, we can feel as though we are stumbling and falling all over the place. But God is patient. He holds your hand when you are learning, and he won't let you fall. When mothers teach their children to walk, they are not only great instructors but also great catchers. So is God. You can trust that he won't let you fall.

A PROTECTING MOTHER

I will attack them
like a bear robbed of her cubs
and tear open the rib cage over their hearts.

—HOSEA 13:8

In verse 8 and the preceding verse, God describes how he will deal with those who continuously turned their backs on him. He uses violent language and compares himself to ferocious beasts (a lion, a leopard, and a bear). However, when he describes how he will meet his adversaries, he invokes maternal characteristics. He knows that mother bears are fierce protectors and defenders of their children and would attack and tear apart any animal or person that would do harm to her children.

How This Truth Heals

God identifies with a mother bear to highlight that in his beauty and *shalom,* there is another aspect of him that is aggressive and violent like a bear whose children are at risk of being harmed. Though this verse isn't directly referring to the attack of God's people, it is comforting to know that he affirms that mothers should be that protective and defensive of their children. You may have been anything other than protected by your mother, but God is not that kind of God. He gets angry and will do whatever is necessary to take care of his children. We are promised that one day he will avenge us and repay anyone who dared to bring us harm. You may not have experienced the justice of God on your behalf in this life, but it is coming. He doesn't play when it comes to you!

What beautiful motherly images of God. They remind me of the great lengths he will go to communicate just how much he knows our deepest needs and how, in him, they are all supplied. God's revealing himself in these mothering capacities affirms just how important human mothers are but also teaches us that because of their weaknesses and limitations, we will never be able to be perfectly mothered by them. He assures us that whenever our mothers fall, however they fail, and to whomever they flee, he never makes a mistake, he perfectly parents, and he provides care and protection eternally. If your mother is gone, by death or choice, have no fear because God's care won't dry up or disappear. His massive mothering love is yours; receive it now, in Jesus's name.

Because of their weaknesses and limitations, we will never be able to be perfectly mothered by them.

REFLECTION QUESTIONS

1. *In what ways does seeing God as a* perfect *parent help you?*
2. *Why is it important and healing for Christians who have mother wounds to see themselves as adopted into God's family?*

3. *Which of the metaphorical mother characteristics of God stands out to you most or brings you the greatest amount of comfort?*

PRAYER

Thank you, Father, for the gift of being adopted into your family. Thank you for being a perfect parent who loves me without limits despite my flaws and cares for me in a motherly way. May I live in greater awareness that I am perfectly parented by you. Amen.

CHAPTER 3

"ARE YOU MY MOTHER?"

Jesus replied, "My mother and
my brothers are all those who hear
God's word and obey it."

—LUKE 8:21 (NLT)

P. D. Eastman's well-known children's book *Are You My Mother?* tells the funny story of a baby bird in search of his mother.[1] In the story, the mother bird is sitting on an egg, then leaves to get food. While the mother bird is gone, her egg hatches. The baby bird comes out of the shell and doesn't see his mother, which begins his quest to find her. The baby bird goes up to a kitten, a dog, a cow, a tugboat, and even a steam shovel, asking them if they are his mother. At the end of the story, the steam shovel puts the baby bird back in the nest, and the mother bird returns. Mother and baby are together and all is well.

From a psychological perspective, I've often wondered how relatable, and maybe even unhumorous, this story is when you consider the real-life disorientation and experience of human children abandoned by their mothers. In this children's book, the baby bird is searching for

1 P. D. Eastman, *Are You My Mother?* (Random House, 1960).

the identity of the mother he has never seen, but in your life, you may be searching for how to identify and classify the woman you have seen and experienced. Have you ever looked at your mother and wondered, *Who are you? What are you? Why are you?* as you tried to make sense of your experience of her?

My goal for this chapter is to help you gain clarity, find language to better understand your mother's behavior, and assure you that you're not being too sensitive and that you're not alone. In this chapter, we will explore seven mother types who wound their children. Although there are multiple ways wounding mothers can be described, with the seven types I've created, my objective is to capture a range of how mothers may present. No one mother will neatly fit into any one type; she may display some, but not all, of the descriptions of a particular type or perhaps appear to fit into more than one type of mother we need to grieve. Why grieve? Because your mother's poor treatment of you does not reflect what God designed a mother to be. You've experienced a loss, and both you and your mother need help and healing.

Abuse, in any form, at the hands of your mother is demonic and devastating, particularly if your mother has never acknowledged her abuse or repented. That violation, betrayal, and injury is not something you just "get over"; that pain requires and deserves healing over time. Forgetting or minimizing the impact of the pain is never the purpose of healing; instead, the aim is to live free, healthy, and whole despite the memory of the tremendous wound. There's an old Zimbabwean proverb that says, "The axe never remembers the tree, but the tree always remembers the axe." You may never forget the abuse, but don't let the abuse have power over you. The axe doesn't have to win.

Forgetting or minimizing the impact of the pain is never the purpose of healing; instead, the aim is to live free, healthy, and whole despite the memory of the tremendous wound.

The safety of this book offers you

a place to learn, process, ask questions, reflect, have aha moments, and maybe even cry. Your mother never has to know you've come to see her more accurately. This isn't about her seeing the information, owning it, being confronted by it, or responding to it; this is for you. You have no responsibility to share your findings with her, and it is not a betrayal of her to gain insight for yourself. As you will notice, some descriptions are longer than others. This is to ensure that issues that are layered and multifaceted, such as abuse, will get the fair nuance and proper explanation they deserve.

If the wounds are still fresh and you're new to this journey, it's okay to skip this chapter and come back when you're ready. If you decide to keep going, pay attention to how you are responding to the material. Take breaks if necessary. Consider working through this section with a trusted family member, friend, or mental health professional. Pace yourself. This isn't a sprint; it's a marathon.

1. The Rejecting Mother

Rejection is defined as "the act of refusing to accept, use, or believe someone or something."[2] Whether you know that formal definition or not, everyone knows rejection because we can undoubtedly feel it when it's happening, and it doesn't feel good. Rejection is responsible for some of the most distressing and consequential events in people's lives, resulting in a myriad of emotional, psychological, and interpersonal consequences. In an article published by *Dialogues in Clinical Neuroscience,* psychologist Mark Leary said, "People not only react strongly when they perceive that others have rejected them, but a great deal of human behavior is influenced by the desire to avoid rejection."[3]

---

2 *Cambridge Dictionary,* "rejection," https://dictionary.cambridge.org/us/dictionary/english/rejection.

3 Mark R. Leary, "Emotional Responses to Interpersonal Rejection," *Dialogues in Clinical Neuroscience* 17, no. 4 (December 2015): 435–41, https://doi.org/10.31887/DCNS.2015.17.4/mleary.

You may have felt the rejection of your mother by experiencing her choose others or her career over you, giving her best efforts and time to everyone and everything other than you. Perhaps she treated you as though you were never enough, with constant criticism of your decisions, appearance, and dreams, especially when you needed her to be physically and emotionally available.

Rejection can also manifest as neglect, conflict avoidance, unwillingness to apologize, and being uncomfortable with physical affection. Mothers who reject their children have a way of making your needs and wants appear unreasonable, negatively needy, or selfish. Maternal rejection is often internalized, leaving those who are wounded by rejection to feel ashamed and guilty and doubt their perception, often wondering if they are feeling too sensitive. In her book *Mothers Who Can't Love,* Susan Forward said,

> The pain in your relationship with your mother keeps turning into fear, which becomes rationalization and self-blame. It's a closed loop that keeps you locked in and unable to change. Our intellects may know what's going on, but our emotions tell us a different story—and most of the time it's our emotions that we listen to.[4]

The irony is that when a mother rejects her children, it damages their self-images and attempts to preserve the mother's image, trapping the children in the false belief that they, not their mother, are flawed.[5] Psychologist Lindsay Gibson noted that rejecting is one of the four signs of an emotionally immature parent and that parents who reject their children "engage in a range of behaviors that make you wonder why they have a family in the first place. Whether their

---

4 Susan Forward, *Mothers Who Can't Love: A Healing Guide for Daughters,* with Donna Frazier Glynn (Harper, 2014), 19.

5 Forward, *Mothers Who Can't Love,* 19.

behavior is mild or severe, they don't enjoy emotional intimacy and clearly don't want to be bothered by children."[6]

2. The Abusive Mother

Child maltreatment is a global problem and is defined as

> the abuse and neglect that happens to children under 18 years of age. It includes all types of physical and/or emotional ill-treatment, sexual abuse, neglect, negligence and commercial or other exploitation, which results in actual or potential harm to the child's health, survival, development or dignity in the context of a relationship of responsibility, trust or power.[7]

It is important to address abuse comprehensively. In fact, research has disproved a common belief that physical and sexual abuse are more harmful than other types.[8] That finding doesn't dismiss the devastation of physical and sexual abuse; rather, the point is to alert us to not overlook or minimize other equally harmful forms of abuse that can sometimes be viewed as less significant. Although it is generally believed that there are five categories of child abuse,[9] I added verbal abuse as well. Verbal abuse has traditionally come under the category of emotional abuse; however, it is important to share the unique features and impact of both. The Bible is emphatic that words are power-

---

6 Lindsay C. Gibson, *Adult Children of Emotionally Immature Parents: How to Heal from Distant, Rejecting, or Self-Involved Parents* (New Harbinger, 2015), 70.

7 "Child Maltreatment," World Health Organization, November 5, 2024, www.who.int/news-room/fact-sheets/detail/child-maltreatment.

8 David D. Vachon et al., "Assessment of the Harmful Psychiatric and Behavioral Effects of Different Forms of Child Maltreatment," *JAMA Psychiatry* 72, no. 11 (November 2015): 1135–42, https://jamanetwork.com/journals/jamapsychiatry/fullarticle/2461738.

9 Kimberly Holland, "Understanding the Causes of Child Abuse," Healthline, December 3, 2018, www.healthline.com/health/causes-of-child-abuse#facts.

ful. They can tear down or build up, they can crush the spirit or soothe it (see Proverbs 12:6; 15:4; 18:21), and we will all be accountable for every word we speak (see Matthew 12:36–37). Here are the categories that abuse falls into:

- **Physical:** hitting, striking, or anything that causes physical harm.
- **Sexual:** molesting, groping, or raping. Traditionally, sexual abuse has been characterized through physical activities, but it can also take the form of willful exposure and giving children access to sexually explicit images or behavior, such as pornography or mothers participating in sexual activity in the presence of their children.
- **Medical:** denying needed medical services or creating fictional stories that put children at risk of neglect.
- **Neglectful:** withholding or failing to provide care, food, shelter, or other basic necessities.
- **Verbal:** using words to control, demean, manipulate, or intimidate. Words are powerful and can be just as injurious as, if not more than, physical abuse. Mothers can wound their children though verbal abuse by criticizing, being combative, threatening, shaming, humiliating, yelling, screaming, using profane insults, comparing children to other siblings or people, making hurtful sarcastic "jokes," speaking negatively about the child's appearance or learning challenges, pushing their buttons, blaming, or characterizing verbal abuse as "tough love." Weaponizing silence in the home can also be a form of verbal abuse. It's important to note that occasional anger or frustration expressed by a mother does not constitute abuse; the key factors are pattern, intensity, intent, and overall impact of the words.

- **Emotional:** withholding emotional connection, belittling, demeaning, or yelling.

EMOTIONAL ABUSE THROUGH MANIPULATION

I want to expand a little more on emotional abuse, specifically manipulation, because it is rarely discussed, but its impact is significant. Manipulation doesn't often come to mind when naming types of abuse, but it is very damaging. Manipulation in relationships describes a person "using mental distortion and emotional exploitation to influence and control others" to get what the person wants.[10] A mother who is an emotional manipulator can use subtle ways to control her children, causing them to question their own sanity. She may or may not even be aware that she is manipulating her kids, but her behavior is nonetheless abusive. The following are several ways you may have experienced your mother being manipulative:[11]

- **Gaslighting:** a covert form of emotional abuse that undermines your perception of reality, causes you to second-guess yourself and your memories, and leaves you feeling blame for something or that you are being too sensitive.[12]
- **Emotional Blackmail:** involves manipulating someone through fear, obligation, or guilt. It can be defined as "a powerful form of manipulation in which people close to us threaten, either directly or indirectly, to punish us if we

---

10 Sheri Stritof, "Seven Signs You're Being Emotionally Manipulated in Your Relationship," Verywell Mind, September 29, 2025, www.verywellmind.com/manipulation-in-marriage-2302245.

11 Adapted from Susan Forward, *Emotional Blackmail: When the People in Your Life Use Fear, Obligation, and Guilt to Manipulate You,* with Donna Frazier (Harper, 1998).

12 Sherri Gordon, "Is Someone Gaslighting You? Look Out for These Red Flags," Verywell Mind, September 29, 2025, www.verywellmind.com/is-someone-gaslighting-you-4147470.

don't do what they want."[13] Here are some categories of emotional manipulation you may experience:

- » *Threats of Retaliation* ("I'm not leaving you any of my money." "I'm never babysitting for you again.")
- » *Threats of Self-Harm* ("I'm going to kill myself and it's all your fault.")
- » *Playing the Victim* ("I'm so sad and it's all your fault; you've always hated me.")
- » *Distorting Reality* ("I'm not hurting you; I've always given you my best and put you first.")
- » *Guilt-Tripping* ("After all I've done for you, how could you be so selfish?" Some believe that guilt-tripping is the first and most common tactic manipulators use, "making you feel guilty, even over the most inconsequential things"[14] or for things you did not do.)

- **Triangulation:** may occur if you are in a disagreement with your mother and she brings in a third person to change the dynamic and maintain control. The goal of triangulation is to tip the scales in her favor and use the third person as the messenger between you and your mom. This tactic often divides you from your social support, makes you look bad, or creates conflict that benefits the mother. Triangulation is usually used to distract from the real issue, reinforce the mother's sense of superiority, attempt to resolve the argument through the third party, or divert some of the stress of the disagreement onto the third person.[15]

---

13 Forward, *Emotional Blackmail,* x.

14 BetterHelp Editorial Team, "Seven Signs of Manipulative Behavior," BetterHelp, September 17, 2025, https://shorturl.at/aTb5w.

15 Maggie Holland, "Narcissistic Triangulation: Definition, Examples, and How to

Another form of triangulation that may occur is called the golden child–scapegoat family dynamic. This happens when the mother "splits their own good self-image and bad self-image into two distinct parts and then projects them onto their children. Consequently, one child becomes the all-good, or golden child, and the other becomes the all-bad, or scapegoat."[16] The golden child is idealized and treated as if they can do no wrong and becomes an extension of the mother's perceived self-goodness. However, the scapegoat is treated as if they can do only wrong and is typically blamed and punished for all the problems of the mother or family. Unfortunately, neither child's humanity, needs, feelings, or personalities are of any consequence to the mother; both are in fact not loved well, as they are pawns in the mother's manipulation.

- **Withholding Affection and Silent Treatment:** simply defined as the mother intentionally withholding hugs, kisses, warmth, care, spending time, and agreed-upon support to gain control. Additionally, this includes employing the silent treatment by refusing to communicate verbally or return texts or calls or using minimal or only necessary words to show displeasure. This form of manipulation is effective if she knows silence hurts you. It's a passive-aggressive form of retribution used for noncompliance and to refuse accountability. The goal of the child then becomes "getting Mom to talk" or "getting Mom back to being

---

Respond," Choosing Therapy, December 19, 2024, www.choosingtherapy.com/narcissistic-triangulation/.

16 Darius Cikanavicius, "Triangulation: The Narcissist[']s Best Play," Psych Central, October 20, 2019, https://psychcentral.com/blog/psychology-self/2019/10/triangulation-and-narcissism#3.

loving or happy," and the issues or concerns the child may have with their mother have to take a back seat or be ignored entirely to restore affection and communication.

- **Love Bombing:** showering you with excessive attention, affection, or gifts for the purpose of gaining trust and control or distracting from your problems and concerns. This may involve the mother giving unexpected gifts, showing up, offering support, smothering with compliments, and being overly generous with words of affirmation, which feels disingenuous but has the intended effect of making you look bad for refusing gifts, not showing gratitude, or wanting to remain focused on what your mother did that hurt you. The love bomb usually goes off to shut you up or shut you down for wanting your mother to take accountability and give attention to your problems with her.
- **Dry Begging:** an exploitive manipulation tactic used to get favors, attention, pity, compliments, material things, and help without directly asking. By doing this, the manipulator never has to look vulnerable or needy and can avoid any sense of debt or gratitude and feel off the hook for showing you any appreciation. "It's a powerful way for them to maintain control and reinforce a dynamic where others are constantly guessing how to please or support them, often to the detriment of their own well-being."[17] Although dry begging is a common manipulation tactic of a narcissist,[18] it's important to remember that narcissism exists on a spectrum—that is, people can have narcissistic tendencies

17 Elizabeth Shaw (@coachelizabethshaw), "Some narcissists won't ask for help directly," Instagram post, November 7, 2024, www.instagram.com/p/DCETJHqsi7Q/?igsh=MXI4aGZ3czQ4cnFzMw==.

18 Elizabeth Shaw (@coachelizabethshaw), "The Narcissist's Dry Begging: How They Subtly Manipulate You into Giving," Instagram post, April 16, 2025, www.instagram.com/reel/DIiFFEzopmw/?igsh=MWZtY3o3cWh2aXkyYw==.

without having a formal diagnosis of narcissistic personality disorder.[19] According to a New York University study, the root of narcissism may be not just an inflated sense of self, as believed, but rather insecurity. Because people with narcissistic tendencies typically lack awareness of self and the impact their behavior has on those they manipulate, their cycle continues until people refuse to be manipulated, which then adds further injury to their lack of self-worth.[20]

3. The Unprotecting Mother

Some have posed this question: Which is worse, the mother who harms her child or the mother who does not protect her child from being harmed? The short answer is that both are terrible. Mothers who passively stand by and allow harm to come to their children are equally as wrong. Scripture tells us that God will protect his people the way a mother bear will protect her cub from being stolen, but not all mothers are like vigilant and protecting mother bears. The unprotecting mother may be the mother who didn't believe her child's reports of abuse or did not intervene when the child reported being bullied by students, neighborhood kids, or even their siblings in their own home. An unprotecting mother often stays with a man in abusive environments to meet her financial or companionship needs. An unprotecting mother may believe that if she is the recipient of the direct abuse and not her

---

19 Narcissistic personality disorder "is defined as a pervasive pattern of grandiosity (sense of superiority in fantasy or behavior), need for admiration, and lack of empathy, beginning by early adulthood and occurring in a variety of contexts. An estimated 1% to 2% of the U.S. population has narcissistic personality disorder"; "What Is Narcissistic Personality Disorder?," American Psychiatric Association, January 30, 2024, www.psychiatry.org/news-room/apa-blogs/what-is-narcissistic-personality-disorder.

20 "Narcissism Driven by Insecurity, Not Grandiose Sense of Self, New Psychology Research Shows," New York University, March 26, 2021, www.nyu.edu/about/news-publications/news/2021/march/narcissism-driven-by-insecurity--not-grandiose-sense-of-self--ne.html.

children, then she is not endangering her children. However, it is extremely traumatizing when children grow up in homes where they observe their own mother being abused, even if the children are never directly physically harmed.

An unprotecting mother may allow her children to pass from home to home with little concern for their welfare. While mothers who are vigilant and protecting cannot always guarantee the safety and welfare of their children, unprotecting mothers show a pattern of blatant disregard for the known or reasonably expected risks to their children's lives. Another hallmark characteristic of the unprotecting mother is that she looks out for her welfare, wants, and needs at the expense of the safety of her children. Lack of protection can also reveal itself in neglect. While it is not an excuse, many mothers who do not protect their kids never learned that skill because they never experienced being protected or no one taught them to protect.

4. The Mentally Ill Mother

The National Institute of Mental Health reports that

> 9.8 million Americans aged 18 or older, or 4.2% of adults, live with a severe mental illness such as schizophrenia, bipolar disorder, or major depressive disorder. . . .
>
> In general, two-thirds of females, and one-half of males who have a severe mental illness, will become parents. Joanne Nicholson, Ph.D., a professor of psychiatry at Dartmouth Psychiatric Research Center, states, "There's a significant number of individuals with some level of emotional distress who are raising children."[21]

---

21 "A Guide to Understanding When a Parent Has a Mental Illness," Montare Behavioral Health, https://montarebehavioralhealth.com/resources/parent-with-mental-illness/.

Some of the challenges and outcomes children of parents with mental illness may face include physical impairment, emotional instability, difficulty with social interactions, feelings of guilt, low self-esteem, difficulty finding and keeping a job, lack of initiating or maintaining interpersonal relationships, and problems parenting their own children.[22] Additionally, some children experience feelings of anger, helplessness, and embarrassment.

Whether or not their mothers have been formally diagnosed, children still feel the effects of what their mothers are going through. There should be much compassion toward both your mother and you, as no mother would want to have a mental illness that compromises her ability to care for her child. While we do not blame mothers who have mental or physical illnesses, the impact on you as the child is still something you may need to grieve. One of my clients who had a mother who struggled with depression said,

> "I love my mom, but I just wished she was normal like the other moms. I would go to visit my friends' homes, and their mothers cooked, kept the home neat, and asked my friends about their day. They also showed up for their kids' games. I remember my mother being in bed most of the time. She wasn't a mean mom; she just was out of it a lot."

Another woman wrote,

> "Throughout much of our childhood, my mother did not get out of bed in the morning; our father took care of the usual household activities, made us breakfast, and sent us off to school. We certainly had furniture in the house, but

22 "A Guide to Understanding When a Parent Has a Mental Illness."

> the house was never decorated with a sense of style and warmth as the homes of some of my friends were."

> "I remember always trying to cheer her up. I would come home from school and regale her with everything that happened—it may be where I acquired a penchant for storytelling (and talking a lot!). She loved it, and my friends loved her. She was engaged and involved in my life but basically quiet."[23]

Growing up with a mother who struggles with a mental illness can be challenging. According to one study, children of mentally ill parents reported that growing up, they felt responsible for their family's well-being; isolated from their families, peers, and larger society; and fearful of inheriting their parents' illnesses.[24] Children often report knowing something was wrong even if they didn't understand it.

Although we have made great strides, there can still be a lingering stigma around mental illness that shuts off communication in the home. Not only may you have needed to grieve your mother being different, but frequent trips to the hospital, the weight of caring for yourself and siblings, and your mother's inability to perform reasonable parenting tasks mean you may also need to grieve the silence and avoidance about her illness. It's okay that having a mother with mental illness was complex for you. Maybe there were times, because of the avoidance, you felt confused, scared, and unloved, but you also enjoyed normal moments that always felt short-lived.

It's possible that even mentioning the grief attached to your moth-

---

23 Carol Bernstein, "My Mother's Mental Illness: A Late-Life Reckoning," Psychiatry Online, March 18, 2020, https://psychiatryonline.org/doi/10.1176/appi.pn.2020.3b22.

24 Vinita Mehta, "What It's Like to Be the Child of a Mentally Ill Parent," *Psychology Today*, September 29, 2021, www.psychologytoday.com/us/blog/head-games/202109/what-its-like-to-be-the-child-of-a-mentally-ill-parent/amp.

er's mental illness can be distressing and potentially make you feel like a bad or insensitive child. Let me help release you from that burden. We aren't blaming our mothers for being sick; we are just telling the truth about how their illness at times affected us. It's okay to love, respect, honor, and grieve a mentally ill mother. It is not her fault, and it is not your fault, but how you process that grief is critical for your own well-being and potentially how you relate to your mother now if she's still in your life.

5. The Immature Mother

It is a reasonable assumption to view adult parents as functioning with more maturity than their children or other individuals much younger than they are, but that is not always the case. Many children have been raised by mothers who were immature and under-functioned in their adult roles. My use of the description *immaturity,* particularly when referring to emotional immaturity, is meant to be not an insult but rather an apt description of the how the mother presents and functions in her relationship with her children. *Immaturity* is defined as "exhibiting less than an expected degree of maturity" or "lacking complete growth, differentiation, or development."[25] Many immature mothers, especially those who struggle with emotional immaturity, likely don't intend to cause harm to their children. That's because "most signs of emotional immaturity are beyond a person's conscious control, and most emotionally immature parents have no awareness of how they've affected their children."[26] An immature mother "under-functions" in regard to an expected standard for someone with her physical and mental capacity. I am not saying that mothers with men-

25 *Merriam-Webster's Dictionary,* "immature," www.merriam-webster.com/dictionary/immature.

26 Gibson, *Adult Children of Emotionally Immature Parents,* 25.

tal or physical disabilities are immature, nor am I making a moral assessment; I am describing mothers who aren't able to rise to the occasion of adulthood and are struggling to fulfill basic functions in parenting roles based on their emotional or spiritual underdevelopment. This assessment is both emotionally and spiritually rooted and functionally measured.

In her book *Adult Children of Emotionally Immature Parents,* Lindsay C. Gibson said this about emotional maturity:

> People who are emotionally mature can function independently while also having deep emotional attachments, smoothly incorporating both into their daily life. They are direct about pursuing what they want yet do so without exploiting other people. They've differentiated from their original family relationships sufficiently to build a life of their own. They have a well-developed sense of self and identity and treasure their closest relationships.[27]

Conversely, Gibson offered an extensive list of personality traits associated with emotional immaturity.[28] The following are a few examples and the likely impact on the child:

> **The mother has low stress tolerance.** This mother will have difficulty dealing with challenging situations, may check out emotionally, and may unravel very easily. She might also request to be cared for and rescued from distressing situations to minimize her discomfort.
>
> > *Impact:* Children feel responsible for the emotional comfort and stress management of their mother.

---

27 Gibson, *Adult Children of Emotionally Immature Parents,* 28.

28 Gibson, *Adult Children of Emotionally Immature Parents,* 29–46.

She does what feels best. This mother is very controlled by her feelings even in the face of wise alternative views and choices.

> *Impact:* Children may find it difficult to disagree with their mother and have conversations based in reality or be respected for an alternate opinion or choice. "Gut" guidance is encouraged rather than thinking and reason. This immaturity can be spiritualized as discernment or a spiritual knowing that is emotional, not biblical.

She is self-reverential, not self-reflective. This mother either will appraise and esteem herself beyond what is reasonable or true or does not have the ability to honestly assess herself, take accountability, or see how her actions affect others. She is characterized by a gross lack of self-awareness.

> *Impact:* Children will never see their mother take responsibility or acknowledge their needs or experiences. She demands respect, obedience, and love despite the ways she injures and invalidates her children. The child likely witnesses their mother blame others for everything and speak badly about other family members or friends, even the child. The child is often forced to agree or acquiesce to the mother's perspective and encourage her victim mentality or grandiose self-perception.

She promotes role reversal. This mother likely will engage in parentifying her children and encourage her being taken care of instead of caretaking.

> *Impact:* Children likely will be taking on non-age-appropriate responsibilities for the care of the mother, home, and other siblings. Children miss childhood ex-

periences and relationships because they are functioning as adults. Additionally, their own needs from the mother are not met.

She is often inconsistent and contradictory. This mother will say one thing and do another. She may give her word but back out at the last minute or express mixed desires.

Impact: Experiences are undependable and unpredictable. It's destabilizing for the children and often leaves them disappointed and blamed for having an expectation of the mother. It leaves the child on edge and not able to feel safe or secure.

She focuses on physical needs rather than emotional ones. This mother may be good at providing basic needs and even can be counted on to fulfill service-oriented tasks, but she will likely be unable to emotionally connect. She may lack empathy and be unable to tolerate her children's negative feelings.

Impact: Children may live with unmet emotional needs, feeling distant and unloved by their mother. The children are left feeling lonely and may crave connection so much that in romantic relationships, they hurry to become emotionally or physically intimate in order to experience a sense of being wanted, heard, understood, and seen. An alternative result is that the children learn to minimize their emotional needs and never learn how to meet others' emotional needs.

Some mothers struggle with emotional immaturity as well as spiritual immaturity. In fact, I'd venture to say that for people who are *spiritually* immature, there will be some areas where they will also be *emotionally* immature.

The Bible references the state of spiritual immaturity as infants in Christ,[29] worldly (fleshly),[30] displaying childish ways,[31] and failing to grow, thereby needing milk and not solid food.[32] There are several ways an immature mother can present. The Bible, particularly in Proverbs, describes three types of people: the wise,[33] the inexperienced,[34] and the foolish.[35] Just in chapter 1 of Proverbs, all three types are mentioned. Biblically, a foolish person is, at the core, defined as someone who rejects wisdom and God's instructions. A mother can deny God and still possess attributes of a good and emotionally mature mother, but the Bible would call that rejecter of God foolish. A mother who unfortunately personifies the foolish person may demonstrate her folly in several ways:

- She denies God in faith or life (Psalm 14:1; 53:1).
- She thinks she is always right and is uncorrectable (Proverbs 12:15).
- She makes a mockery of sin (Proverbs 14:9).
- She conceals hatred with lying lips and she slanders (Proverbs 10:18).
- She takes pleasure in shameful behavior (Proverbs 10:23).
- She has deceitful and perverse speech (Proverbs 19:1).
- She trusts in herself over God and wisdom (Proverbs 28:26).
- She vents all her anger and says whatever is on her mind (Proverbs 29:11).

---

29 See 1 Corinthians 3:1–3.
30 See Galatians 5:19–21.
31 See 1 Corinthians 13:11.
32 See Hebrews 5:12–14.
33 See Proverbs 1:5.
34 See Proverbs 1:4; some translations (such as ESV, NIV, and NLT) say "simple."
35 See Proverbs 1:7.

- She cannot control her tongue and is more interested in giving her opinion than understanding a matter (Proverbs 18:2).
- She is slow to trust and accept the gospel (Luke 24:25).
- She is lazy, unfocused, and without purpose. She makes up excuses for why she can't do hard work (Proverbs 24:30–34; Ecclesiastes 4:5).
- She is reckless and careless (Proverbs 14:16).
- She is dangerous and hard to deal with (Proverbs 17:12).
- She will inherit disgrace, not honor (Proverbs 3:35).

A mother who exhibits the characteristics of a fool will likely be void of wise biblical counsel, act in ungodly ways, be stubborn, or be too permissive in her parenting and desiring to be a friend instead of an instructive and caring parent. Also, she may disrespect the child's father, encourage the child to live in an ungodly way, despise correction, and refuse to submit her life to the Lord. Immature mothers lack godly wisdom. True wisdom is the application of Scripture, not just the knowledge of Bible verses. Biblical wisdom informs all our decisions and influences our behavior. We become wise by growing up and maturing in Christ. The truth is, all of us have been and can be like this fool. It is only by the grace of God and our cooperation with the Holy Spirit that we can be wise in Christ.

A child who experienced having an immature mother may struggle with relationships and reciprocity in relationships, as their mother modeled relationships that were characterized by her neediness, her selfishness, and a chronic inability to show up for others and give rather than just take. A child may also experience struggles with self-esteem, goal setting, and achieving, because they had an immature mother who complained more than completed goals, pointed the finger and blamed rather than took accountability, and had defeating self-talk instead of determination and resilience.

Many women with emotionally immature mothers report they didn't learn basic life skills regarding self-care, managing money, handling puberty, maintaining relationships with men, or building friendships. Like their immature mothers, these women may have knowledge of God and biblical principles but are unable to translate and appropriate that power and information into their own lives. Children of immature mothers may struggle with adult readiness because they have witnessed their mothers' constant cycles of crash-outs, broken promises to do better, little to no healthy relationships with others, no follow-through, and normalized self-centeredness and dependency on others for basic adult responsibilities. Some mothers have aged but not matured, and their children are experiencing the consequences of that maturity deficit.

6. The Jealous or Competitive Mother

Nothing is more confusing than when a parent is jealous of their children. You expect parents, especially mothers, to want the best for their kids and always look for ways to make sure the children have better lives than they had. Isn't each generation supposed to be stronger and more prepared than the previous? Many mothers believe that their children thriving and surpassing their own success and achievements is a noble and right goal, but for a variety of factors, other mothers, who would wholeheartedly say they love their children, are unable to stave off feelings of jealousy. *Jealousy* is defined as "the feeling of anger or bitterness that someone has when they wish that they could have the qualities or possessions that another person has."[36]

---

36 *Collins Dictionary*, "jealousy," www.collinsdictionary.com/us/dictionary/english/jealousy.

While we often use the words interchangeably, envy and jealousy are not the same. Envy is wanting *what* someone has, but jealousy is the negative attitudes and feelings because they have it and you don't or can't. Jealousy is a sinful emotion and evidence that we are being controlled by our own fleshly desires (see 1 Corinthians 3:3, ESV) and reveals that we are not satisfied with what God has given us (see Hebrews 13:5). But thankfully this is nothing like his jealousy. He is righteously jealous as an expression of his commitment to his covenant with his people and his expectation of their faithful devotion to and worship of him alone (see Exodus 20:4–5; 34:14). Additionally, there is godly jealousy, which the apostle Paul describes in 2 Corinthians 11:2, which is righteous and protective zeal for God's glory and the well-being of his people. God is the perfect parent!

Some actions from a jealous mother are her minimizing or ignoring your successes; constantly criticizing your choices, appearance, or friends, which makes you feel insecure about your decisions; giving backhanded compliments; acting disinterested when you share exciting or positive news; controlling access to or speaking negatively about your opportunities for personal advancement, such as a new job, travel, school, or additional training; and limiting your independence and social life. Dr. Nikki Martinez says another sign that your mother may be jealous is her overreacting. Moreover, "she may be sarcastic, angry, give the silent treatment, or resort to personal attacks. . . . These are very impulsive reactions, and often your mother is not even aware of why she is behaving [that] way. It just comes out."[37]

One of the most striking examples of a jealous mother is her desire for the spotlight at her child's expense. This could show up in her resentment toward your relationship with your father or other family members and friends, and because a jealous mother is constantly com-

---

37 Nikki Martinez, quoted in Carolyn Steber, "Signs Your Mom Has Jealousy Issues," *Bustle*, July 7, 2017, www.bustle.com/p/11-signs-your-mom-might-have-jealousy-issues-how-to-deal-with-it-68216.

paring herself to others, she will use you as a benchmark for comparison. She may begin to change her appearance, hair, or style of dress to look more like you or change her look in some way that doesn't reflect her age or personal style. If you take up a new activity or adventure—such as photography, running a marathon, starting a new diet or eating plan, taking an advanced class, joining a book club, or dancing—you may notice that your mother is following close behind.

That may not be inherently malicious. However, a jealous mother will not show support for what you are doing; she will withhold compliments and encouragement. Perhaps she may even pretend that she thought of the idea on her own. Your mother's actions might make everything you both are doing feel like a competition.[38] The agony and confusion created by the jealous mother is a double-edged sword: On one hand, the child is raised to "make Mother proud," but the mother's jealousy communicates, "Be great, but don't outshine me." Why maternal jealousy occurs is complex and likely related to the mother's past wounds, insecurities, mental health issues, or fear of not being enough. But the Bible is clear that jealousy is destructive to one's mental state and relationships (see Proverbs 14:30; James 3:16, ESV). As Proverbs 27:4 says, "Wrath is cruel, anger is overwhelming, but who can stand before jealousy?" (ESV).

7. The Religious-Hypocrite Mother

The Greek translation of the word *hypocrite* is "actor," which is exactly what children experience: a great performance from their mother onstage before the audience of the public, church members, co-workers, and even family. Children of mothers who are religious hypocrites relate to Jesus's frustration. We see him strongly rebuke the Pharisees for their hypocrisy in Matthew 23:27–28. However, once the curtain falls,

38 Steber, "Signs."

children see the real person beyond the religious veneer. The wound is the distance between her professed orthodoxy (belief) and orthopraxy (how to live out one's faith). This mother may also engage in spiritual abuse and misuse Scripture to wound and control her children. Here are some examples of how a mother may present as a religious hypocrite:

- Praising her child in public to make the mother look good but in private not showing love or support or being proud of the child.
- Appearing kind, helpful, and available to others but not to the child. The child feels the frustration of their cold mother being loved and praised by others who don't know "the real woman."
- Exhibiting hyper-religious behavior such as contriteness, humility, worship, prayers, and repentance in public, but not in the home.
- Blaming her children for her unhappiness and telling them they are demonic, used by the devil, and evil. "God doesn't like ugly" or "God is going to get you" is the retort for everything and a tool of discipline and control. Mothers may be spiritually abusive and manipulative with Scripture, saying such things as, "God said you must honor me or he's going to kill you." Additionally, the mother treats her children as the opposition in her spiritual warfare.

The harsh reality is that many of these kinds of mothers may be leaders, disciple makers, teachers, preachers, and pastors who teach, challenge, counsel, and correct other mothers, applying biblical principles regarding parenting and family that they do not personally practice.

There are several potential impacts on children of a religious-hypocrite mother. One is resentment toward others and the church for falling for the mother's performance and benefiting from the kind, religiously committed version of their mother they don't experience. Children may also feel like they aren't enough if they aren't able to elicit the good spiritual side of their mother. They may begin to believe they are evil and the cause of problems in the family or even that God doesn't love them and is against them.

In addition to the low self-esteem and spiritual confusion that creates, the children may also grow to distrust God, the Bible, and the church. The mother's fake and performative behavior can deeply injure the children's ability to feel safe in church or even desire a relationship with God. In essence, in the child's eyes, the mother's hypocrisy soils Christianity and God himself, robs them of experiencing the true love of God and care of the church, and paints Christianity and its disciples as angry, mean, combative, and sick.

It is important to note that the children may not ever understand the behavior of the mother as hypocritical, as she is shaping their understanding of God and faith. It may not be until early adulthood that they realize their mother was wrong, but even then, their injuries are experienced as originating from both the mother and the church. Many times, such children become agnostic or atheistic or opt for a version of spirituality that is divorced from organized religion. It is important for children of religious-hypocrite mothers to deconstruct and reconstruct their faith in a healthy, safe, and sound community.

It is important for children of religious-hypocrite mothers to deconstruct and reconstruct their faith in a healthy, safe, and sound community.

I pray that this chapter was helpful in providing not only needed psychoeducation but also the biblical wisdom to assist you in better understanding some of your experiences with your mother. It is often life-giving to have someone put into words what you couldn't explain, and hopefully your soul bears witness and feels validated, understood, and cared for as you continue your journey to healing. Remember, no matter what type of mother you had, God is your perfect parent. His perfection and love surpass even that of the best of mothers, and he can be trusted. I hope that in your search to find and understand your mother's type, you have had an encounter with a God who will never fail.

REFLECTION QUESTIONS

1. *What mother type best describes how you've experienced your mother? Is there a type not reflected in the chapter that you would name?*

2. *What did you learn from reading this chapter that was helpful? What did you learn that raises more questions for you?*

3. *Remember, the point of this chapter is not for you to go to your mother and name her behavior or label her as a specific type of mother; this information is solely for you. Given that, what will you do with this information? Are you motivated to pray differently or talk through some of your self-discovery with a professional?*

4. *If you are a mother, how did this chapter provoke personal introspection or conviction?*

PRAYER

Lord, thank you for helping me have language to describe what I've experienced with my mother. Please guide me in what I do with this information to better grieve, heal, and make peace with my mother wounds.

CHAPTER 4

AFTERSHOCKS

FEELING THE IMPACT OF MOTHER WOUNDS YEARS LATER

They will say, "This land that was laid waste
has become like the garden of Eden;
the cities that were lying in ruins, desolate
and destroyed, are now fortified and
inhabited." Then the nations around you
that remain will know that I the LORD have
rebuilt what was destroyed and have
replanted what was desolate. I the LORD
have spoken, and I will do it.

—EZEKIEL 36:35–36 (NIV)

Everyone is familiar with the power and potential devastation of an earthquake, but did you know that aftershocks are smaller earthquakes that occur in the same general area during the days and even years after the initial big quake? Aftershocks are unpredictable and can cause damage of their own. The impact of a mother wound is similar to an aftershock; it may be days or years since you sustained injuries from your relationship with your mother, but your life can still be shaken up a bit as a result of what you've experienced.

As we dive into this chapter, we must be careful not to quickly attribute every negative characteristic, dysfunctional behavior, failed relationship, or life struggle to our mothers. In modern pop psychology, there is a growing trend to blame our parents, particularly our mothers, for our dissatisfaction with our lives. Sometimes our lives reflect our underdevelopment, spiritual immaturity, poor choices, and sin issues. It is undeniable that children learn what they live and are shaped by their primary caretakers, and because of that, there are some connections to our childhood experiences and past mother wounds that are important to make in order to grow and heal. People from all walks of life are influenced by their mother wounds well into adulthood. Though you've grown up, graduated from college, maybe started a family, have a successful career, and serve faithfully in the church, you still may be sick (not feeling well or living well) in various ways that you didn't know to attribute to mother wounds. Your current choices, perceptions, relationships, fears, lack of boundaries, low self-esteem, insecurities, anger, relationship patterns, and perpetually feeling stuck in life could be groans after years of digesting explicit and implicit lessons your mother served you.

> We must be careful not to quickly attribute every negative characteristic, dysfunctional behavior, failed relationship, or life struggle to our mothers.

Identifying the wound and understanding how it has affected you can be a starting place for lasting change and open the door for you to finally show up in the world the way you've always wanted to and live the life you've always dreamed of having: the abundant life God promised. Together, let's investigate the effect of our mother wounds on our present lives and learn the truth of God's Word, which reminds us who we really are and the life that is possible in Christ. In this chapter, I want us to explore three main areas where mother wounds have the greatest impact: emotional awareness, insecurities, and relationships.

Emotional Awareness

You may struggle to notice and feel your emotions, name them, and healthfully respond to them. Doing those three things make up emotional awareness/intelligence. Psychologist and author Daniel Goleman views emotional intelligence as a much more important predictor of good decision-making, thinking, and success than traditional measures of intelligence (for example, an IQ test). He offers five characteristics of emotional intelligence (EI):[1] knowing our emotions, managing our emotions, motivating ourselves, recognizing emotions in other people, and handling our relationships.

Having emotional awareness helps you understand how your feelings relate to your thoughts and actions. Emotional awareness also helps you accurately label your emotions with a word (such as *happy, sad, frustrated, confused, lonely,* or *angry*), understand the causes and consequences of the emotion, express the emotion appropriately, and if necessary have a healthy stress response to regulate the emotion.[2] There are two significant ways your mother may have negatively influenced your ability to be emotionally aware.

1. YOUR MOTHER MET YOUR PHYSICAL NEEDS BUT NOT YOUR EMOTIONAL ONES

Not all mother wounds are abusive or even rooted in malice for the child. For instance, your mother may have fed you, changed your diapers, provided a house for you, and made sure you got to school and had clean clothes and a packed lunch, but she may not have given you

---

1 Daniel Goleman, *Emotional Intelligence: Why It Can Matter More Than IQ* (Bantam, 2005).

2 Modern Recovery Editorial Team, "Emotional Awareness: Definition, Benefits, and Techniques," Modern Recovery Services, July 6, 2023, https://modernrecoveryservices.com/wellness/coping/skills/emotional/emotional-awareness/.

comfort, warmth, attention, and emotional safety. If your mother was unavailable to your emotional needs, she likely was or is uncomfortable with your sharing negative emotions and may have scolded you for expressing your unpleasant feelings.

2. YOUR MOTHER HAD A PATTERN OF INVALIDATING YOUR FEELINGS

If your mother invalidated your feelings, she likely had a critical mindset toward you, particularly when it came to your emotional expression. She may have dismissed, minimized, or denied your feelings, causing you to believe that what you felt was wrong or insignificant. Statements like "You're a big baby," "You're too sensitive," "You're overreacting," and "You make a big deal out of nothing" or, in the case of boys and men, saying things like "You're being a sissy," "Toughen up," "Be a man," or "Stop acting like a girl" (which also implies that girls are inherently weak and overwhelmed by their emotions) may have affected your ability to trust, own, and respect your feelings or have an expectation that other people should respect them. Invalidation can happen through nonverbal cues such as your mother ignoring you, rolling her eyes, smirking, grunting, walking away, or changing the subject. Individuals who are chronically invalidated are at risk for increased mental health issues such as depression, anxiety, and low self-esteem as well as worsening mental health issues that already exist.[3]

If your mother has unprocessed trauma, it will be difficult for her to be emotionally available to you. She may also be avoiding accountability and responsibility for the pain she caused you. In her mind, minimizing your feelings about her treatment of you reduces her obli-

---

3 Brittany Carrico, "What Is Emotional Invalidation?," Psych Central, July 19, 2021, https://psychcentral.com/health/reasons-you-and-others-invalidate-your-emotional-experience#consequences.

gation to see her faults and respond appropriately with humility, empathy, and an apology.

HOW TO IMPROVE YOUR EMOTIONAL AWARENESS

Rest assured that you can increase your emotional awareness and enjoy all the benefits that come with greater emotional intelligence. It is important to remember that the goal of emotional awareness is not to deny, control, or suppress your emotions but instead to gain an understanding of yourself, empathize with others, and manage your responses in a healthy way.

Let's first start by understanding the brain science behind emotional awareness. Emotional awareness is a function involving the brain, specifically the limbic system.[4] It works in three core ways: initial response, emotion identification, and emotion management.[5] Our senses send messages to the amygdala (emotional response center) part of the brain, which processes emotions, particularly fear and anxiety. The amygdala quickly assesses the situation and triggers an emotional reaction. The amygdala is responsible for the fight, flight, freeze, or fawn response and is named by some as the "jumpy superhero" who goes into overdrive to protect us from perceived threats.[6]

The prefrontal cortex is responsible for decision-making and behavior regulation and helps us identify and label our emotions. Once our amygdala is responding to a perceived threat, the prefrontal cortex can step in to analyze the situation and regulate the amygdala's alarm,

---

4 The limbic system is a group of interconnected brain structures that help regulate our emotions and behavior. The parts of the limbic system (amygdala, thalamus, hypothalamus, hippocampus) work together with other brain regions by processing our memories, thoughts, and motivations and then tell our bodies how to respond.

5 Modern Recovery Editorial Team, "Emotional Awareness."

6 Lauren Spigelmyer, "The Amygdala: The Decision Maker of Your Emotional Brain," Medium, June 9, 2021, https://thebehaviorhub.medium.com/the-amygdala-88149dc66cfd.

preventing an impulsive reaction. The prefrontal cortex is the part of the brain that plays a major role in our emotional awareness. With increased emotional awareness and practice, we learn to manage our reactions to our emotions. When we recognize our feelings, we can pause, reflect, and decide how we should react.

There are several practices you can do to improve your emotional awareness and regulation.

Strengthen Emotional Regulation

When a person can regulate or manage their emotions, they are able to experience calm and happiness, even in moments of stress. Improving people's ability to regulate their emotions can happen in a number of ways. For some, psychotherapy will be helpful; that is when a person works with a mental health professional to address the underlying trauma or other mental conditions that may be contributing to the individual's emotional dysregulation as well as learn skills and coping strategies for self-soothing in response to stressful or triggering events. Diet and exercise, along with counseling, is beneficial, and psychotropic medications can help.[7]

Use a Feelings List or Wheel

If you've been to therapy, your therapist may have given you a feelings list or wheel to help you in learning to identify and name your emotions. Many times when I ask patients to name what they are feeling, they give me a thought instead of a feeling. For example, I would ask, "Lisa, tell me what you are feeling right now as you talk about your last phone call with your mother." She would respond, "I don't understand

---

7 Keri Wiginton, "What Is Emotional Dysregulation?," WebMD, November 3, 2025, www.webmd.com/mental-health/what-is-emotional-dysregulation.

why she can't be happy for me." That's a thought, not a feeling. When I referred Lisa to her feelings list, she was able to figure out that she felt sad. She may very well have been confused by her mother's inability to show happiness for her, but the reality that Lisa was experiencing made her feel sad. Take some time to try it for yourself. When you think about your relationship with your mother, how do you feel? Are you able to differentiate a feeling from a thought? With practice, you can improve your ability to access your feelings.

Practice Mindful Meditation

This involves paying attention to your thoughts and feelings. It's a way to train your attention, choose where you want to direct your attention, and improve your ability to monitor yourself. That is achieved by sitting still, closing your eyes, and not judging your thoughts and feelings, just noticing them. It is a revolutionary step for those who have been consistently told that what they feel or think doesn't matter. You can make time to focus on yourself because you are worthy to be noticed by you. God sees you, but do *you* see you? He knows what you are thinking and feeling, but do *you* know what you are thinking and feeling?

Pay Attention to Your Bodily Sensations

Depending on how we feel about our bodies and our ability to connect to them, this may require a lot of tenderness and patience. You can practice this with an exercise called a body scan, where you sit or lie down in a quiet place, take deep breaths, and imagine a warm, comforting light that you control is scanning your body. Starting at the top of your head, move the light slowly from head to toe, front and back, and as the light moves over certain body parts, notice if you feel any tension, pain, lightness, calm, or distress. We don't pay attention to our bodies until unbearable pain forces us to.

You can also simply start a conversation with your body by asking it, "How do you feel?" I am not saying your physical body is going to verbally speak back to you, but it is a way to lovingly respect it and consider how it is feeling. This is a good practice for when you notice you are experiencing an intense emotion. Pausing to also notice what your body is feeling (rapid heart rate, upset stomach, hand tremors, heavy breathing, chest tightness, jitters, clenched jaw, muscle tension) is very helpful when emotions get intense. What does your body feel like doing? Screaming, crying, punching something, walking, running, sleeping, going numb?

Notice Others' Emotions

Once you are in the habit of checking in with yourself, start noticing the emotions of others around you. Be careful not to assume you know how someone else is feeling. Pay attention to people's body language, facial expressions, and voice intonation. You may even practice noting others' emotions by closing your eyes. Interestingly, research suggests that people are better at identifying others' emotions when they are not looking at the person.[8] Closing your eyes to listen may be challenging in a social situation, but try practicing when "watching" television; close your eyes and see if you can pick up on how the characters in a show are feeling. If you're in a public space like a bus, a café, or a shopping center, I think you'd be fine to close your eyes and practice listening to the emotional states of people talking. (They may even think you are sleeping.)

8 "Best Way to Recognize Emotions in Others: Listen," American Psychological Association, October 10, 2017, www.apa.org/news/press/releases/2017/10/emotions-listen.

Share Your Feelings with Others

It may be a scary thought to begin intentionally sharing your feelings with others if you are not used to doing it, but finding a safe person to be vulnerable with is helpful in your increasing your emotional awareness and strengthening your connections with others. The benefit of sharing is learning. First, someone may agree with your perceptions, which gives you an experience of validation, but they also may disagree with you and challenge your perceptions in a way that isn't disrespectful or harmful. Gentle disagreement helps you consider other perspectives without invalidating your feelings.

Track Patterns of Feelings Associated with Your Behavior

This requires you to observe your feelings in response to various settings, people, and experiences. For instance, when you're at the gym, work, church, or a group dinner or social setting, what feelings show up and what feelings lead to specific behavior? For example, in certain settings, do feelings of shame, low worth, or insecurity cause you to retreat or try to make yourself small or invisible? Or perhaps you notice that these same feelings may cause you to engage in histrionic attention-seeking behavior or become critical and competitive with others. Do some feelings lead to what you would consider positive or negative behavior, and does that behavior reflect your stated values and goals? Ask yourself, *What feelings motivate me, and what feelings inhibit my ability to take action?*

Observe Additional Feelings That Surface When You Have Certain Ones

Not only do our feelings elicit certain behavior, but they can also arouse other feelings. For instance, if you are feeling sad or angry in response to something your mother did or said, you may notice that the sadness and anger provoke you to feel guilt and shame for feeling that way. You may be so used to having your emotions invalidated or having been responsible for your mother's emotions that you quickly feel as though it is wrong for you to have strong emotions toward her. You may begin to tell yourself, *She doesn't mean it, She can't help it,* or *She did give me life, so I should be more grateful.* Noticing this is very helpful in your becoming more emotionally aware and beginning the process of healing from your mother wounds.

Write in a Journal

Writing in a diary or journal is a well-known technique for connecting with and processing emotions. Some people also enjoy creating a video journal that allows them to freely express themselves and talk about their days, experiences, and feelings. Don't put pressure on yourself to attend to your journal every day, but work at being as consistent as possible so you can see the evolution and growth of your expression, vulnerability, insights, and emotional awareness. You can free-flow journal or use prompts. There are several accessible journal prompts for your convenience online.[9]

Try Expressive Art Therapy

Expression therapy can help you process feelings and memories and offers techniques and mediums to encourage you to share your emotions.[10] Engaging in dance, art, music, or drama therapy have all shown positive outcomes for increasing people's emotional awareness and

---

9 "Thirty Journal Prompts for Emotional Awareness and Self Care," Calming Grace, August 2020, www.calminggrace.com/wp-content/uploads/2020/08/Emotional-Awareness-Journal-Prompts.pdf.

10 Jeremy Sutton, "What Is Emotional Awareness? Six Worksheets to Develop EI," PositivePsychology.com, November 24, 2021, https://positivepsychology.com/emotional-awareness/.

overall mental health. Therapy modalities that encourage expression or just implementing these practices into your own life can be helpful.

Take Your Emotional Pulse

Throughout the day, take a moment to check in with yourself and ask, *How am I feeling?*[11] This doesn't have to be only in response to a dramatic event, but rather you want to build the habit of considering, noticing, and identifying your feelings. You can do that several times a day even. You are constantly receiving stimuli that you are reacting to, and checking in with your feelings increases your emotional awareness and gives you invaluable data on who and what make your feelings change and when that takes place.

Practice Self-Compassion

Practicing self-compassion helps you acknowledge your full humanity. It also involves acknowledging that we all have flaws and weaknesses and make mistakes and that we are not alone in our feelings. When we have a mother wound, either we are tempted to retreat or overlook any personal weakness because we have been taught that weakness means we are bad, or we embrace seeing ourselves as only all bad and harshly judge ourselves with no grace.

Having self-compassion isn't about being nice to yourself; it's more about being honest about yourself, which is one of the kindest things you can do for yourself. Honesty opens the door for accountability, growth, and grace. Over time, increased emotional awareness leads to increased emotional regulation, thereby replacing your feelings as the boss of your life with important data. As you learn to steward your

---

11 Bernard Golden, "Ten Ways to Increase Your Emotional Awareness," *Psychology Today,* October 9, 2023, www.psychologytoday.com/us/blog/overcoming-destructive-anger/202310/10-ways-to-increase-your-emotional-awareness/amp.

emotions, you'll get better at making healthier and wiser executive decisions that reflect the person you desire to be.

Insecurities

Insecurity is defined as "a feeling of inadequacy, lack of self-confidence, and inability to cope, accompanied by general uncertainty and anxiety about one's goals, abilities, or relationships with others."[12] When insecurity is chronic, it impedes daily life functioning, one's mental health, and relationships. Early childhood mother wounds can play a particular role in an adult's insecurities. They can cause instability, low self-worth, and being paralyzed by fear. Identifying the remaining effects of your mother wound and working to make significant changes in those areas can help free you from debilitating insecurities. With each one I share in the following pages, I'll also provide solutions.

LOW SELF-ESTEEM (I'M NOT GOOD ENOUGH)

Low self-esteem means not having a positive view of oneself. Some common signs and symptoms of low self-esteem include the following:[13]

- "Lack of confidence
- External locus of control
- Negative social comparisons
- Trouble asking for help
- Worry and doubt
- Difficulty accepting compliments

---

12 *APA Dictionary of Psychology*, "insecurity," https://dictionary.apa.org/insecurity.

13 Kendra Cherry, "Eleven Signs of Low Self-Esteem," Verywell Mind, December 1, 2025, www.verywellmind.com/signs-of-low-self-esteem-5185978.

- Negative self-talk
- Fear of failure
- Poor outlook for the future
- Lack of boundaries
- Being a people-pleaser"

On the other hand, high self-esteem allows people to develop strong coping skills, handle adversity, improve mental health outcomes, and have success with school, work, and relationships.

Below are some suggestions for how you can begin to improve your self-esteem. Remember, different things work for different people, so be open to trying new things and find what works best for you.

- Challenge negative self-talk and your inner critic.
- Replace the lies with the truth of God's Word.
- Build a positive support system.
- Recognize and celebrate your strengths and accomplishments.
- Take care of your physical health.
- Take on age-related developmental tasks.[14]
- Strive for moral integrity and consistency.
- Challenge yourself by taking calculated risks.

When I had my fourth child, I asked myself a life-changing question: *Sarita, what is one thing you don't think you can do?* I had accom-

14 Kim Maertz, "Strategies to Build Healthy Self-Esteem" (McGill University, August 2020), www.mcgill.ca/counselling/files/counselling/self-esteem_helpful_hints_0.pdf.

plished a lot in my life up to that point—I had two doctorate degrees, a successful private practice, and leadership skills—but I wasn't feeling challenged. When I asked that question, the first answer that popped into my mind was "Run a marathon." As quickly as the thought came, I regretted asking the question. But I said, *Sarita, don't walk the earth feeling like there's something you can't do.* So this non-runner began to walk, then train, and a few years later ran a 5K (3.1 miles), a Broad Street Run (10 miles), the Philadelphia half marathon (13.1 miles), and then the main goal, the Philadelphia marathon (26.2 miles). I can't tell you what that did for my self-confidence. You don't have to run a marathon, but find something to push yourself, and then smash the goal! It will be a game changer for your self-esteem.

INDECISIVENESS

Research suggests that approximately 20 percent of the population is indecisive and that this is a learned behavior.[15] The fear of making the wrong decision weighs heavily on indecisive people, but refusing to make a decision helps them avoid responsibility and blame.[16] While the research is limited for helping us understand the root cause of indecisiveness, for many, the impact of a demanding, controlling, critical, or dictatorial mother can play a role, such as the child's doing what only the mother wanted even if it wasn't what the child wanted. This likely breeds insecurity in decision-making because the child is never taught that their feelings and wants matter, so they learn to rely on only the decisions of their mother for a sense of stability. Although mothers may be the primary decision-maker in early childhood, one

---

15 Laura Hanrahan, "Calling All Indecisive People: Why Are We Like This?," Wondermind, September 15, 2022, www.wondermind.com/article/why-am-i-so-indecisive/.

16 Hanrahan, "Calling All Indecisive People."

of the most important developmental tasks of the child is healthy differentiation, where the child is discovering who they are as a person and forging their own identity. When mothers don't support this natural and necessary growth process, many adult children are left feeling stressed, insecure, and indecisive because they have "the ache of unfinished differentiation business."[17]

One of my former clients was a very successful intensive care unit nurse, whose job required her to make countless life-and-death decisions every day. But when it came to her own life, she was paralyzed by doubt and indecisiveness. Things that seemed less consequential than the decisions she made for patients sent her spinning and desperate for approval and permission. She couldn't decide if she wanted to cut her hair or buy a new car, if she should get a pet, if she really liked the guy she was dating, or what to do for her summer vacation. I noticed that as she processed normal and mundane decisions, she would say such things as "My mother would hate that" or "My mother says I waste money on dumb things." We later unpacked how she grew up in a house where her mother controlled so much of her life that she never learned independence in decision-making and instead just did whatever her mother wanted. That led to her not being able to trust her own thoughts or feel empowered to make her own decisions without someone influencing her. That overflowed into her friendships, too.

Mother wounds rob you of autonomy, your own voice, and a secure self-concept. But there is hope! Think of decision-making as a muscle: The fewer decisions (or reps) you make, the weaker that muscle is. In the case of my client, she had a strong decision-making muscle related to her job performance but a weak one when it came to her personal life. Here are a few practical steps you can take to become less insecure and indecisive.

---

17 Tina Gilbertson, "Differentiation: 'Normal' Estrangement from Parents?," Tina Gilbertson, LPC, March 22, 2014, https://tinagilbertson.com/differentiation/.

Just Say No by Discovering the Power of Differentiation

One of the critical steps of working through insecurities such as indecisiveness is developing a separate will. The first muscle that needs to be strengthened is the "no" muscle because we can't really know who we are until we know who we aren't; that's why babies go through the "no" stage first.[18] You've likely spent many years agreeing in order to be accepted or withdrawing to avoid conflict, so this might be a challenging muscle to develop because it requires you to say no, disagree, or state a different opinion from people you are close to.

Say Yes to You by Getting to Know the Real You

Who am I? is one of the most important questions of life. As Christians, we have a bestowed identity given to us from the Lord; the core of who we are as God's children has been given, secured, and empowered by him. However, that is not all of who you are. He blessed us with a personality, gifts, and callings, and though we are one body in him, we have uniqueness. Strengthening the "say yes to me" muscle isn't about self-centeredness or even saying no to God; rather, it's about embracing all of you, even the parts that you've suppressed, ignored, or minimized to cope with your mother's will dominating your life. Have fun getting in touch with the life you want to live. Get it out of your heart and head and onto paper. Give yourself permission to create a judgment-free zone and just dream.

Realize That All Decisions Aren't Either Good or Bad

We are told that, in Christ, we have a lot of liberty (see Galatians 5:1, 13; 1 Peter 2:16). Everything we choose isn't easily categorized as either

---

18 Henry Cloud and John Townsend, *The Mom Factor* (Zondervan, 1998), 112.

sinful or good. Many choices we have may be God-glorifying options, and we have the privilege of choosing from them. Focus on whether a decision is acceptable to God, not your mother, and explore the numerous options available to you. Prayer is an amazing start to decision-making. When in doubt about what to do, you can always ask God (see James 1:5). Wanting him to give you wisdom for decision-making and seeking his purpose for you turns your focus from the approval of your mother. The controlling and enmeshed mother, whether she intends to or not, places herself in the position of authority and priority over God. Doing his will is what is most important. That is a revolutionary concept for people whose lives were centered around doing the will of "thy mother," and it's possible that your mother's influence has kept you away from God or wary of his goodness in answering and guiding you. Romans 12:2 empowers us to "discern what is the good, pleasing, and perfect will of God." We can trust his will because it is good, pleasing, and perfect. The less we project our feelings about our imperfect and controlling mother onto a perfect God, the easier it will be for us to embrace how his will should influence our own (see Colossians 3:17).

Don't Be Afraid to Make the Wrong Decision

An old adage says, "A bad decision is better than no decision." Indecisive people have a fear of making the wrong decision. They have never been allowed to try new things, test the strength of their choices, or learn to recover and move on from mistakes in decision-making. It is normal to not always make the right choice, but the wisdom gained from failure helps us mature and build character and confidence for better decisions in the future. We've heard the saying "No risk, no reward," but no decision is usually a life with little reward as well.

Give Yourself a Time Limit

Normally, I would discourage rushing a decision, but for those whose indecisiveness can lead to analysis paralysis, the initial strategy of setting a deadline to decide can retrain people to avoid making decisions without the co-signing of others. The Bible teaches us that there is safety in a multitude of counselors (see Proverbs 11:14), but that Scripture doesn't mean to depend on others' opinions without ever trusting your own discernment and God's Spirit to lead and guide you. There is wisdom in consulting wise and reliable friends and leaders if needed, but the goal is also to get you in the habit of not fearing making a final decision. You want to strengthen your self-leadership capacity, which doesn't have to mean rebelling against being led by God; rather, self-leadership for the Christian is using God's wisdom to make decisions for one's life. Seeking accountability by setting a firm deadline on less risky decisions will be helpful as you build your confidence to think for yourself.

Relationships

At the core, mother wounds are relational injuries. The mother or mother figure is the most impactful relationship in your life, and the quality of health in that relationship has significant ramifications for all your other relationships. Identifying and understanding how it's affected you is essential for beginning the process of unlearning, personally growing, and strengthening all your relationships in the present and future. That's the goal of this section: to figure out what's contributed to some of your relationships being unwell and to begin the process of introducing truths and practices that will help you live better. We will discuss how our mother wounds affect our relationships with romantic partners, our children, other maternal or authoritative figures, and God. Many of the lessons I will write about can be helpful in other types of relationships as well.

ATTRACTING PEOPLE LIKE OUR MOTHERS

Almost every person I've ever talked to about their mother wounds expresses having moments when they said something like this to themselves: *When I get away from my mother [or out of this house], I will never let someone treat me like she did.* The vows we make to ourselves often help us survive situations that feel unending, stifling, and painful. They also encourage hope for a time in the not-so-distant future when we will get the opportunity to experience an intimate, trusting relationship in which we are loved, protected, and valued and our needs matter to the other person.

We don't get to choose our mothers, but we do get to choose our significant others, and if you have been wounded by your mother, typically her characteristics are not exactly what you are looking for. However, while they may not be what you are looking for, they may be what you are mysteriously attracted to. Often there are parts of her and her dysfunctional relational style that you experienced growing up that are in the person you choose to like, love, or marry. How could this be?

I want to anchor our understanding of this phenomenon in science. Lindsay C. Gibson has described how our brains interpret safety, which causes us to attract people most like our mothers:

> The most primitive parts of our brain tell us that safety lies in familiarity. . . . We gravitate to situations we have had experience with because we know how to deal with them. As children, we don't recognize our parents' limitations, because seeing our parents as immature or flawed is frightening. Unfortunately, by denying the painful truth about our parents, we aren't able to recognize similarly hurtful people in future relationships. Denial makes us repeat the same situation over and over because we never see it coming the next time.[19]

---

19 Lindsay C. Gibson, *Adult Children of Emotionally Immature Parents: How to Heal from Distant, Rejecting, or Self-Involved Parents* (New Harbinger, 2015), 11–12.

The following chart I created provides some examples of how a partner's behavior similar to one's mother's behavior can be displayed in the romantic relationship:

MOTHER TRAIT	PARTNER TRAIT	PARTNER BEHAVIOR
Emotionally Unavailable	Emotionally Unavailable	Isn't vulnerable. Minimizes their own experiences of trauma and tragedy. Considers it a strength to avoid or adopt a "move-on" mentality. Doesn't prioritize time and attention despite requests. Complains about or has a low tolerance for your emotions. Doesn't prioritize talking and sharing deeply. Blows up or feels accused if you share difficult emotions. Does acts of service, buys things, cooks, but struggles to connect in a deep, meaningful way. Only connects sex to intimacy and affection.
Controlling	Controlling	Wants you to dress and wear your hair a certain way but doesn't embrace your style or desires. Shows displeasure if you have a different opinion from them. Plays the victim or accuses you of not loving them if you don't do what they want. Tracks your movements and demands you check in with them, calling it "safety," but it feels controlling.
Verbally Abusive	Verbally Abusive	Calls you names, belittles your life and choices, screams, curses you out, makes fun of your appearance and ideas.
Angry/ Abusive/ Emotionally Dysregulated	Angry/ Abusive/ Emotionally Dysregulated	Avoids conflict, hits, kicks, slaps, grabs, pinches, shakes, or insists on painful "play fighting." Acts one way in public, but behind the scenes it's another person. Doesn't believe someone can rape their spouse. Ignores your refusal of sex. Gives the silent treatment and doesn't return texts or calls. Throws things, intimidates with their words and actions. Reactions are overblown or disproportionate.

MOTHER TRAIT	PARTNER TRAIT	PARTNER BEHAVIOR
Manipulative	Manipulative	Withholds affection to get you to do what they want. Plays the victim, makes you responsible for their feelings and happiness. Threatens to harm themselves. Wants you to normalize very quickly and receive them warmly after an argument or disagreement. Gaslights you by blaming you for the relationship problems without ever taking responsibility.
Immature	Immature	Not dependable and expects you to be the caretaker of their feelings and life. Frequently complains, looks for pity and rescuing, doesn't make mature or reasonable decisions, is unable to handle age-appropriate tasks.
Jealous	Jealous	Unable to celebrate your success, gets quiet when you share positive news about your life, makes you reassure them that your success won't go to your head or cause you to leave them. Speaks negatively to others about what you are doing. Talks about what they couldn't achieve in their life and constantly compares themselves to you. Is more engaged when you struggle, something doesn't go well, or you are disappointed by a failure or dream deferred but unable to engage when you succeed. Makes you feel like you had an unfair advantage or privilege when you accomplish something instead of honoring your hard work and efforts.

We might not date or marry people who are totally like our mothers, but often the significant ways we were wounded, if not acknowledged and healed, will show in what we attract into our lives. We re-create in our romantic partners the types of relationships we desperately think we want to avoid.

BECOMING LIKE OUR MOTHERS

What many people loathe to face or admit is not so much when we have attracted our mother but rather when we've become her in our romantic relationships. Author Kara-Leah Grant describes her journey of noticing ways she had become like her mother:

> One of my strongest memories of my mother as a child is her passionate declaration that she would never bring us up the way her mother brought her up. She grew up with an Angry Mother and coming home from school, she never knew what she would find upon entering the house. My mother described it as walking on eggshells and always being in fear of triggering the anger.
>
> To her credit, my mother kept her word. She didn't bring us up like she was brought up. Instead, she suppressed her own anger and her own needs and, not knowing what she really felt, she was often emotionally distant. . . .
>
> No, she wasn't the angry mother—she was the flipside of that, the emotionally repressed mother.
>
> And in turn, I too never wanted to turn into my mother because I saw her as a fearful victim—afraid of what other people thought, afraid of life and afraid of having to take care of herself and three children post-divorce.
>
> I prided myself on being strong, confident and independent and most *definitely* not afraid. Yet I too couldn't escape the patterning of the psyche. I too was just burying my fear so deep I couldn't feel it anymore, just as my mother buried her emotions so deep she couldn't feel them.
>
> I discovered, bit by bit, the buried truth of my being as soon as I got into a romantic relationship—I would turn into my mother, and hate myself for it.[20]

---

20 Kara-Leah Grant, "Is the Mother-Wound Ruining Our Romantic Relationships?,"

I had a client whose story resembled Kara's. Her habit of swallowing her emotions came from her mother, who had done the same to survive an abusive relationship. However, after years of repressing her emotions, my client was beginning to explode in out-of-control anger like a shaken soda can that was opened. She wasn't in an abusive relationship (although she had unresolved trauma from witnessing the abuse of her mother), but she did not feel safe expressing herself freely. She was increasingly having trouble processing and expressing anger appropriately, and that began to affect her relationship with her husband and kids. Thankfully, my client was able to see great improvements when she prioritized learning to name and healthily respond to her feelings and accept anger as an important and useful emotion that deserved to be attended to and expressed properly. She did that by journaling, unpacking her beliefs about anger (she grew up believing that she didn't have the right to be angry and that feeling anger was dangerous), learning not to see her husband as her enemy when she was angry (which created space for her to safely talk to her husband about her needs and disappointments), and developing the awareness that she'd lived most of her life believing she would be penalized or harmed and lose those she loved (as her mother had feared) if her authentic feelings, particularly anger, were on display.

And while it will take work, you can become a healthier version of yourself. Surveying your relationships in the past and present, looking for patterns of issues that show up, and working to address them are the only ways to change. That is what I call "performing a relationship autopsy." Take time to dissect your previous relationships to discover why they were sick and died. Look for common illnesses, dysfunctional patterns, and diseased parts (communication, intimacy, trust, safety, respect, joy, freedom, violence, control, spirituality) to better see what you were subconsciously complicit in attracting and creating. It

---

Elephant Journal, April 13, 2014, www.elephantjournal.com/2014/04/is-the-mother-wound-ruining-our-romantic-relationships/.

takes time, intentionality, and most likely additional support from trained professionals to help you identify and heal the wounds, reprogram your mind, and work on behavioral change. Healing is not a destination but rather a lifelong process of growth: increasing one's capacity, development, wisdom, and skills building.

It is also a work of the Spirit to bring about the healing and transformation we need. A part of lasting change is learning the kingdom's culture, taking off the old (including the culture your mother created for the household), and putting on the new. It involves being submitted to a new leadership structure (where God is the head), learning a new language through Scripture, following a different set of rules, being made to look less like your natural self and more like Christ, and relating to others in a new way.

Maybe you feel overwhelmed by that challenge, but the good news is you don't fully do the work on your own (see Galatians 2:20). Instead of feeling as though you are running from the actions and attitudes of your ancestors, focus your attention on running toward Christ (see Colossians 3:1–10). We are made new in him, and if we pursue him and his Word for direction and are in healthy community filled with godly discipleship, leadership, and friendship, we will have the counsel, help, resources, accountability, and examples we need to avoid repeating the negative patterns of our past.

It is . . . a work of the Spirit to bring about the healing and transformation we need.

IMPROVING OUR RELATIONSHIPS WITH OUR CHILDREN

How you were mothered will likely play a role, for better or worse, in how you show up as a parent. We've heard it before that "you learn what you live." The implicit and explicit lessons from our childhood are downloaded information for how we think about ourselves as parents and about the children we are called to love and raise. The potential impact on children is substantial. As a result of our becoming one or more of the types of mothers mentioned in chapter 3, we might also engage in one or both of the following two forms of parenting.

1. Anger-Based Parenting

A painful or difficult childhood experience can be a strong motivator for healing and intensify your desire to guard your own children against having to go through what you did. However, when we treat them as measuring sticks of how much better parents we are than our mothers, we unknowingly use their young lives as proof that we haven't fallen short or failed like our mothers. Instead of focusing on raising your children, you are fighting the ghost of your mother, proving that not only did you survive her, but you didn't become her. Anger-based parenting can show up in a number of ways. Here are two of them:

1. **Performing in front of your mother.** If your mother is still living and bearing witness to your family, you may subconsciously be getting in digs at her, showing her through your upstanding parenting what she didn't provide. If your child is crying in front of her, you might say, "It's okay to cry, sweetie; I was never allowed to cry when I was your age, but I want you to know that crying is okay." Or if your child asks to hang out with friends or get a piercing, you might say, "Absolutely you can; I want you to enjoy your life and try new things since I never got to do that when I was your age." Perhaps you want your mother to see you apologize to your child for some minor wrong you did that upset your child. The point is you want her to witness your giving your child what your mother didn't give you, letting her know you believe she was wrong or withheld something from you that you needed.

2. **Critiquing your mother in front of your child.** This might take the form of sharing examples of how your mother was not a good mother in your view, getting your child to agree, and getting your child to see how you are vastly different from your mother. In essence, you are encouraging your child to compare you to your mother. You might say, "Your grandmother has a terrible temper, but I'm much calmer than she is, don't you think?" Or "When your grandmother buys you things, she's trying to make up for what she didn't do for me." It may also be more subtle, such as undermining the grandmother's discipline of the child by your being permissive and saying, "That's just how she is; she's always been like that."

That kind of parenting is the outgrowth of your anger. The sad consequence of it is the impact on your child. Instead of your parenting being fueled by love for your child, it's fueled by resentment for your mother. Consequences that your child may face may include anxiety about having to choose whom to love—you or your mother—when the child likely loves both. This behavior promotes triangulation, requiring your child to take your side and show you ultimate loyalty at the expense of their relationship with their grandmother. This can cause psychological distress for the child; it may also encourage the child to see their grandmother in only a negative light, which could enable dishonor and disrespect of their grandmother. Children are also much more astute and observant than people often give them credit for. This behavior teaches a passive-aggressive conflict style and can have the opposite effect of what you desire, which is to present yourself as the healthy and evolved parent. You may instead fuel resentment from your child toward you.

Change is possible. It first starts with owning whether anger-based parenting is something you do. Besides getting help for your painful relationship with your mother, you can improve your parenting by deciding what kind of mother you want to be instead of opposing her. Dream of and pursue who you want to be and what God calls women to be as mothers so that truth can be your guide. Also, begin to make note of how much you think about your mother when you make decisions for your family or engage with your child. If your mother is always on your mind, that is a clue that you've centered her in your parenting experience instead of centering Christ. Along with following Christ, it may be helpful to find mother mentors who can be great examples for you to aspire to. These women can encourage your parenting to be powered by their strengths instead of angered by your mother's weaknesses.

Anger is often a secondary emotion. That doesn't mean it is unimportant; rather, it means the anger often acts as a shield that covers more vulnerable and distressing feelings. Anger is often the part we can see; however, it is important to get to the root cause. It will be helpful to acknowledge the anger that shows up in your own parenting (and other relationships, for that matter), sit with it, listen to it, and over time try to identify some of the primary emotions (rejection, sadness, grief, shame, anxiety, loneliness, powerlessness) that we cover or have a difficult time accessing or expressing.[21]

Galatians 6:8 tells us, "Whoever sows to please their flesh, from the flesh will reap destruction; whoever sows to please the Spirit, from the Spirit will reap eternal life" (NIV). Sow into your child from a pure place where your child (not your mother) is the focus. Sow the seeds that produce the fruit of the Spirit. Sow commitment to them and their happiness and well-being instead of using them as a comparison trap with your mother.

---

21 Gabrielle Ilagan, "Anger as a Secondary Emotion: What's Important to Know," Manhattan Center for CBT, August 19, 2024, https://manhattancbt.com/anger-secondary-emotion/.

Can I keep it real with you? It's a big waste of time to try to show your mother you are better than she is. Most likely, if you have a very unhealthy mother, she is not aware of her faults and failures to the degree that you may hope. Her lack of insight into her own psychopathology and the pain she causes, as well as her limited emotional awareness, is exactly why she injured you in the first place. Say these words out loud, in the kindest voice you can muster: "I have nothing to prove to my mother, but I do have beautiful children God gave me to raise." My dear sister, I am sorry for what your mother didn't give you, I am sorry for what she did, but just keep doing your very best to love yourself and your child. Give it to God.

2. Fear-Based Parenting

Unlike anger-based parenting, fear-based parenting is rooted in anxiety and worry that you as a parent will somehow injure your children the way your mother injured you. Fear-based parenting is ruled by an excessive pursuit (even to the detriment of your children) to escape what feels like unavoidably being a repeat of your mother. For example, if your mother never attended your sporting events, you may feel pressure to attend all your kids' events or more than are reasonable with your work schedule. If your mother was harsh with her discipline, you may become very permissive or avoid discipline altogether. If your mother always dismissed your feelings, you may feel pressure to let your children vent for an excessive amount of time because you were never able to. If your mother didn't buy you many things other than necessities, you may go overboard with spending money on material items for your kids.

Fear-based parenting may also look like frequently asking your children for feedback on your parenting. Perhaps you are consumed with being perfect or your parenting practices can be characterized as unhealthily overcorrecting for the pains of your childhood. Fear-based parenting can also lead to overprotecting and stifling our children by trying to manage and limit their exposure to pain. When adults are afraid of turning into their mothers and thereby injuring their children, they may opt out of the duties of parenting and just become their children's friends. Some avoid parenting altogether by refusing to have kids.

In an attempt to avoid being like our mothers, we might underprotect since we're blinded by our anger toward our mothers, or we parent from fragility and self-judgment, overprotect, or avoid parenting fully to escape the chance of failure.

Both anger-based and fear-based parenting reveal a lack of healing from your own mother wound. However, you are able to become more self-aware, resilient, intentional, self-assured, and proactive instead of reactive in parenting.

We cannot escape the reality that our mothers have had a powerful influence on our lives, but here is the beautiful truth about people who've survived earthquakes: After an earthquake, the damage is assessed, repairs are made, and structures are reinforced to protect against new earthquakes or aftershocks in the future. The people affected choose to move on without living in constant fear of what's coming next.

There is a healthy acceptance that when pain comes, the ground of your life may shake, but it doesn't have to paralyze you or rob you of joy. No matter what the residual impact of your mother wound is, you must face the truths that you can cling to: that you can heal, you can change, and you can be the person God created you to be. You may look like her, you may sometimes sound and act like her, but say it with me: "I am not my mother."

REFLECTION QUESTIONS

1. *What suggestions from this chapter on strengthening emotional awareness will you try? What practices are you already doing?*
2. *In what ways have you struggled with insecurity and indecisiveness?*
3. *Have you ever attracted a partner who had similar behavior to that of your mother? In what ways can you see yourself reflecting similar thinking or behavior to your mother? How does that make you feel?*
4. *In what ways have your mother wounds influenced your parenting?*

PRAYER

Lord, help me grow in my emotional awareness and identify the ways my relationship with my mother influences my life and relationships with others. Thank you that I know you can rebuild and repair any damage that was done. In Jesus's name, amen.

CHAPTER 5

THE FUNERAL

GRIEVING THE MOTHER YOU NEVER HAD

Blessed are those who mourn,
for they will be comforted.

—MATTHEW 5:4

A few years ago, I was a guest speaker at Jackie Hill Perry's Glory Conference in Dallas. During our question and answer session, a woman unassumingly approached the microphone and calmly asked, "I was just wondering if you all have thoughts or wisdom for people who don't have strong relationships with their mother." She also asked how to honor her mother (although that was edited out of the video clip that was on social media). Jackie shifted her eyes over to me as if to say, *You take this one.* Sometimes she and I would smirk as we passed off questions to each other, but this time she felt the weight of the moment; it was no laughing matter. I took a deep breath, whispered a prayer to the Lord, and did my best to empathically sit with this sister as the grief oozed from her question. It wasn't just a question; it was a cry for help.

Every woman in the room seemed to lean in as if they'd asked the question for themselves. The thing about Q&A sessions is that one person stands and asks for thousands. (Later, this question was asked for over a million people as the video clip of this moment went viral on social media, and no one response I could ever give has the power to reach and heal diverse hearts and hurts unless heaven sends the answer.) I felt the Lord with me in that moment. I lowered my voice to almost a whisper, slowed my pace, and locked my eyes on her face, as if she were the only person in the room. What follows is a portion of my response to her:

> I don't ever think you grow out of needing your mom. Even people who have lost their mother in terms of they're deceased—that's a deep, deep pain. But it's also painful to have your mother alive and feel like you don't have her and for you to be full grown and there's like a baby in you, there's a little girl in you, that still wants to be cared for and encouraged and affirmed [and] still needs attention. I want to affirm that that desire you have is good. . . . When we say . . . , "Honor your mother and father so that your days may be long upon the earth," . . . this is the only command given with a promise. Parents like to quote that for disobedient children, . . . but I think it's also important for us [to consider], What does that look like when you're an adult? What does it look like to honor your mother when sometimes they haven't even lived an honorable life? So, first thing I would say in order for you to love your mom well and build a relationship with her and to honor her is to first grieve the loss of the mother you wish you had, and in some ways, many of us . . . have to have . . . a funeral in our own hearts and mind for the fantasy mom that [we] have to bury because she does not exist. . . . I think grief, real grieving, has to precede your ability to really love, because sometimes we're loving a ghost [of a mother] and we're not loving the actual woman and who she really is.[1]

---

1 Jackie Hill Perry (@jackiehillperry), Instagram video, September 26, 2023, www.instagram.com/reel/Cxp-ocNLv2n/?igsh=MWY1bGM0Z3ZhM2prZg==.

I say the same thing to you: Grief is the necessary first step of healing and continues to be an integral part of the process. We may not understand grief or know how to grieve well. Some truths about grief are universally accepted: Grief shows up at unexpected times, has no expiration date, can't be rushed, must not be avoided, can be a teacher though is often disguised as an enemy, is evidence of love, and is a language we should be fluent in.[2]

Grieving the mother you never had is indeed challenging, but on the other side, you will experience a more authentic, liberated, and Spirit-empowered life.

I won't restate the many faces and experiences of grief here. What I will aim to do is dive deeper into what I believe is one essential step of grief for those who have a mother wound: grieving the mother you didn't have by having a funeral for her.

In the ritual of a funeral as a metaphor, each funeral element and corresponding action step will help you answer these liberating questions:

- Why does holding on to the fantasy mother not serve you or your relationship with your real mother?
- What do you need to do to let the fantasy mother go?
- What are the blessings and open doors of opportunities that emerge when the fantasy mother is allowed to die?

Grieving the mother you never had is indeed challenging, but on the other side, you will experience a more authentic, liberated, and Spirit-empowered life.

---

2 Sisters Network Inc. (@sistersnetwork), Instagram video, November 18, 2025, www.instagram.com/reel/DRNSI5cDuj3/?igsh=OWt2OXFjcHc4MDNz. The idea that grief is a language is taught by John Onwuchekwa.

The Fantasy Mother

The "fantasy mother," as I call her, is not your real mother. She is the mother you create from an amalgamation of the mothers you wish you had: your friend's mother, a television mother, the mother you may not even know you deserved to have, and even the type of mother God would want for you based on the biblical standards for mothers we see in Scripture. I am not suggesting the fantasy mother is a form of a delusional disorder; rather, she's the mind's coping mechanism that either denies the reality of who your real mother is or gives you boundless hope for a better day ahead. She is the personification of your childhood needs, and there is a part of you that believes, despite evidence or reason, that one day this mother will walk into your life, sounding sort of out of breath from her long and disoriented journey, and explain her absence, like in these examples:

> "Ooh, child! Sorry I've been gone so long. I was kidnapped and tied up in a basement."

> "I was in a coma."

> "I was stranded on an island, but I prayed to God to help me get back to my baby."

> "I fell at work and bumped my head, and I've had amnesia all these years and couldn't find my way home."

> "I was drugged and started acting insane, and the cops locked me up. It was a case of mistaken identity."

> "Now I'm back, I'm well, and I'm ready to be the mother you need. I love you, and I missed you. This is a miracle to see you again."

We find creative ways to show our real mothers who they could be or demand they become, and we are constantly giving them lines to speak in the mother-child dramas of our imaginations. Every time our real mothers fail by going off script or exiting stage left when they haven't finished their scenes, we are frustrated, angry, and afraid. But if fantasy mothers continue to live in us as a possibility of what our mothers could be, we will keep trying, like Dr. Frankenstein, to make the monsters of our nightmares into the mothers of our dreams. We helplessly stare at our battered, barren, and broken mothers and inside cry or scream like wet, starving babies, "Just try to be like this [fantasy] mother and everything will be fine." Our tight grip on the fantasy mother creates a secondary, self-inflicted wound. It's like standing in front of your favorite restaurant, waiting to be served, and ignoring the sign on the door that reads, "Permanently Closed for Business." Please understand this: Your creation of the fantasy mother makes sense. It seems like a noble idea to the aching heart of the wounded child. The fantasy mother isn't bad; she just isn't real.

The Funeral Ritual

The word *funeral* comes from the Latin root word *funus,* meaning "dead body," so a funeral is the ritual that involves taking care of the dead body. Unlike the natural death of a person, which happens and is beyond your control, the death of the fantasy mother begins with your decision to allow her to die. In fact, it begins with the realization that she was "alive" only through your sheer will, imagination, desperation, and avoidance of suffering. You can't have a funeral for the living.

I know the pain of the death decision all too well. I didn't have to let my fantasy mother die, but I did have to let my real mother die. I will never forget the days leading up to January 13, 2024, when we released her. The doctors gave us all the bad news in the gentlest way possible, and, frankly, it annoyed me. It tugged me between hope and despair. I remember in one of those team meetings, where I heard my father share the gospel with the doctors and tell them what he knew our God could do (all of which I believe too), I was at a point where I just couldn't take it anymore and I blurted out in the meeting, "Give it to me straight: Is my mother ever going to get off the ventilator and breathe on her own?" The room grew cold and silent. The younger doctors and nurses were staring at the ground, waiting for the doctor in charge to tell me the truth. The one with gray hair cleared his throat, leaned in, and said, "We can't say with 100 percent certainty, but all her vitals, her underlying cancer, and her inability to breathe without assistance for this many days all point to the fact that your mother will likely not be able to breathe on her own."

My dad quickly jumped in and said what I expected him to say: "Thank you for your superb care of my wife and your medical opinion, but Jesus has the final say." I just said, "Amen." Two days later—after much prayer, many tears, and a private conversation my dad had with my mother that consisted of her responding to his questions by blinking her eyes and shaking or nodding her head—my father and I made the decision to take my mother off the ventilator and let Jesus have the final say. In truth, we didn't make a death decision; rather, we made a ventilator decision, and Jesus was in control of the rest. Making a decision that could usher someone you love into death is brutal. Although I cannot compare the death of the fantasy mother to taking a loved one off a ventilator, I won't minimize someone's pain. A loss is a loss, and how someone responds to it is none of our business. What I've learned is that the deeper the losses you've suffered, the less arrogant you become in your opinions of grief. If your fantasy mother keeps you from grieving what you have already lost in your real mother, then letting her go may be heart-wrenching for you.

I want to tenderly offer you a blueprint for how you perform a funeral that takes care of the dead body of the fantasy mother and frees and empowers you to live with what is real. As with natural funerals, there are certain rituals that help the living accept death and move through the fire of grief.[3]

WRITE THE OBITUARY

An obituary that is printed in the funeral service program provides a summary of the deceased's life. It includes the person's accomplishments, interests, and family and tells the glowing story minus any negative details that would detract from an honorable tribute. I want to suggest that you write an obituary for your fantasy mother. Take all your hopes, dreams, desires, and expectations you've demanded from and projected onto your real mother in the form of the fantasy mother and write them down. Transfer the conscious and subconscious[4] thoughts and desires about your fantasy mother out of your heart and mind and put them on paper. (This process may take a while, so there's no need to rush.) The goal is to begin to write or speak what you wish you could write about your real mother in an obituary. We often carry hopes and desires, wants and expectations, in us but aren't always aware enough to name them. Writing the obituary puts "meat on the bones" of the abstract fantasy mothers in our heads. But remember, we aren't funeralizing actual women; we're funeralizing ideas. We aren't burying mothers; we're burying dreams (see Proverbs 13:12).

---

3 The funeral ritual is a metaphor for grieving the mother you didn't have.

4 The subconscious mind is also referred to as the nonconscious mind and represents the part of the mind that operates outside our conscious awareness but significantly influences our thoughts, emotions, and behavior. The subconscious mind is made up of a range of mental processes that are not actively in focus, including automatic actions, habits, and deeply ingrained beliefs. Journaling is one tool often suggested to help access the subconscious mind; therefore, consider the task of writing an obituary for the fantasy mother a journaling exercise to see what thoughts and feelings come up for you. If you are more of a verbal processor, begin by freestyling the obituary—that is, "talking" yourself into learning and discovery.

VIEW THE BODY

News of the death of a loved one is always somewhat abstract until you see their body in the casket. That's why many people often avoid viewing the body, saying, "I don't want to see them like that [dead]; I want to remember them the way I experienced them [alive]." I get it. Viewing the body is a jarring wake-up call. It helps and it hurts. It helps snatch us from the denial of death, and it hurts because often it is the first significant heart singe from the fire of grief.

Visualizing the fantasy mother as deceased is helpful for releasing her; it will help and it will hurt. The fantasy mother may look different than your real mother, depending on how you constructed her in your mind, or she may look like your mother, just with untrue, incomplete, or exaggerated character traits and experiences attached to her. Viewing the body isn't meant to be morbid; rather, it's an exercise to create distance from what is not real. That can be accomplished through visualization, but instead of imagining a physical body in a casket, you can imagine the obituary that you write and place in the casket. Or you can draw a box to represent the casket and write inside all the characteristics, narratives, and longed-for interactions and experiences that are not your actual mother or never occurred. Writing out the imagined or incomplete story of your mother wound is important. We can carry imagined or exaggerated stories about the living and the dead that aren't helpful. My father did that with his deceased mother. It wasn't until my father was well into his fifties in seminary for a doctor of ministry in Christian marriage and family therapy that he came face-to-face with the buried anger and grief he carried about her.

After it was discovered that my father's father had an affair with his mother's friend, my father's mother left the family (this was in the 1950s) and never came back. She left her cheating husband (who my father was also angry with) and her six children, two girls and four boys, ages six, eleven, thirteen, fifteen, seventeen, and nineteen. But my dad rarely told that story about his mother, and when he did, he would leave out the suffering he experienced from her abandonment. Growing up, the stories I'd heard about his mother were only of how wonderful, loving, supportive, and kind she was and what a great cook and seamstress she was. Those things may have been true experiences my dad had with his mother.

However, if my father was only eleven years old when his mother left him, his memories were incomplete stories. What he left out were the pieces that drastically affected my dad and his five siblings, who all manifested their mother wound of abandonment in various ways. Using the empty-chair technique,[5] my father's professors in his counseling program helped him dig deep into his pain, resurrect the truth, and bury the lie of who his mother was. He said it was gut-wrenching yet freeing. Now my father can tell a truthful story about his mother, mixed with the heartache and the real love he has for a woman who for so many years he was unable to speak honestly about.

We often think telling the truth about someone who hurt us means we don't love them, but what is more loving than being willing to see people accurately? My dad is eighty-three years old and says he's forgiven his mother. He still loves her and thinks about her every day. The version of his mother that was a fantasy died, and he was free to love his real mother by embracing the reality of the pain she caused and holding on to the beautiful accurate memories he has.

The body of your fantasy mother may represent the whole story of a narrative you've sanitized by leaving out the bad, the positive characteristics your real mother doesn't possess, or the longed-for experi-

---

5 The empty-chair technique is "a technique originating in gestalt therapy in which the client conducts an emotional dialogue with some aspect of themself or some significant person (e.g., a parent), who is imagined to be sitting in an empty chair during the session. The client then exchanges chairs and takes the role of that aspect or of that other person. This technique is now sometimes also referred to as the two-chair technique"; *APA Dictionary of Psychology*, "empty-chair technique," https://dictionary.apa.org/empty-chair-technique.

ences she didn't provide. Here are some examples of longed-for experiences:

- Your unfulfilled dreams of traveling together, her babysitting your children, or her getting you gifts for your birthday that reflect she knows what you like and wants to see you happy
- Your longing to have seen her in the audience at your graduation, athletic events, wedding, dance recitals, or baptism
- The daydreams of having long conversations over tea, snuggled on the couch, where she tells you stories of her childhood, passes on wisdom, and tells you she's proud of you
- The text messages of Scripture, prayers, and words of encouragement you wanted to receive as you started your day
- The memory you wish you had of her in labor and delivery, holding your legs and telling you to push as you birthed your child or her holding your hand as you recovered from surgery
- The home movies and pictures you don't have
- Smiles, words of encouragement, hugs, cooking lessons, shopping trips, and Mother's Day teas and prayer breakfasts

Is this body viewing necessary? you may wonder, especially if you are a Christian. It isn't an affront to the gospel; in fact, it forces us to really confront what we believe about the power of God. Sure, he can heal, but what are we asking him to heal if we don't tell the truth about what is sick? Jesus said that the well don't need a physician (see Matthew 9:12). Sure, God can resurrect dead things back to life, but what are we asking him to resurrect if we don't admit that something in our mother and between us has died?

If we don't bury the fantasy mother, we will never give the Lord the opportunity to ask us the faith question he asked Ezekiel in the middle of hopelessness: "Can these bones [my relationship with my real mother] live?" (Ezekiel 37:3). If we don't view the body of the fantasy mother, we will never view the life of the real mother. If we never view the body of the fantasy mother, we won't enter the fire of grieving the mother we never had. And if we never enter that pain, we will never dare enter the valley of dry bones, where we can get a vision of God's power to restore hope and life to lifeless situations.

EULOGIZE THE FANTASY MOTHER

The eulogies of the dead are an important part of the funeral. Eulogies tell the story of the person's life and impact. However, we all have heard eulogies that leave out negative data about the dead. To effectively eulogize the fantasy mother, it may be helpful to write what the fantasy mother protected you from and provided you with that made her existence necessary. Remember, the fantasy mother is a construction of our wants and needs that buffer us from the reality of what we didn't have. You can write out the eulogy in list form, or you can write it in paragraph form like a typical eulogy. For example, portions of your eulogy may read like one of these examples:

> "My fantasy mother is a safe and doting grandmother, but that's not who my real mother is. And because I've always wanted my real mother to have a relationship with my children, I have at times unwisely endangered my children's emotional or physical safety by giving my real mother access to them that she hasn't earned. I've related to my mother as my safe fantasy mother despite her unchanged behavior."

> "My fantasy mother is a good listener and always gives me great counsel with my best interests in mind; however, that is not who my real mother is. I've wanted my real mother to love me in this way so badly at times that I've unwisely shared sensitive information with her or made myself extremely vulnerable and have been hurt by her inability to show up and care for me."

Who is the woman you always hoped, believed, and prayed would show up but never did? Tell her story and what she means to you and process how you believe your life and relationship with your real mother will change when you say goodbye to the fantasy.

MOURN

Dr. Alan Wolfelt, death educator and grief counselor at the Center for Loss and Life Transition, describes our society as an unfortunate "mourning-avoiding culture" but believes that the more we participate in the rituals of funerals, the more we will normalize a very natural and important aspect of death.[6] Mourning is not limited to only the funeral day and may happen over multiple events, days, and years. My experience has been a little different. Maybe it's a cultural thing, but for the most part, Black people are not averse to mourning; we've been mourning since we entered these shores. I've been to more funerals than I care to remember. Having a father as a pastor and a mother as a church clerk meant we stored obituaries in our home like books and precious artifacts. So many faces of the dead (whom I never knew) were neatly organized and stacked in my parents' china cabinet for safekeeping.

---

6 Alan D. Wolfelt, "Why Is the Funeral Ritual Important?," Center for Loss and Life Transition, December 21, 2023, www.centerforloss.com/2023/12/funeral-ritual-important/.

At the numerous funerals I've attended, I've seen people buckle their knees and pass out under the weight of grief. I've heard the volume and pitch of the ear-piercing screaming, with them stomping and yelling "No!," "Why?," "Mommy," "Daddy," or "Oh God." I've even heard people yell, "Wait!" as the casket is about to be closed. No amount of tissue the ushers passed out could collect all the tears; the anguish of the loss, even of a life well lived, is just too much for some to take. Those, might I add, were Christian funerals where people were grieving with hope (see 1 Thessalonians 4:13). Funerals where the people mourning don't know God and they don't know what comes next are especially heavy, as they don't have the hope that comes in knowing Christ. In all the various forms mourning can appear, it is a necessary part of grief. As hard as it is, it is healthy to feel.

The goal for funeralizing your fantasy mother is to allow yourself to be emotionally aware and feel the emotion, name it, and express it, whether it's anger, anxiousness, sadness, exhaustion, or some other feeling. Allow yourself to mourn as you give up the fantasy mother. You are letting go of her, but you are also letting go of your preferred and idealized image of yourself. Your real mother didn't just cost you access to a great mother; she cost you access to how you wanted your life to look and feel. Her choices—trauma responses, unhealed pain, and possibly the things she could not control that wounded you—changed your life. You lost your dreams and desires for yourself as a child. Mourning hurts but is a prerequisite to healing. Mourning allows you to come face-to-face with what has never been and feel the heat of the hell of grief. If you mourn honestly, the gift it gives is protection from the proclivity to pretend that what you lost doesn't matter. If you need to mourn now, do it. Do whatever you need to do to feel the pain and remind yourself that your loss matters. Please don't rush to keep reading; instead, take a moment and feel the fire. God is with you.

If you took a moment to mourn, what was that like for you? If you need to reach out to a support person, do so. You don't have to go through this without human care.

WORSHIP GOD

Worship is a hallmark of Christian funerals. In the Black church tradition, we have what we call staple funeral songs, such as "I Shall Wear a Crown," "It Is Well with My Soul," "I'll Fly Away," "Yes God Is Real," and the one that always breaks me down into a sobbing mess, "Goin' Up Yonder," because it is the song they often play as the casket is wheeled out of the sanctuary.

Christian worship is a soul soother because we believe that God is good, his will is perfect, and he is in control and worthy of praise. We worship him at funerals because we believe he is due exaltation in every season of life and we know he is the conqueror of sin and death. We know as believers that death does not have the final say and that even in our grief and loss, he is a God of comfort and the troubles of this world have an expiration date.

We worship through song as we elevate our eyes and hearts from the present pain to affirm the goodness and majesty of God. We sing songs that remind us that earth has no sorrow that heaven cannot heal. We worship through the reading of the Word because it reminds us that "weeping may endure for a night, but joy comes in the morning" (Psalm 30:5, NKJV). We set our hope in the gospel, and we let the Epistles order our steps on this Christian journey. Worshipping God in the middle of our grief helps us let go of the fantasy mother, freeing our hands to grab hold of him in a new way. Releasing the made-up parent allows us to cling to the perfect parent, who never fails: "When my father and my mother forsake me, then the LORD will take care of me" (Psalm 27:10, NKJV).

RECEIVE COMFORT FROM OTHERS

Funerals are community projects. No one is supposed to be at a funeral alone. Funerals are for the living, not the dead. Funerals help mourners cope with grief and loss and acknowledge the death of a loved one. The most notable comforters at a funeral are the people who travel near and far to come alongside the family in a time of grief. What you hear at almost every funeral is people saying, "It's so good to see you, but I wish it was under better circumstances," or, "We shouldn't wait until someone dies to come together." Then they trade promises of staying in touch that usually fade over time. However, it is undeniable that there's beauty and power in people showing up with cards, flowers, money, food, hugs, tears, and their presence to help others walk through the pain.

As you prepare to grieve the mother you didn't have, it is important to bring your community in. Trusted people who love you need to know much more than "My mom and I don't get along." When possible, some should be invited into the grief to bear your burdens with you: "Carry one another's burdens; in this way you will fulfill the law of Christ" (Galatians 6:2). Sometimes people know there is trouble between you and your mother but don't know or understand there is loss. Sometimes people know you have been trying to work things out and maintain a relationship but don't know what it's cost you because you were relating to your fantasy mother instead of your real one. Sometimes people experience your anger about your mother but not your sadness, loneliness, confusion, and pain. One of the consistent things I've heard from people living with a mother wound is they feel alone and don't know of anyone else dealing with that kind of injury. Give people a chance to comfort you. When you invite them into the valley of your vulnerability and into the fire of your grief, you may be surprised that some of them have walked through the mother-wound fire like you. They know the path of grief, and perhaps you will get to hear the story of how they survived. The apostle Paul sums up the comfort the Lord gives:

> Blessed be the God and Father of our Lord Jesus Christ, the Father of mercies and the God of all comfort. He comforts us in all our affliction, so that we may be able to comfort those

> who are in any kind of affliction, through the comfort we ourselves receive from God. (2 Corinthians 1:3–4)

BURY YOUR FANTASY MOTHER

The hardest part of my mother's funeral was seeing my mother's casket being lowered into the earth. The committal was the part of the funeral I dreaded the most. It was the finale of my connection to her in the physical and it felt cruel. My mother wasn't perfect, but Etta Mae King Taylor was good. Even though my theology was intact and I knew that what was in the grave was just the shell, that was still the shell that combed my hair, cooked my food, walked me to school, and hugged me. I knew that very soon that body would deteriorate and return to dust. It was the final step of my saying goodbye to my mother on this side of eternity. I liken it to the final cut of the umbilical cord. When we are born from our mothers' wombs, we are still connected to them and must be cut away so that we can live separate lives. I believe the death of a mother is the final invisible umbilical cord that God cuts, this one more painful than the first.

The act of going through the emotional burial for your fantasy mother is like cutting the umbilical cord on your connection to her. No matter how cozy, safe, and protective the womb of your imagination feels, it is necessary for individual growth and flourishing to separate. Burying your fantasy mother aids acceptance and increases your willingness to do life without her. You must separate from the fantasy mother and send her to the deep and dark grave so you can grow in the light—the truth.

Burying your fantasy mother frees you to see your real mother, whether living or dead, in whatever shape or emotional state she is in. It allows you to make peace with the reality of your real mother, even if what you buried seems better. The beauty in burying the fake is that there are always greater possibilities for the real mother. The possibility of an honest but hard conversation, the possibility of repentance and forgiveness, the possibility of time and touch, tears and laughter. Even if it's uncomfortable, there's the possibility of growth, change, and rebuilding of trust or even the possibility to accept that your real mother will never change. The fantasy mother was constructed only to love you, but you were never actually loving her, because she was a lie. Like I said to the woman at the Glory Conference, many of us think we are trying to love our real mothers well by relating to them as fantasy mothers, but we are loving only figments of our imaginations.

Whomever your real mother is revealed to be, remember that the gift of walking through the fire of grief is that what is left will be only what is real. An old, bruised, brown banana is always better than a bright, shiny, plastic fake one. The angels said to those who came to see Jesus's dead body, "Why do you look for the living among the dead?" (Luke 24:5, NIV). Now you, too, will not look for your real mother among the decaying flesh of the fantasy; you can look for your mother in this life. And no matter what you find, no matter how hard it will be, I want you to know that God will be there. May your mother-wound grief sanctify you and make you more like Christ.

PREACH THE GOSPEL

Even though this step isn't in the correct order of the typical funeral program, I saved it for the end. Eulogies are part of most funerals, but what makes Christian funerals different is that the gospel is preached. The eulogy talks about the life of the dead, but the sermon talks about our living God. One of the reasons many Black church traditions call funerals homegoing celebrations is that our faith informs our understanding of death. When a person dies in Christ, their body goes back to the dust of the earth through burial or cremation, but their spirit goes home to be with God (see 2 Corinthians 5:8).

In the case of having a funeral for your fantasy mother and grieving the mother you never had, the gospel still needs to be preached to your soul. The gospel message is one of hope, salvation, and restoration from what sin destroyed. It promises that there is new life coming and an abundant life to be experienced right now. It lifts our heads, wipes our tears, encourages our hearts, and reminds us that our lives are not over, even when everything ends down here on earth.

When you hear the gospel or preach it to yourself, you can transcend the pain of this life. It reminds you that you have victory because Jesus secured it for you when he died in your place on the cross and rose from the dead. Though not all churches do it, one of the reasons I love when the funeral director closes the casket after the viewing before the worship and sermon portions begin is that it symbolically tells the griever to stop looking at who's gone, stop looking at what's dead, stop looking at what you lost, and look to Jesus: your deliverer, sustainer, healer, comforter, savior, redeemer, and friend.

When you hear the gospel or preach it to yourself, you can transcend the pain of this life.

The gospel doesn't ask you to pretend you don't hurt; it just wants to infuse that hurt with hope. As you walk through the fire of grief, remember that Jesus is not afraid to get into the fire with you. Let the Scripture preach the gospel to you. Go to church and hear a Bible-soaked sermon and let the gospel preach to you. Yes, you are called to be an evangelist and ambassador, called to "go tell it on the mountain" (see Luke 2:8–20), but I want to remind you to also tell it to yourself.

We have to grieve that our mothers weren't able to be the kind of mothers we needed, but keeping our fantasy mothers alive will always impede our ability to heal and embrace what is real. If your real mother is deceased, that is a compounded grief that the Lord wants to help you through. Grieving your fantasy mother opens you up to inviting Jesus into that situation, applying the balm of the gospel, and being filled with hope that God can heal, change, and repair what is broken, starting with your heart and also your relationship with your mother.

REFLECTION QUESTIONS

1. *Describe times when you've wanted and related to a fantasy mother you created and not your actual mother. What was the result?*
2. *What aspects of the ritual of a funeral stood out to you, and how does it feel to be encouraged to let the fantasy mother die?*
3. *Have you given yourself permission to lament and grieve that the mother you wish you had is not your real mother? Why is that an important step in your healing?*
4. *How does the good news of the gospel bring hope and peace when burying the fantasy mother?*
5. *What next steps are you willing to take to bury the fantasy mother?*

PRAYER

Lord, thank you that I can live in the truth,
no matter how painful it may be. Thank you for the freedom
to let go of a fantasy mother so I can face with grace
and strength the mother you ordained for me to have.

CHAPTER 6

CAN YOU FEEL A BRAND-NEW DAY?

HEALING YOUR MOTHER WOUNDS STARTS IN THE MIND

Then shall your light break forth like the dawn,
and your healing shall spring up speedily;
your righteousness shall go before you;
the glory of the LORD shall be your rear guard.

—ISAIAH 58:8, ESV

The 1978 film *The Wiz* (an adaptation of *The Wizard of Oz*) is set in an urban environment with a Black cast. There is a famous celebratory scene near the end of the movie in which the Wicked Witch of the West, named Evillene, is defeated. Evillene gets outsmarted by Dorothy (played by Diana Ross) after Dorothy and her friends (Scarecrow, Tin Man, Lion, and Toto) are captured by Evillene's flying monkeys and brought to her sweatshop to be tortured. The goal is for the witch to retrieve Dorothy's magical silver slippers. Evillene was known for terrorizing her captives by stomping through the aisle of her sweatshop and slinging a whip while shouting, "Work, work, work!" and singing her signature upbeat song, "Don't Nobody Bring Me No Bad News."

Dorothy eventually defeats Evillene by using the witch's weakness: water. After the wicked witch is destroyed, you begin to see beautiful people slowly emerge as they strip off the dark, dingy masks and work clothes of the sweatshop, squirming their way into the light like a butterfly escaping its chrysalis. The lighting in the room changes, moving from dusk to dawn, and a dark haze gives way to the brightness of a noon sun as the music hesitantly transitions into an upbeat freedom song.

This celebratory song asks a liberating but introspective question to all those who've been freed from the witch: "Can you feel a brand-new day?" What a profound question. It assumes freedom and a new chance at life has come, but the song asks the freed, "Can you feel it?" God asks a similar question in Scripture: "I am doing a new thing, don't you see it?" (see Isaiah 43:19). As you read those words, wherever you are in the process of healing from your mother wound, take a moment and imagine that your healing may be closer and more achievable than you think.

When your healing "springs up," you will be like the freed cast members in *The Wiz*. The light of your life will get brighter; you will disrobe from the darkness and heaviness that cloaked you like guilt, shame, low self-worth, sadness, isolation, anxiety, victimization, and bitterness; and you will fearlessly and more freely move through the world. That's exactly what the gift of healing offers: an opportunity for the saving light of Christ to break forth. Our healing will spring up quickly, our righteousness will go before us, and the Lord will watch and protect our backs. That's healing—a literally brand-new life! Don't you want that?

I have intentionally wanted healing to be interwoven throughout this book to bring hope and give you strength and care along the way. This chapter, though, will focus more specifically on the *mindset* needed for healing, as "the work" (as we often call it in therapeutic circles) is made up of what we believe, how we choose to think, and then what we do with that new thinking. Having the right mindset is paramount to our healing.

A needed step in our healing is making sure to ask ourselves the right questions. We can turn to Jesus for examples. One thing I love about him is that he often asked a lot of questions. He asked approximately 305 questions that are recorded in the Gospels.[1] In fact, he often asked questions before he performed healing:

- "Who touched me?"—healing the woman who bled for twelve years (see Luke 8:43–48).
- "Do you see anything?"—healing the blind man from Bethsaida (see Mark 8:22–26).
- "Why are you thinking evil things in your hearts? For which is easier: to say, 'Your sins are forgiven,' or to say, 'Get up and walk'?"—healing the paralytic (see Matthew 9:2–8).
- "Do you believe that I can do this?"—healing the two blind men (see Matthew 9:27–31).
- "What do you want me to do for you?"—healing blind Bartimaeus (see Mark 10:46–52).
- "Didn't I tell you that if you believed you would see the glory of God?"—raising Lazarus from the dead (see John 11:38–44).

These questions weren't for his own understanding; he used them as tools for revealing people's faith, unbelief, or underlying emotional or spiritual needs that they may not have been aware of. Sometimes Jesus asked questions prior to healing to engage those in need, invite them to be active participants in their healing, give them agency and responsibility in their healing, and encourage obedience to God.

I want you to begin by asking better questions as a necessary aspect of your healing and notice and attend to the questions Jesus may be

---

1 Zach Zehnder, "The 305 Questions Jesus Asked with One Shocking Discovery," Red Letter Living, November 17, 2022, https://redletterchallenge.com/the-305-questions-jesus-asked-with-one-shocking-discovery/.

asking you from the pages of Scripture. I want to encourage you to not be passive in your journey of healing. One important and active thing you can do is become very curious. Perhaps you, like many others, typically rush to the "healing" chapter of any book because you want to cut straight to the chase and you hope authors will give you a list of things to do to feel better. But what if I told you that healing is not usually formulaic and that checking off a healing to-do list isn't where the most power and transformation are gained?

What is consistently seen in Scripture is that God is always involved in the healing, he is not bound by doing it one way, and he is often doing much more than healing the obvious issue that people see or request his help with. His methods are as diverse as the people, and his providential intervention into human suffering is more than meets the eye. I once heard that "God is always doing 10,000 things in your life, and you may be aware of three of them."[2] That is a powerful and comforting revelation and an important mental shift to make. The idea is that when we think we can see what God is doing in our lives, he is usually never doing just what we can perceive. We don't have perfect knowledge of the past, present, and future to understand his mind and his ways (see Isaiah 55:8–9). In addition to healing your mother wound, could God also be doing the following?

- Growing your faith and dependence on him
- Inviting you to spend more time with him in prayer and Bible study
- Affirming his love and care for you as his child
- Exposing sin in your life that you need to repent of
- Preparing you for future ministry

2 John Piper, "God Is Always Doing Ten Thousand Things in Your Life," Desiring God, January 1, 2013, www.desiringgod.org/articles/god-is-always-doing-10000-things-in-your-life.

- Stirring your gifts and awakening a calling you weren't aware of or abandoned
- Giving you courage to make a change you've been avoiding
- Affirming you aren't alone and allowing you to sense more of his presence
- Encouraging you to go back to therapy or start it for the first time
- Nudging you to reach out to or check on someone (your mother or someone else)
- Giving you strength for a greater challenge ahead
- Healing your grieving heart
- Helping you become a better friend, spouse, or parent
- Prompting you to share your story to help someone else
- Encouraging you to rest
- Telling you to end that relationship you've been holding on to
- Prompting you to forgive someone you swore you could never forgive
- Increasing your gratitude
- Inviting you to bring your questions and doubt to him
- Reminding you of your need for friendship and community
- Developing empathy and understanding for a sibling or another family member
- Prodding you to start discipling someone who's been on your mind but whom you didn't think you had the capacity to take on
- Answering a prayer that you thought he didn't hear or ignored

- Revealing himself to you and inviting you to receive salvation through Jesus

I'm asking you to try a new way of thinking about healing your mother wound, and I want you to become more inquisitive about what else Jesus may be up to in your life as you seek wholeness, clarity, relief, and freedom from what's had you broken and bound.

That's why this chapter is ditching the "ten steps to healing the mother wound" approach and instead tilling the ground of our minds and spirits to ready us for comprehensive healing and total *shalom*. We will address two imperative areas where we need a mental shift for healing. First, we will ask an important but often unasked and presumed question: "Do you *want* to be healed?" Second, we will explore the importance of not avoiding discomfort and why our willingness to increase our capacity for distress is helpful in our healing process.

Do You Want to Be Healed?

I have always been struck by Jesus's interaction with the disabled man by the pool of Bethesda. Scripture teaches us that there were many disabled people with various disabilities (blindness, lameness, paralysis). This man had been disabled for thirty-eight years and had been by this pool for a long time waiting for someone to put him in it. This invalid man apparently held to a popular superstition that the pool periodically was stirred with divine healing power but you had to be the first to enter the water to be miraculously healed.[3] Jesus didn't just *see* this man; he also *knew* he'd had this condition for a long time (see John 5:6, NASB). While some commentators suggest Jesus found out about this man from inquiry or reports from others, the Greek participle *gnous* suggests he also used supernatural knowledge, and unlike

3 D. A. Carson, *The Gospel According to John,* The Pillar New Testament Commentary (Eerdmans, 1990), 243.

the paralytic man who was lowered in front of Jesus through a hole in the roof (see Mark 2:1–12), this man at Bethesda is the recipient of God's sovereign initiative because Jesus came to him.[4]

That is the beauty of Jesus's role in our healing. From the beginning of time, God has always made the first move toward us to offer us the healing we need. Jesus left glory on a rescue mission to save us; he comes after us when we are lost. He sees us, knows we need healing, and is ready and willing to provide it.

From the beginning of time, God has always made the first move toward us to offer us the healing we need.

Jesus doesn't offer the paralyzed man money, food, or a piggyback ride to the pool; rather, he asks him a direct and seemingly ridiculous question for a disabled person: "Do you want to be healed?" (John 5:6, ESV). I always wondered why Jesus doesn't just heal him since it's clear he needs healing and the man has positioned himself by a pool he believed could give him that healing. But Jesus isn't mocking him; he's revealing a mindset that is one of the core issues often connected to our lack of healing.

I believe Jesus's question "Do you want to be healed?" is twofold. First, it establishes that the first step to wholeness is to recognize your deep need for healing and have a desire for it. Second, it reflects Jesus's style of elliptical offers[5] that we see throughout the gospel of John (4:10; 6:32–33).[6] That means Jesus is asking the man to consider if he wants to be well, possibly exposing that if he does want healing, he is in the wrong place and depending on the wrong people. Jesus is offering himself to him as the only one who can make his body well but

---

4 Carson, *Gospel According to John*, 243.

5 An elliptical offer of Jesus refers to the way he presents his teachings, or truth, in a concise or potentially indirect manner that invites the listener to engage more deeply and discover the meaning behind his communication.

6 Carson, *Gospel According to John*, 243.

also deal with his true malady: his sin. What is shocking about this exchange is that Jesus asks this desperate man a question about healing and the man's answer is not affirmatively "Yes, I want to be healed"; rather, the disabled man responds by calling Jesus "Sir,"[7] a clue that he does not recognize him as the Messiah. Instead of following with "Yes, I want to be healed," he responds by complaining. The man tells Jesus that he never has anyone to help him get into the pool at the right moment and that when he does try to get in, someone jumps in front of him, blocking his chance to be healed.

That makes me think about how many of us can act similarly when we need healing. Instead of taking advantage of the access we have to Jesus, our hope is in another plan, path, potion, pool, or person. Perhaps you really want to be healed but have spent so many years in this emotional condition, so many years disappointed, that your "mat"—a symbol of your problem, burden, and perceived helplessness—has become your comfort zone and you are unwilling to try something new. Has your mat become your identity? Is it so hard for you to imagine yourself apart from your sickness, emotional pain, and narratives about the struggles with your mother that parting with the mat would feel like losing yourself? Maybe your identity as a wounded mat dweller gets you attention, pity, and spare change (empathic onlookers who you've shared your story with a million times). I understand the resignation. I understand the disappointment. I also understand that when the healing is available and the Healer is right in front of you, you may not even recognize or want the healing.

What I love about Jesus is that even though the lame man gave no answer to his actual question, that didn't stop Jesus from healing him. Jesus didn't say anything about how the man avoided his question; he just said, "Get up. . . . Pick up your mat and walk" (John 5:8). Then Scripture tells us, "Instantly the man got well, picked up his mat, and

---

7 Carson, *Gospel According to John,* 243.

started to walk" (verse 9). I can't help but notice that in every word-for-word translation of the Bible, there is a three-part result described in the healing. First, he instantly got well, then he picked up his mat, and then he started to walk. I just wonder if when the man "got well," it was healing for not only his body but also his mind. What if Jesus had just instantly healed his legs but the man did not believe or was so emotionally broken and discouraged that he refused to trust and obey God's command to "get up"? Maybe Jesus healed the man's body *and* his mind. Maybe a healed mind led to him trusting Jesus enough to follow his instructions to pick up the mat and get up. Maybe he had to let go of some things mentally, such as blaming others for his condition, resignation to sit on the mat, or avoidance of direct questions from someone who had the power to help him.

In addition to the pain you have about your relationship with your mother, what aspects of your thinking may Jesus need to heal? If he healed your emotional pain right now, would there still be anything in the way that would hinder your ability to get up and walk—that is, live your life as God has called you to live? Jesus is willing and able to heal your mother wounds, but maybe before you can get up, he must first heal that part of your mind that gave up.

Are you, in any way, like that lame man at the pool of Bethesda, struggling with your "want to"? Do you need healing? Is Jesus asking you about your desire to be healed, and are you avoiding his question by blaming someone else for your not being healed? Are you struggling to directly answer the question "Do you want to be healed?" If Jesus asked you, "Do you want to be healed of your mother wound?" which of the following statements would you use as excuses?

- *I have tried to talk to her so many times, but she just doesn't see herself.*
- *I offered to go to counseling with her, but she didn't want to go.*
- *I tried therapy, but it didn't work.*

- *I just decided to be the bigger person and stop talking about how she hurt me.*
- *Things will never change.*
- *She had a hard life, and I feel sorry for her. I can live with what she did to me.*
- *I will never trust her again. I will not speak to her again.*
- *Every time I try bringing up issues to my family, I'm treated like the bad guy, so I'm not going to try.*
- *She will never apologize, and even if she does, it's just a matter of time before her real self resurfaces.*
- *She never abused me, so it's not that bad.*
- *My own siblings know she treats me worse, but they don't defend me or talk to her about her behavior.*
- *My father/aunt/uncle just says, "You know how your mother is."*
- *I'm fine; it is what it is.*

Has the hurt, despair, and longevity of the problem bruised your desire to want healing for yourself? Do you associate your potential for healing with whether your mother heals? Are you afraid to hope and awaken the desire to be healed because you don't want to be disappointed again? Have you over-spiritualized your pain and engaged in spiritual bypassing, believing Jesus must want this suffering for you since he didn't stop it? Have you resigned to living on your mat with the brokenness of your relationship with your mother and with a broken heart, broken dreams, broken self-image, and broken future because you can't imagine it could get better?

Here is the good news: Even if you have given up, even if your desire to heal has been injured, that doesn't stop Jesus. I pray in his mighty name that you will get your "want to" back. I pray that you will recognize who Jesus is and the power he has a lot sooner than that lame man on the mat who at first only called him "Sir." I pray you can hear Jesus asking you a question he already knows the answer to: "Do you, ________ [insert your name], want to be healed?" Notice in the text that Jesus doesn't say, "Get up and throw your mat away." He just says, "Pick up your mat." That may be symbolic of us having to learn how to walk and live with our issues. Our problems may not immediately go away (if ever), we may still struggle with emotional difficulty as we are healing, but we can still walk. Healing takes time, it's a process, it's messy, it's nonlinear, we make progress, and we slide backward as we are healing. That's all normal. Being stuck sitting on a mat and walking with a mat are worlds apart; you can hold your struggles instead of your struggles holding you. I'd rather get up and go with my mat than be glued to it. What about you?

Are You Willing to Have Discomfort and Challenges as You Heal?

As Christians, we talk a lot about the Cross and Jesus's sacrifice on Calvary, and rightly so. It is the apex of the gospel message, and our faith hinges on his dying for our sins and being raised on the third day. That is why we celebrate and feel tremendous gratitude to our Lord. But one thing he did that we all know about but gets far less attention is what happened in the Garden of Gethsemane. My faith is rooted in what happened on the cross, but my willingness to endure and align my will to the Father's has been encouraged by what happened in the garden.

If Jesus had not exchanged his will for the Father's and made peace with accepting the bitter cup of death, he never would have finished the mission he came to earth for. There would be no Golgotha if there had been no Gethsemane. It was in the Garden of Gethsemane that Jesus made the decision to embrace suffering and submit to the Father's will even though he didn't want to. It was in the Garden of Gethsemane that Jesus increased his willingness to do the hard thing

> My willingness to endure and align my will to the Father's has been encouraged by what happened in the garden.

for the greater good. He wrestled but did not retreat. He asked for another way but stayed the course. He agonized but did not abort the mission. He kept praying until the Father's will was his will, and then and only then was he willing to go all the way. Our healing from our mother wound does not require us to die on a cross, but it does require us to pick up our crosses, die to ourselves, and follow Jesus (see Matthew 16:24). Our healing will not be a cakewalk, but if we are willing to do some hard things, the fruit is sweet.

One important mental shift that must take place for your healing process is to increase your willingness to have challenging feelings and experiences. The trauma or heartache of being wounded by your mother may make you averse to feelings of distress, which means you likely have adopted avoidance strategies for pain that may not always be helpful or allow you to be fully present to feel and respond in an emotionally healthy way. Here are some examples:

- Avoiding conflict
- Not saying or doing anything that could cause necessary introspection and accountability
- Steering clear of feedback even if from a friend
- Staying in comfort zones for work
- Avoiding therapy that requires the exploration of current and past pain
- Never taking risks like asking for what you want, going back to school, or developing your skills and gifts if the growing pains for mastery feel too overwhelming

- Avoiding experiencing pain that feels like sadness, depression, anxiety, and stress associated with critique, correction, challenge, and the work of change
- Having a low tolerance for distress, all pain and discomfort that may be categorized in your mind as bad, and even the discomfort that is helpful for your growth and healing
- Not being willing to experience discomfort or realize that not all pain is trauma

Healing your mother wound requires you to revisit unpleasant memories, talk about difficult experiences, evaluate your role in the mother-child feud, and feel what's real in the moment as well as connect with buried feelings from the past. If you aren't willing to go there, healing is typically stalled.

As I was training in my doctoral clinical psychology program, I studied third-wave behavioral science treatments called acceptance and commitment therapy (ACT). The creator of ACT, Steven C. Hayes, has said, "If you're not willing to have it, you've got it," which is also called experiential avoidance.[8] Most people erroneously believe and tell themselves, *If I don't think about my pain, if I ignore my past, if I push down my unpleasant memories and feelings, I will outsmart my pain and distance myself from having to feel it.* But ACT teaches that if you aren't willing to have pain, you ironically will have more of it; the fight against what's real tends to magnify the experience. For instance, if I said, "Don't think about a pink elephant; don't think about a pink elephant; don't think about a pink elephant," you will likely be thinking about that pink elephant more than you'd like. The attempt to suppress a thought can paradoxically make it more prominent and persistent in your mind.

---

8 Steven C. Hayes, "Chasing Joy Without Losing It: The ACT Way to Happiness," Medium, July 28, 2025, https://medium.com/@stevenchayes/chasing-joy-without-losing-it-the-act-way-to-happiness-ff9d00595ab6.

If you are trying to avoid something (painful memories or feelings, confronting the difficult aspects of your mother and having a relationship with her), you may unintentionally increase the pain you are desperate to avoid through your resistance. There is a second warning from ACT, called experiential attachment, that suggests, "If you're not willing to lose it, you've lost it."[9] Both admonitions require an adjustment in our thinking. We can't avoid distress, and we can't demand positive feelings and experiences as if they never fade. The goal is increased psychological flexibility, which Hayes defines as

> the ability to feel and think with openness, to attend voluntarily to your experience of the present moment, and to move your life in directions that are important to you, building habits that allow you to live life in accordance with your values and aspirations. It's about learning not to turn away from what is painful, instead turning toward your suffering to live a life full of meaning and purpose.[10]

Here are five things we should do to support our healing:

1. **Increase our willingness to have discomfort and to lose comfort.** As we previously discussed, the process of healing may at times be uncomfortable. Doing the emotional work of healing, like tearing a muscle in weight training, will result in temporary pain that leads to growth. Stay the course and find a support system, especially other people who have already done the work of healing, to encourage you to keep going.

---

9 Hayes, "Chasing Joy."

10 Steven C. Hayes, quoted in J. W. Bertolotti, "The Art of Being Wise: How to Pivot Toward What Matters," Medium, March 24, 2023, https://medium.com/perennial/the-art-of-being-wise-1143ab3395ec.

2. **Increase our willingness for pleasure.** That may sound surprising, but many people struggle to enjoy life and to find pleasure all around them because they have been so accustomed to suffering and living with despair. But pleasure is a biblical principle: God brought us pleasure in the person of Christ, and he intends for us to experience numerous outlets for pleasure as an extension of what we find in him. But it's not just to be found; pleasure must also be cultivated and practiced. We must *want* pleasure; we must learn to recognize, invite, and enjoy it. It is important to survey your life and assess if you are more pain-averse or pleasure-averse.
3. **Increase our willingness to have community.** We need to increase our willingness to be around diverse types of people. Some people can be challenging, scary, off-putting, fickle, or struggling with their own low volume of willingness. When we aren't willing to be with people, we constantly avoid them. But we need people to heal. We need friends, mentors, models of healed people for us to aspire to, and people who will test our progress by triggering or provoking our old wounds. This may seem counterintuitive, but the blessing of doing life with difficult people is we get to practice the skills we've learned and change the stories we've told ourselves about who and what we can't handle. People in our lives who test our progress and healing remind us that avoidance of stress is no longer the only prescription for peace. We'll see that having those knee-jerk reactions to frustrating people gradually increases our response time and that perhaps unpleasant feelings will get extinguished through exposure over time. Growing in our ability to navigate diverse people makes us more psychologically flexible to be successful at work, at church, in public spaces, and with our families, where we can't neatly

curate our relational interaction. Thankfully, we don't have to fear what doesn't have power over us, and how will we test our newfound strength if we only choose a life or community that guarantees ease? Being around difficult people is an opportunity to bear witness that we are stronger, developing, healing, and increasingly unbothered.

4. **Increase our willingness to name and work toward our stated values and goals.** A part of healing is growth and forward movement to the lives we want for ourselves and believe God has planned for us. There is some utility in processing the past, but too often we think the secret to healing is to determine why the pain happened and who caused it. As we ready our hearts and minds for healing, much of the work we'll need to do won't have anything to do with the past; rather, it will relate to the future. Some of our healing is deeply connected to forward thinking, goal setting, and learning about ourselves. Take time and make a list of what you value in life, what your goals are, and what it will practically take to get there, including any specific barriers.[11] That is not selfish ambition; it's wisdom. As you develop your list of values and goals, ask yourself, *Do I believe everything has to be right and all my pain completely healed before I set myself on a course for the future?* The goal of true healing is being able to say, *I am willing to live out my stated values and work toward my goals, even if everything isn't perfect. I am willing to move into my future, even if I am sad and even if some days I struggle with anxiety. I am willing to work on myself and work toward my future, even if disap-*

---

11 Steven C. Hayes et al., "Acceptance and Commitment Therapy and the Third Wave of Behavior Therapy," *Dutch Journal of Behavior Therapy,* 12, www.actmindfully.com.au/upimages/acceptance_and_commitment_therapy_-_an_overview.pdf.

pointment and grief are my companions. Our future doesn't have to wait on the effects of our past to disappear.

5. **Increase our willingness for humility and curiosity.** When we increase our humility and curiosity, we are more open and flexible to exposing ourselves to people and information that may challenge our presuppositions, long-held opinions, and dogmatic ways of doing things. It's true that we don't know what we don't know, but sometimes we are too confident in things we think we know for sure. For instance, there are many helpful tools that have been written off as unbiblical without any research or proof, including meditation (it depends on what you're meditating on), mindfulness, breath work, body work, psychotropic medication, and psychotherapy. We don't want to heal through ways that offend our conscience or are antithetical to our faith, but if you have rejected a particular treatment modality, do you know why? Or we may have misunderstood or misinterpreted Scripture and therefore made decisions about forgiveness and reconciliation, what it means to heal or suffer, our relationship with our mothers, our own parenting and relationships with others, and what God expects of us that are based on a faulty understanding of the biblical text. What I've learned as both a clinician and Bible teacher is that those who know the least tend to have the most grandiose confidence in their lack of knowledge, but those who study, seek truth, and love learning are most in touch with how little they know. When you increase your willingness to be humble and curious, it is not a call to throw away Christ or the Bible but rather to be sure of what we believe and why we believe it, be able to defend our choices, and not cut ourselves off from a means of grace that God would willingly provide.

Healing, growth, and change are possible. No matter how tough it is, today isn't the end of your story. Before the practical work and process of healing begin, remember the mindset shift that needs to happen. Healing is often so focused on "What do I do to heal?" that we neglect perhaps the most important question: "How should I think to heal?" I hope that you will investigate your "want to" regarding healing and explore what it would look like for you to increase your "willingness to" be challenged, stretched, uncomfortable, and open to learning something new.

REFLECTION QUESTIONS

1. *Based on the list provided on pages 125–28, what other things might God be inviting you to do? Consider how they might be connected to your healing and making peace with your mother wound.*

2. *Why is "Do you want to be healed?" a profound question Jesus is asking you? Is there any evidence in your behavior and thinking that might reveal that you have not declared you want to be healed or that you're possibly working against your healing? What is your "mat"?*

3. *To work toward healing, what do you need to increase your willingness for?*

PRAYER

Lord, help me discern the questions you are lovingly asking me. Show me the mental roadblocks that keep me from pursuing healing. Thank you for always being up to so much more than what I can see. Please give me greater spiritual sensitivity to the other things you are inviting me into, and help me cooperate with all you have planned for me. I know your plans are good.

CHAPTER 7

WARFARE AND WEAPONS IN HEALING YOUR MOTHER WOUNDS

The weapons of our warfare are not of the flesh, but are powerful through God for the demolition of strongholds.

—2 CORINTHIANS 10:4

One of the most profound revelations the Lord has ever given me is that healing is spiritual warfare! Yes, the very act of healing is itself resistance against the kingdom of darkness and the schemes of the enemy, who often uses our various pain points to distort our understanding of God, distract us from our purpose, diminish our value, and discourage us from living the lives God has called us to live. The enemy has plans for our hurt that don't involve our healing or God's glory.

Spiritual warfare is the invisible inward and outward battle Christians are engaged in against the enemies of God. These enemies are defined for us by the apostle Paul when he instructs Christians to go to war against the sin in themselves (see Romans 6; 7:21–24) and oppose the schemes of the devil (see Ephesians 6:10–18). Despite the many conflicts with people that we have on earth, the Bible is clear that "our struggle is not against flesh and blood, but against the rulers, against the authorities, against the cosmic powers of this darkness, against evil, spiritual forces in the heavens" (verse 12). People tend to make two mistakes when thinking about and identifying spiritual warfare: Either they overemphasize it, believing that every sin, relational conflict, sickness, or problem is because of a demon that needs to be cast out, or they underemphasize it, completely ignoring the kingdom of darkness in the unseen spiritual realm despite God telling us our battle is against spiritual powers.

> The enemy has plans for our hurt that don't involve our healing or God's glory.

Healing is spiritual warfare because it also fights against the hopelessness that the enemy wants to take root in our hearts regarding our mother wounds and the possibility of true personal healing and restoration of relationship.

Generational Curses

Many Christians may think the struggles they face, particularly with their mothers, are generational curses, but that is not true for the believer under the new covenant of grace. Jesus's death and resurrection have broken the curses that could be against us (see Exodus 20:5; 34:7; Numbers 14:18; Deuteronomy 5:9). The trend in some churches to blame all sin and problems on a general curse is not biblical.[1] The cure for a generational curse is repentance. Yes, God promised to visit Israel's sin with a curse upon the third and fourth generations, but we can't forget that in the very next verse, he says he would show love to a thousand generations of those who love him and keep his commands (see Exodus 20:5–6). That means "God's grace lasts a thousand times

1 "What Does the Bible Say About Breaking Generational Curses?," Got Questions, April 6, 2022, www.gotquestions.org/generational-curses.html.

longer than His wrath."[2] If you have ever been concerned about an inherited generational curse from your mother's actions or the actions of any of your other ancestors, let me affirmatively say, let that go! As a Christian, you are a new creature in Christ and unable to be under a curse (see Romans 8:1; 2 Corinthians 5:17). On the cross, Jesus took on the curse to free us from it (see Galatians 3:13).

Most assuredly, if you are a Christian, you are not dealing with generational curses, but you may be dealing with strongholds. These strongholds that disrupt our thinking and life don't leave us hopeless; they can be cast down and destroyed. But the weapons of our warfare are not carnal. Carnal weapons have no divine power in our spiritual battle; the weapons God has given us come with his authority and power.

Divinely Powerful Weapons

When Moses was anxious about God's assignment for him to go to Egypt, he felt empty, weak, incapable, insufficient, small, and powerless against the mighty Egyptians (see Exodus 3:11; 4:1). God directed Moses to notice what was in his hand (see 4:2). The stick he was holding may have seemed insignificant to Moses at the time, but it was a divinely empowered staff that God intended for Moses to use in battle against his enemy. As you consider your worries and doubts about healing your mother wound, can you imagine God asking you the same question he asked his servant Moses? "What is in your hand? What do you already have access to that may seem familiar, unimpressive, simplistic, and common but certainly doesn't seem to be a weapon to aid you in your healing?" God promised us that we have "divinely powerful" (2 Corinthians 10:4, NASB) weapons, in which the effective-

---

2 "What Does the Bible Say About Breaking Generational Curses?"

ness of the weapon is established by the one empowering it. The following are some of those weapons.

THE VICTORY

If you had to engage in a fight and knew you were already declared the winner, wouldn't that make the walk to the battlefield easier? I would run if I knew I couldn't lose. If you are a Christian, you can run to the front line of battle too because we all have the unique privilege to fight every spiritual battle on the side of the predetermined winning team. It's a fixed fight, and we already won the war; we fight not *for* victory but *from* it, and that victory has been secured in Christ (see Revelation 20:7–14). Knowledge that the ultimate battle has been won by Christ is a weapon, as it aids in our confidence, boosts our boldness, and strengthens our resilience. Read these verses to shore up your weapon and remind yourself the victory is yours in Christ Jesus:

- "I have said these things to you, that in me you may have peace. In the world you will have tribulation. But take heart; I have overcome the world" (John 16:33, ESV).
- "Thanks be to God, who gives us the victory through our Lord Jesus Christ" (1 Corinthians 15:57, ESV).
- "He disarmed the rulers and authorities and put them to open shame, by triumphing over them in him" (Colossians 2:15, ESV).
- "In all these things we are more than conquerors through him who loved us. For I am sure that neither death nor life, nor angels nor rulers, nor things present nor things to come, nor powers, nor height nor depth, nor anything else in all creation, will be able to separate us from the love of God in Christ Jesus our Lord" (Romans 8:37–39, ESV).

- "The Lord will fight for you, and you have only to be silent" (Exodus 14:14, ESV).
- "The Lord your God is he who goes with you to fight for you against your enemies, to give you the victory" (Deuteronomy 20:4, ESV).
- "What . . . shall we say to these things? If God is for us, who can be against us?" (Romans 8:31, ESV).
- "You equipped me with strength for the battle; you made those who rise against me sink under me" (Psalm 18:39, ESV).
- "All this assembly may know that the Lord saves not with sword and spear. For the battle is the Lord's, and he will give you into our hand" (1 Samuel 17:47, ESV).

God has promised us victory, but here's the thing (a very frustrating thing): There is a present reality where believers are called to engage in a series of battles in our earthly lives, though the ultimate war has been decided in the heavens. You don't have to be skilled at boxing; you don't need an arsenal of guns, knives, grenades, and bombs; you don't need to be a brilliant military strategist; and you don't have to be rich and bribe your opponent or have a mouth on you to win verbal arguments. Those weapons are useless in a spiritual battle. What you possess is spiritual, and what you are possessed by is the power and presence of God. You have spiritual weapons for a spiritual fight, and believe it or not, they will greatly aid you in the battle to heal your mother wound. God has already handed them to you in Christ, so know them and use them. There are several offensive and defensive weapons that have been outlined in Scripture (most notably what Paul describes for us in Ephesians 6), and all of them are important to understand and use. Let's continue with a few weapons that I think are essential in our spiritual battle of healing. But don't wait until the battle is over; shout now, because you've already won!

THE WORD OF GOD

The Word of God is perhaps the most well-known but underutilized spiritual weapon. Paul tells us in Ephesians 6:17 that the sword of the Spirit is the Word of God. We must learn to swing against and stab the mental assaults from the enemy with skill and confidence. Hebrews 4:12 reminds us that the sword, unlike earthly weapons, is "living and effective and sharper than any double-edged sword, penetrating as far as the separation of soul and spirit, joints and marrow. It is able to judge the thoughts and intentions of the heart." Jesus wielded the Word of God when he was tempted in the wilderness by the devil (see Matthew 4:1–11). When he was vulnerable due to being weak and hungry after fasting for forty days and forty nights, he was approached by the tempter, who questioned his identity to try to manipulate him into satisfying Satan's desire by abandoning God's plan and misusing his power.

But look how Jesus, who is the Word (see John 1:1), valued and used the written Word of God to fight against the temptations and accusations of the devil: "He answered, 'It is written: Man must not live on bread alone but on every word that comes from the mouth of God'" (Matthew 4:4). In that moment, his vulnerability was hunger, so the devil wanted him to abort the mission and make bread, but throughout the exchange, the devil tempted him to put God to the test. Satan absurdly offered Jesus something he already owned (all the kingdoms of the world) if he would bow down and worship the devil. Jesus responds not with his opinions, feelings, or suggestions but rather with the Word of God. He basically declares, "No matter what you are saying or offering, what matters is what is written!"

What mental and emotional attacks are you facing? What does the voice of the enemy sound like as you think about your mother wounds? You can recognize it because it will not sound like the voice of God, which you will be able to identify based on only what is written. Jesus did not say, "My therapist told me . . . ," "I read in a book . . . ," "I saw a

TikTok . . . ," or "I watched a YouTube video . . ."; rather, he said, "It is written." That suggests that we must read, study, memorize, and become very knowledgeable of God's Word if we are going to use it in our battle of healing. When we know his Word, we can discern if another voice or counsel is off. Everything we need in our spiritual battle may not be directly stated in the Word, but it should be compared against the Word to see if there is any conflict with what is written.

The devil left at the command of Jesus, who used Scripture to shut down every lie and suggestion from him (see verses 10–11). Then the angels came to minister to Jesus, who was strong in his spirit but weak in his flesh, and God will send *you* help too. This same account in Luke 4:13 gives us additional insight into our spiritual battles: "When the devil had finished every temptation, he left Him until an opportune time" (NASB). The devil does not give up. He will respond to the Word of God as the sword of the Spirit does damage to his schemes and runs him off, but he will return. And when he does, keep coming back at him with Scripture.

Last but certainly not least, the Word of God is a healing agent that we can receive and apply. Psalm 107:19–20 affirms this: "[The fools] cried out to the LORD in their trouble; he saved them from their distress. He sent his word and healed them; he rescued them from their traps." It is so important for you to speak the Word of God over your life. Meditate on the following scriptures and know that God not only has the power to heal you but actually wants to do so.

- "Beloved, I pray that all may go well with you and that you may be in good health, as it goes well with your soul" (3 John 1:2, ESV).
- "Do not be wise in your own eyes; fear the LORD and turn away from evil. It will be healing to your body and refreshment to your bones" (Proverbs 3:7–8, NASB).

- "LORD my God, I cried to You for help, and You healed me" (Psalm 30:2, NASB).
- "Heal me, LORD, and I will be healed; save me and I will be saved, for You are my praise" (Jeremiah 17:14, NASB).
- "Surely he has borne our griefs and carried our sorrows; yet we esteemed him stricken, smitten by God, and afflicted. But he was pierced for our transgressions; he was crushed for our iniquities; upon him was the chastisement that brought us peace, and with his wounds we are healed" (Isaiah 53:4–5, ESV).
- "He said to her, 'Daughter, your faith has made you well; go in peace and be cured of your disease'" (Mark 5:34, NASB).
- "God anointed Jesus of Nazareth with the Holy Spirit and with power. He went about doing good and healing all who were oppressed by the devil, for God was with him" (Acts 10:38, ESV).
- "We rejoice in our sufferings, knowing that suffering produces endurance, and endurance produces character, and character produces hope" (Romans 5:3–4, ESV).
- "He himself bore our sins in his body on the tree, that we might die to sin and live to righteousness. By his wounds you have been healed" (1 Peter 2:24, ESV).

Those God-breathed words are still alive, active, effective, and powerfully speaking through the entire counsel of Scripture. Know them, speak them, soak your heart in them, apply them to your pain like ointment, and have faith that God will heal. In addition to the ones listed, what are some of your favorite or go-to scriptures related to healing or that serve as reminders for you of the power of God's Word in spiritual battle?

FAITH

I often wonder if my faith is as strong as I think or hope it is. I've learned that suffering can build our faith, but first suffering reveals it. What is faith, and what does it have to do with healing mother wounds? Faith is a core aspect of the Christian's life and can be tricky to define. It extends beyond mere belief in God to a deep trust of him: "Genuine faith involves abandoning all human reliance on self-efforts and placing total dependence upon God's character, His actions, and His promises, as revealed in His Word."[3] If you recall the story of the centurion, you'll remember that Scripture shows us that Jesus was astonished at the soldier's faith. "Hearing this, Jesus was amazed and said to those following him, 'Truly I tell you, I have not found anyone in Israel with so great a faith'" (Matthew 8:10). Wow! That hits me so beautifully in my heart. God wants to be amazed by our faith in him, his authority, and his power to heal.

The writer of Hebrews tells us, "Faith is the assurance of things hoped for, the conviction of things not seen" (11:1, ESV). Similarly, "biblical faith takes present-day possession of things not yet seen with our eyes but hoped for in the future."[4] I love that sentiment. Isn't that one reason faith is so important when it comes to healing our mother wounds? The battle is about robbing us of our faith by deceiving us into believing that whatever we can see about our current reality, whatever we can feel now, that's all that will ever be. Weak or nonexistent faith is limited by human observation bankrupt of hope.

The Bible instructs the Christian to "walk by faith, not by sight"

---

3 "What Does the Bible Say About Faith?," Got Questions, July 30, 2024, www.gotquestions.org/Bible-faith.html.

4 "What Does the Bible Say About Faith?"

(2 Corinthians 5:7). However, faith is not blind, uninformed wishful thinking; rather, it is assurance not just in what can happen but in the person who has the power and can make it happen. Faith in Christ is the foundation. Faith is always rooted in the person, work, and promises of Jesus as revealed in Scripture. As you heal, your faith cannot be in you, despite the world telling you to have faith in yourself. Pop psychology rooted in humanism centers on you and your determination and will to manifest the reality you want, but biblical faith resembles what the psalmist said in Psalm 62:5–8:

> For God alone, O my soul, wait in silence,
> for my hope is from him.
> He only is my rock and my salvation,
> my fortress; I shall not be shaken.
> On God rests my salvation and my glory;
> my mighty rock, my refuge is God.
>
> Trust in him at all times, O people;
> pour out your heart before him;
> God is a refuge for us. (ESV)

So often in Scripture, we see people's faith in God preceding their healing.[5] Your faith in God's ability to heal your heart, change your situation, and give you a brand-new life and relationship is a powerful weapon against the lies from the devil and your own anxiety and fear that nothing will ever change. Meditate on the following passage on faith as you heal:

> Everyone who has been born of God overcomes the world. And this is the victory that has overcome the world—our faith.

---

5 See Matthew 8:13; 9:22; 15:28; Mark 5:34; Luke 7:50; 17:19; 18:42.

> Who is it that overcomes the world except the one who believes that Jesus is the Son of God? (1 John 5:4–5, ESV)

PRAISE

Praise is not just an activity that kicks off a Sunday gathering; it's also a heart posture, expression, and lifestyle that is done both individually and corporately and is a potent weapon in spiritual warfare. Among the diversity of tools in battle, we see several scriptures elevating praise as a formidable weapon.

One of the most notable examples of praise being used as a weapon in concert with God's plan to give his people victory is King Jehoshaphat's battle against the Moabites and Ammonites. In 2 Chronicles 20:21–22, we read,

> [King Jehoshaphat] consulted with the people and appointed some to sing for the LORD and some to praise the splendor of his holiness. When they went out in front of the armed forces, they kept singing:
>
> Give thanks to the Lord,
> for his faithful love endures forever.
>
> The moment they began their shouts and praises, the LORD set an ambush against the Ammonites, Moabites, and the inhabitants of Mount Seir who came to fight against Judah, and they were defeated.

This passage shares accounts of praise being metaphorically compared to weapons in battle:

> Hallelujah!
> Sing to the LORD a new song,
> his praise in the assembly of the faithful. . . .

> Let the exaltation of God be in their mouths
> and a double-edged sword in their hands. (Psalm 149:1, 6)

> About midnight Paul and Silas were praying and singing hymns to God, and the prisoners were listening to them. Suddenly there was such a violent earthquake that the foundations of the jail were shaken, and immediately all the doors were opened, and everyone's chains came loose. (Acts 16:25–26)

When people are injured emotionally, the last thing they feel like doing is participating in any form of praise. Many erroneously believe we must be in the mood to praise, but the truth is, we just need to have a mind to do it. Praise does several things to aid you in your healing:

1. **Praise invites the presence of God.** When you are hurting, you need God. Praise invites him to rest his presence on your praises amid your pain and problems. Read Psalm 22:3.
2. **Praise encourages a thankful heart.** It can be challenging to be thankful when you are feeling low and disappointed that your life and relationship aren't improving. Praise reminds you of God's worth and goodness. Praise transforms a complaining heart into a thankful one. Read Psalm 138.
3. **Praise fixes your focus.** As you heal your emotional wounds, the enemy would rather you navel gaze more than focus on God. Sometimes we even make our pain the center of our attention, which makes it impossible to see God: his goodness, faithfulness, perfect track record, and promises. When we don't see God, we won't seek him. Seasons of healing are when we most need to see and seek his strength, wisdom, and reminders of his love and his commitment to us. Praise lifts your eyes to the one who can do something about the hard circumstances the enemy hopes

will occupy your vision. When you focus on God, you increase your confidence in him. Read Psalm 105:1–8.

4. **Praise shifts your emotions.** I think of Isaiah 61 as announcing the mission of the Messiah. Have you noticed that not only did Jesus come to set the captives free and heal the brokenhearted, but he also came with gifts and tools for us to gain relief from pain? One of the things he will "grant to those who mourn" is "the garment of praise instead of a faint spirit" (Isaiah 61:3, ESV). When you are struggling, in despair, or feeling weak and helpless, God is telling you through the prophet Isaiah to put on that outfit Jesus brought you called praise. Dress yourself in praise to change and get relief. Read 2 Chronicles 5:11–14 and Isaiah 61:3.

Praise invites the presence of God, and when he is present, it is undeniable. Change the temperature and atmospheric pressure of your life through your praise.

PRAYER

Many people mistakenly view the sword of the Spirit (Word of God) as the only offensive weapon detailed in Ephesians 6. However, a well-known spiritual discipline that isn't often viewed as a weapon is prayer. After the call to put on the full armor of God (see verses 11–17), we're told in verse 18 to "pray at all times in the Spirit with every prayer and request, and stay alert with all perseverance and intercession for all the saints."

Prayer is one of the most powerful spiritual weapons in the believer's arsenal. This weapon is often missed in the text because unlike for the other weapons, there was nothing in the soldier's arsenal for Paul to compare it to. All the other weapons related to actual weapons the soldiers had in their possession (helmet, shield, breastplate, belt, sword, shoes). If Paul were to write about the armor and weapons we have at our disposal today, he would have something to compare prayer to. Prayer is like an army's air support in that when a platoon is under heavy fire, soldiers get on their radios, give the coordinates where they need a bomb dropped to take out the enemy, and provide their location where they've taken cover so they can be rescued.[6]

Prayer has no limitations; it's the Christian's long-range weapon that can lock in on a target and go to work on our behalf while we are taking cover in the secret place of the Most High God. When we talk to God, we have a direct line of communication to petition him for intervention, direction, protection, and strength for ourselves and others as we face life's challenges and battles. Pastor H. B. Charles, Jr., said, "There are a lot of things you can do to fix your situation after you pray. But there is nothing you can do to fix the situation until you pray. Whatever it is you need God to do in your life, it happens after prayer."[7] God has invited us into a relationship with him, and no relationship is strong or intimate if communication is absent.

He already knows what you need, but he wants you to exercise your dependency on him by asking him. He already knows how you feel, but he wants you to exercise your intimacy by telling him. God already knows what problems you have, but he wants you to exercise your faith by inviting him in to solve them. If you have trouble in your relationship with your mother, if you are having trouble healing, if you are having trouble grieving and finding peace, I have good news for you: "Prayer is of great value to trouble."[8] If prayer is like calling in an air strike or a rescue mission from air support in spiritual battle, it is important to understand the power of our prayers. E. M. Bounds de-

---

6 Jeremy Myers, "Ephesians 6:18—Prayer: The Secret Weapon," Redeeming God, January 18, 2026, https://redeeminggod.com/sermons/ephesians/ephesians_6_18/.

7 H. B. Charles, Jr., *It Happens After Prayer: Biblical Motivation for Believing Prayer* (Moody, 2013), 23.

8 E. M. Bounds, *E.M. Bounds on Prayer* (Whitaker House, 1997), 312.

scribed how prayer moves God to work on behalf of his own people, in his own way.[9] God has ordained that we pray, and he will do things through and for people as they pray that he would not do if they didn't. Prayer puts him to work on our behalf in his own way.

Prayer is never only about defeating our enemies, protecting us from danger, or changing our circumstances; prayer should change us.

Prayer is never only about defeating our enemies, protecting us from danger, or changing our circumstances; prayer should change us. In the following scriptures, notice how God works for those who pray and wait for him to answer. Also notice the conditions he places on us when we pray. He is trying to move us, not just move for us.

- "From of old no one has heard or perceived by the ear, no eye has seen a God besides you, who acts for those who wait for him" (Isaiah 64:4, ESV).
- "On your walls, Jerusalem, I have appointed watchmen; all day and all night they will never keep silent. You who profess the LORD, take no rest for yourselves; and give Him no rest until He establishes and makes Jerusalem an object of praise on the earth" (Isaiah 62:6–7, NASB).
- "Call to me and I will answer you, and will tell you great and hidden things that you have not known" (Jeremiah 33:3, ESV).
- "Call upon me in the day of trouble; I will deliver you, and you shall glorify me" (Psalm 50:15, ESV).

9 Bounds, *E.M. Bounds on Prayer,* 533.

- "The LORD appeared to Solomon in the night and said to him: 'I have heard your prayer and have chosen this place for myself as a house of sacrifice. When I shut up the heavens so that there is no rain, or command the locust to devour the land, or send pestilence among my people, if my people who are called by my name humble themselves, and pray and seek my face and turn from their wicked ways, then I will hear from heaven and will forgive their sin and heal their land. Now my eyes will be open and my ears attentive to the prayer that is made in this place'" (2 Chronicles 7:12–15, ESV).
- "I will do whatever you ask in my name, so that the Father may be glorified in the Son. You may ask me for anything in my name, and I will do it" (John 14:13–14, NIV).
- "If you remain in me and my words remain in you, ask whatever you wish, and it will be done for you" (John 15:7, NIV).
- "You shall call, and the LORD will answer; you shall cry, and he will say, 'Here I am.' If you take away the yoke from your midst, the pointing of the finger, and speaking wickedness" (Isaiah 58:9, ESV).

Prayer works for us and on us for the glory of God. Our prayers don't control or manipulate God, but they do move him by inviting him in to do what we cannot do in our own strength. I want you to consider one thing you hoped would change by now on your journey of healing. Where have you seen little to no success in your emotions, thinking, behavior, or relationship with your mother? What's something that just doesn't seem to change about your mother wound? Be honest and remember these words of encouragement from Pastor Charles: "Have you used all of your strength? No, you haven't if you have not asked for God's help and prayed about it sincerely, diligently, and persistently."[10] Prayer is your stealth weapon; call in air support and watch God work.

We are not defenseless and empty-handed in spiritual battle; we have offensive and defensive armor and weapons, and we have much more than weapons in our hands. For those of us who have put our faith in Jesus Christ, we now have a weapon in our hearts. God is in us and we cannot fail. The Holy Spirit is a weapon because Jesus told us we would receive power when he showed up. Jesus is a weapon "by His stripes" (Isaiah 53:5, NKJV); even when we don't feel like we can pray, he sits on the throne and prays for us. His name is a weapon:[11] At his name, demons flee,[12] and there is power—wondrous working power—in the blood of the Lamb.[13]

We have victory both now and in the future over every spiritual battle: "They conquered him by the blood of the Lamb and by the word of their testimony; for they did not love their lives to the point of death" (Revelation 12:11).

REFLECTION QUESTIONS

1. *Describe why healing your mother wound is spiritual warfare. Does seeing healing from that lens change your thinking or approach to healing in any way?*
2. *What weapons are you using or underutilizing in healing your mother wound?*

---

10 Charles, *It Happens After Prayer,* 24.

11 See 1 Samuel 17:45; Proverbs 18:10; Philippians 2:9–11.

12 See Matthew 10:1; Mark 16:17; Acts 16:18.

13 See Romans 5:9; Hebrews 9:14; 13:12; 1 John 1:7; Revelation 1:5.

3. *Make a note of the Bible verses in this chapter and throughout the book that you will meditate on as a part of your spiritual arsenal. What is one verse you want to commit to memory?*
4. *How does sitting with the truth of the spiritual weapons and armor we have as Christians give you hope for healing from your mother wounds?*

PRAYER

Thank you, Jesus, for not leaving us defenseless in spiritual battle. As I incorporate many good, natural tools for healing, remind me not to abandon my most important armor. I am excited to spiritually strap up in the fight for my healing, with the confidence of knowing the ultimate victory has already been won by you!

CHAPTER 8

THE POWER OF SPIRITUAL MOTHERS

When Jesus saw his mother and
the disciple he loved standing there,
he said to his mother, "Woman, here is
your son." Then he said to the disciple,
"Here is your mother." And from that hour
the disciple took her into his home.

—JOHN 19:26–27

Many of us have a vision and understanding of mothering that is too small. Could it be that we've measured and defined the outcomes of our lives based on the action or inaction of just one woman? What if the hurt that was caused by one woman could be healed by the actions of many? While no one can ever replace your birth mother or the mother who raised you, I want to assure you that the mother-shaped hole you carry does not have to remain deep, dark, and deserted forever. God wants to fill it first with himself, but because he made us for relationship to meet a variety of spiritual and natural needs, he also has a plan to abundantly fill the hole with the love, presence, guidance, care, and discipleship of other women who serve as spiritual mothers.

This may be surprising to you, but God never intended for your mother to provide all the mothering you would ever need. In fact, no one woman, not even a great mother, can give you everything you need. If you endured getting far less than what one would reasonably expect a mother to provide, don't be discouraged: You are not a tough case to God, and he's got you covered. You can take a deep sigh of relief and say, *My mother was never supposed to give me everything, and God has other women in the kingdom who can help me. Selah.*

When we are adopted by God, we become his children and immediately gain not only a new perfect parent in God but also, according to Scripture, other family relational connections. We receive and become sisters and brothers. We see in Scripture people being parents of non-blood relatives, which also means we can become parents of or become someone else's sons and daughters. Adoption into God's family creates new siblings, children, and parents. That's a major revelation to receive. It means that when we are "in the faith," we are "in the family."

Paul referred to Timothy and Titus as his children in the faith though he had no biological children (see 1 Timothy 1:2; Titus 1:4). Not only did the apostle see himself as a spiritual father to his sons in the faith, but he also honored one of his spiritual mothers, the biological mother of Rufus (see Romans 16:13, ESV). Yes, Paul, who we see as a major spiritual father and writer of the majority of the New Testament through the Holy Spirit, had a spiritual mother. There were other women who played roles in Paul's life and ministry. In Romans 16, Paul starts by naming twenty-eight individuals who were prominent in the church, ten of whom are women (Phoebe, Prisca, Mary, Junia, Tryphaena, Tryphosa, Persis, Rufus's mother, Julia, and Nereus's sister) (see verses 1–15). Although most of the women Paul names and honors are listed for their ministry and financial contributions, their hard work, and risking their lives for the sake of the gospel, Rufus's mother is named among those women not for her direct co-laboring but for her gift of maternal love to someone who was not her biological child. It seems to Paul that being a spiritual mother is as significant a ministry as any other and worthy of honor.

Maternal Corrective Experience

In their book *Our Mothers, Ourselves,* Henry Cloud and John Townsend describe five basic needs of a child that must be met by a mother: safety, nurture, basic trust, belonging and invitation, and having someone to love.[1] Are you doomed to live the rest of your life without ever having those needs met and never having necessary skills developed in you from having a mother who gave you what you needed to thrive? Absolutely not. There is hope and there is another way. The answer is through spiritual mothers, and that can be in the form of discipleship or someone who is willing to take you under her wings.

To understand this more, I coined the term *maternal corrective experience.* The key in understanding the maternal corrective experience is that not just one person but multiple people can provide what you need over a short- or long-term period. It consists of one or more healthy experiences in which a person gets a core human need fulfilled by another maternal figure that would ordinarily be received from the mother or primary caretaker. You are not looking for one surrogate supermom to take your mother's place. (They don't exist anyway.) Rather, the goal is to become more aware of surrogates that may have been in your life in the past, are a part of your present, or may show up in the future.

> [The maternal corrective experience] consists of one or more healthy experiences in which a person gets a core human need fulfilled by another maternal figure.

A maternal corrective experience not only will supply you with some of what was missing in your own mother-child relationship, but

---

1 Henry Cloud and John Townsend, *Our Mothers, Ourselves: How Understanding Your Mother's Influence Can Set You on a Path to a Better Life* (Zondervan, 2015), 25–27.

over time—as needs are met more consistently—will have the power to help you heal. It can also help you unlearn negative things you've inherited from an unhealthy relationship with your mother as well as create new pathways of learning. The experience can reshape your beliefs, values, and understanding of yourself, the world, and motherhood.

A maternal corrective experience can function similarly to what we see in the field of psychotherapy, where the therapeutic alliance[2] between clinician and patient is what some describe as a key to therapeutic effectiveness. Dr. Allen Frances said one of the most impactful lessons he learned from his mentor early in his training was how

> the main and unifying goal of all psychotherapies is to help patients have new and better experiences. . . . Such experiences could heal wounds from the past, change perceptions and attitudes in the present, and result in healthier behaviors and virtuous cycles in the future.[3]

It is believed that a *corrective emotional experience* happens when someone experiences a healthier interaction with a therapist than they did with significant figures in their past, such as parents or caregivers. This new experience and relationship with the therapist allow patients to revisit painful emotions in a safe, supportive environment,

---

2 "The therapeutic alliance refers to the strength of the relationship between a therapist and a client. It is defined by mutual trust, honest communication, and a feeling of safety within the confines of treatment. A client who feels a strong alliance with their therapist is more likely to engage in the work of therapy, and a therapist who feels a strong alliance with their client is more likely to understand their challenges and help create a treatment plan that works for that individual"; "Therapeutic Alliance," *Psychology Today,* January 18, 2026, www.psychologytoday.com/us/basics/therapeutic-alliance.

3 Allen Frances, "Corrective Emotional Experience Is the Key to Therapeutic Effectiveness," Psychotherapy.net, March 15, 2022, www.psychotherapy.net/blog/title/corrective-emotional-experience-is-the-key-to-therapeutic-effectiveness.

which has the result of promoting healing and growth.[4] Here's an example:

> A patient whose parents were overly critical may find comfort in a therapist's compassionate and nonjudgmental approach. Conversely, someone raised in an overly permissive household might benefit from a therapist who sets clear boundaries. These therapeutic adjustments help patients reframe their understanding of relationships and develop healthier emotional patterns.[5]

Sándor Ferenczi, a clinician in the 1920s, introduced this experiential way of viewing psychotherapeutic change. Though a radical assertion at the time, he suggested that emotional experiences in therapy, not intellectual insights, are the real drivers of change. Later, the process was defined this way: The patient, in order to be helped, must undergo a corrective emotional experience suitable to repair the traumatic influence of previous experiences. It is of secondary importance whether this corrective experience takes place during treatment in the transference relationship or parallel with the treatment in the daily life of the patient.[6]

Information and insight alone aren't sufficient for bringing about healing and lasting change. People with mother wounds can greatly benefit from therapy, but they also need to have an encounter and experience through a trusted, safe relationship to foster real healing and change. As much as we can learn about God, it is a relationship with him that changes us. As much as we can learn about mother wounds—

---

4 Staff Writer, "Corrective Emotional Experience: A Pathway to Emotional Healing," Chicago Psychoanalytic Institute, April 22, 2025, https://chicagoanalysis.org/blog/elements-of-psychoanalytic-technique/corrective-emotional-experience/.

5 Staff Writer, "Corrective Emotional Experience."

6 Staff Writer, "Corrective Emotional Experience."

their impact and healing techniques—nothing will be as powerful as a corrective experience with a mother figure to heal wounds, reshape thinking, and build confidence that was lost in painful encounters with one's actual mother.

Here is how a maternal corrective experience should function in everyday life, especially in the life of the church and among the family of God:

- A person who wasn't allowed to make mistakes can have a relationship with a maternal figure who tells them it will be okay (such as reassuring the individual that they can try again if they fail their licensing test for nursing).
- A person who had a mother who made them feel guilty if they wanted to do something different than what the mother wanted can have a relationship with a maternal figure who welcomes their unique opinions and desires and encourages their agency.
- A person who had a mother who didn't teach them much about being an adult woman (such as basic financial literacy or caring for their home and body) can find a great teacher in a maternal figure who will take the time to explain those life lessons without judgment or critique.
- A person who had a mother who rarely said "I love you" or engaged in physical touch could benefit from a maternal figure who comfortably says "I love you" and provides hugs and freely expresses love.

You can probably name many examples from your own life where a maternal figure doesn't have to replace the significance of your mother or caregiver while also offering you something you need and didn't receive.

Challenges in Embracing a Maternal Corrective Experience

Mother wounds can make it difficult for us to trust others, particularly other women. This can impede our ability to get re-parented and repaired through maternal figures. Often, we have access to women who are willing and ready to pour into us, show up for us, and be at least one surrogate in helping meet some of our basic needs. I've experienced that many times both as a clinician through a process called transference[7] and in discipleship relationships in the church.

I remember when one woman, whom I'll call Melissa, asked me to disciple her, as she had experienced abandonment by her mother and generally had trust issues with other people. She was very clear that she wanted me to be part of her life, walk with her, help her grow as a Christian, and navigate her sanctification process. She consistently reached out via phone or text, always made her way to speak to me and give me a hug in church, and would frequently share things she was learning from Scripture. But when I met with her to discuss her request for discipleship and agreed to take on the role of spiritual mother, something changed: She became hard to reach, I never saw her around the church, it would take her days to return my calls, she would arrive late for our meetings, she was less serious in our discussions, she wasn't doing the readings I'd given her, she was unavailable to grab coffee, and she began to treat the relationship very cavalierly.

I started to feel confused and like she was wasting my time. However, instead of being annoyed, I said to myself, *Sarita, put some language to what you are experiencing with her. How does it make you feel?* Immediately, my thought was, *I feel like she's pushing me away. I feel like she's rejecting me and testing me. How much annoyance will I take before I*

---

7 In psychology, transference is when a client redirects or transfers their feelings from a significant other or person in their life to the clinician. It can be a helpful intervention tool when the therapist is aware that it is happening. For instance, a client who is extremely angry toward their mother will then transfer that anger to the therapist as if the therapist is the mother. This process is not typically part of the client's awareness.

return the treatment she's giving me? The next time I met with Melissa, I brought to her attention how I was experiencing her and simply asked, "Melissa, what's going on? Do you notice a change? You seemed enthusiastic about building a relationship and learning from me." The tears filled her eyes, and she dropped her head and cried. I gave her a moment to sit with the feelings and didn't talk over her emotions. She finally said, "I'm so sorry, but I just didn't believe you really wanted to spend time with me. I expected at some point you wouldn't want me anymore, so I was protecting myself by rejecting you first. I'm so scared." Boom! She'd nailed it.

What amazing insight she had. But not everyone can so quickly realize the truth of what's going on with them, and perhaps the people in your life aren't trained clinicians who can help you become aware that something deeper may be going on. I want to encourage you to become curious about how your mother wound influences how you relate to other women, particularly older women, women in authority, leaders, therapists, and women who are nurturing and ready and available to provide a corrective experience.

How do you respond to maternal figures in your life? Sometimes we may relate to them in the same unhealthful ways we learned to relate to our mothers in hopes of keeping ourselves safe and securing love, attention, and approval by caring for our mothers' emotions, denying our own, or over-functioning through parentification. Sometimes our chronic disappointment from our mothers has taught us we have to depend on ourselves and not anyone else. Sometimes we feel safer being the friend who advises, protects, celebrates, and shows up to support others, but we don't like feeling vulnerable, so we never ask for help or show any signs of weakness.

If you've been injured by your mother, do strong, secure, healthy women make you feel disoriented and maybe uncomfortable because you've always had to manage a mentally ill mother or caretake for an immature one? Does a woman pastor, preacher, leader, or Bible teacher trigger you or provoke distrust because your mother was a religious hypocrite who performed at church and abused at home? Does a woman supervisor or professor intimidate or frustrate you? Do you find yourself avoiding, shrinking, stressed to win their approval, or crushed by their critique? Do you struggle to receive nurturance and care from other women because it makes you feel childlike and dependent and those feelings are uncomfortable for you because those primary years were filled with instability and pain?

Sometimes we are so used to harsh talk, struggle, being called names, being gaslit, and criticism that words of kindness, loving behavior, and relationships filled with freedom and peace are repulsive to us and deemed fake. Ask yourself, *Do I let myself be celebrated, complimented, built up, supported, and graciously corrected by other women? Does a maternal corrective experience feel like disloyalty to my mother? Does having a disciple maker or a spiritual mother seem offensive to my mother?*

I know a woman whose mother struggled with addiction but is now, by God's grace, clean and sober, walking as a Christian and with a completely changed life. But during the mother's addiction, her child (the woman) grew to form necessary bonds with other women. One woman became a beautiful disciple maker and spiritual mother to help her receive many of the needs she never got during her mother's addiction. But once sober, her mother resented the spiritual mother and, in several ways, demanded that her daughter not think of the spiritual mother as a mother figure. The adult daughter has been torn regarding how to embrace, forgive, honor, and make a new life with her biological mother while also maintaining a relationship with the woman who helped her in so many ways. Sometimes we avoid the maternal love of another woman because we think we are wronging, dishonoring, or giving up on our birth mother, whom we love.

I believe that women who consistently say they don't get along with other women, avoid community with women, struggle to make new female friends, say they would rather hang out with men, and love to learn from and be around older men are labeled as having daddy issues. But what if it was a mother wound driving those beliefs and behaviors? As you come in contact with other women, one powerful question you can ask yourself is, *What about this person reminds me of something about my mother or provokes discomfort in the way my mother created discomfort?* It could be a signal worth paying attention to because while not all willing surrogates may be healthy or a good fit for you, you might have a fear-based concern that is extinguished when brought into the light and processed.

Review the italicized questions from the last few pages, really sit with them, and ask yourself more questions regarding your openness to a maternal corrective experience. I also don't want to neglect to mention that if you have a mother wound and desire a maternal corrective experience or discipleship, you may run into women who say they don't have time to mentor you or whose behavior reinforces the mother wound you already have. Not all older people you think would be able to provide a maternal corrective experience are willing to. That can cause additional harm and make you resistant to building relationships with other women, but don't give up.

I will always advocate for professional counseling as a major intervention and support for your journey of healing, but we cannot forget that these guiding relationships, too, can heal relational wounds from our mothers.

Discipleship

Notice what Paul says to Titus, the one he called "my true son in our common faith" (Titus 1:4), when he gives him instructions to be shared with women and men in the household of faith:

> Older women likewise are to be reverent in behavior, not slanderers or slaves to much wine. They are to teach what is good, and so *train the young women* to love their husbands and chil-

> dren, to be self-controlled, pure, working at home, kind, and submissive to their own husbands, that the word of God may not be reviled. (2:3–5, ESV, emphasis added)

Paul is writing to Titus to give him instructions on how to guide different groups within the household of faith to live in a way that aligns with sound doctrine, reflects the grace of God, and promotes health among its members.

He uses the phrase "train the young women," which is similar to the scripture intended for parents when they're raising their children (see Proverbs 22:6), language used in the New Testament regarding parents raising children (see Ephesians 6:4), and how Paul commends Timothy to remember what his mother and grandmother taught him[8] (see 2 Timothy 3:14–15). Paul is announcing to Titus that women in the family of faith have a shared responsibility in having good character so they can teach what is good and train younger women in godliness and good works.

This charge and calling is discipleship. Discipleship involves coming alongside another Christian to help them in their process of progressive sanctification. The aim is for all disciples to look less like themselves and more like Christ, which is called Christ formation, spiritual maturity, spiritual growth, or spiritual formation. This is a lifelong work of the Holy Spirit in which Christ is being formed in the life of the believer (see Romans 8:29; 2 Corinthians 3:18; 1 John 3:2).

> Discipleship involves coming alongside another Christian to help them in their process of progressive sanctification.

The disciple maker serves as a godly example for the younger, less

8 In 2 Timothy 1:5, Paul emphasizes that Timothy's faith first lived in Timothy's grandmother Lois and his mother, Eunice. Paul correctly assumes that because of their faith, they trained him well and that same faith "dwells in" him as well (ESV).

mature Christian to follow for instruction as they follow Christ. The goal of discipleship is for the trainer or spiritual parental figure to teach in words and deeds through up close, consistent relationship so lessons needed for maturation are both explicitly taught and caught over time through proximity.

Some spiritual mothers will be excellent at teaching you Scripture, some may help you with being a wife or mother, and some will be great at helping you navigate work in the marketplace as a Christian or managing your home and stewarding your money. Others will have skills in helping you work through pain and relational issues, others will be great for helping you take care of your physical body, and still others will be amazing at discerning your gifts and helping equip you for your ministry call.

Some women will have multiple abilities and strengths, but not any one woman will have everything, and when it is your turn to make disciples, you won't have everything either. That is the benefit of the household of faith with members who have diverse gifts. Remember, I started this chapter by saying that our view of mothering and motherhood is too small. If your definition of motherhood involves only your loving and nurturing the children you've birthed from your womb, you don't understand God's plan for motherhood. Discipleship gives each woman the unique opportunity to birth children who didn't form in her womb but formed in her heart. All women—married, single, widowed, divorced—have a special call to be mothers to other children in the faith.

We've discussed what discipleship is from a biblical perspective, but it's also important to discuss what it is not. What follows are several wrong or incomplete views of discipleship and spiritual mothering on the part of the disciple:

- *Discipleship requires me to find one singular "super saint" willing to give me everything I need for my Christian journey, or I will simultaneously collect numerous women with different skill sets and build one supermom experience even though I won't go deep with any of them.*

- *Discipleship is free professional therapy.*
- *A disciple maker will replace my biological mother; I can just move on from my mom and get a new mother in my spiritual mother.*
- *Discipleship is about finding a cool godly older woman, like a big sister to hang out with, vacation with, and call for prayer when I am tempted.*
- *Discipleship is my opportunity to tell a mature woman what I want her to do for me and give me; I can customize my curriculum.*
- *A disciple maker is the one I confess to, but she just listens and advises me, not corrects me or holds me accountable.*
- *Discipleship is one-sided. I receive and she gives because she is the teacher; I am the only one receiving in the relationship.*

Additionally, women open to being spiritual mothers can get it wrong too:

- *Discipleship will be a way for me to get a second chance at being a good mom since my relationships with my biological children are so bad.*
- *Discipleship means being the judge of this woman's life. My job is to point out everything that is wrong with her. Tough love is the overarching theme of the relationship.*
- *Discipleship is a way to get my own emotional needs for friendship met. I don't have many friends, and I don't have any kids.*
- *Discipleship requires me to prepare Bible lessons all the time.*

- *Discipleship means I now have a younger person to babysit my children, clean my home, and run errands for me.*
- *Discipleship means I have to devote more time and attention to this individual than to my own family.*
- *Discipleship requires me to know everything about the Bible and have the answers to all the disciple's questions.*
- *Discipleship makes me the ultimate authority in my disciple's life. She must get permission from me to do anything and owes me absolute loyalty.*

Those wrong assumptions about discipleship can hinder the experience, compound a preexisting mother wound, or make people avoid it altogether. Discipleship should be a prayerful decision for both parties. Discipleship should be mutually beneficial. Although the disciple maker is doing the heavy lifting in training, effort should be put in by the disciple to show interest and a willingness to submit to the leadership and wisdom of the disciple maker. The discipleship relationship is a beautiful context for women who desire to grow in their relationship with the Lord and who have not had healthy relationships with their biological mothers. I am so grateful for the women who have poured into my life over the years, and I am also blessed to have paid forward and replicated that love in training the many spiritual daughters the Lord has blessed me to mother in a variety of ways.

I Needed a New Pair of Shoes

I remember the first time I formally met with the woman who discipled me. I had my eye on Sister Martina Lambert for months as I watched her teach the Bible at the women's ministry of the church we were attending in Philadelphia. Her mastery of it was something I had never seen. No matter what question she was asked, she was able to walk people through Scripture for an answer.

In my mid-twenties, I recognized how much I needed to learn and was hungry for growth. I was more consistent in my church attendance and Bible study at home and was even serving in youth ministry, but something felt missing and uncomfortable in my life as a Christian and I wanted more. Also, I knew God wanted more for me, but I just didn't know how to get there. Have you ever felt like that? It was like I was going through a spiritual growth spurt but still wearing the same tight shoes.

Sister Martina has always helped me spiritually shoe shop. She was able to watch me walk, help me select the right fit for the season, and help me size up. There is nothing worse than trying to walk or run the race of life with the wrong shoes for the journey and terrain. That is why discipleship is so helpful: We have someone to help us see if we are wearing a shoe that is too big for where we are or too small for where we are soon going.

Sister Martina's deep biblical knowledge initially attracted me, but her genuine love for people, including my family and me, is what kept me. She had a unique ability to make everyone feel special, showing compassion and a servant's heart, especially toward those considered rough around the edges. She was wise, humble, and committed to the Lord, with a gift for exhortation that always uplifted me and reinforced my identity in Christ.

Our relationship began after a women's ministry Bible study when I nervously asked her to lunch. She graciously accepted, even letting me know how honored she felt to be asked. We met at a diner, and despite my initial nervousness and overpreparation, she immediately put me at ease with her warmth and humility. Our conversation flowed naturally, marking the start of a discipleship relationship (though we never used that term). Over the years, she profoundly influenced my spiritual and personal growth and how I parent, maintain friendships, and approach my ministry.

Sister Martina became a second mother to me. Our relationship evolved into a reciprocal friendship filled with prayer, laughter, and mutual support through life's challenges. She was there for me during my mother's passing, honoring her memory while becoming a vital part of my life. Our friendship and bond exemplified the essence of spiritual mothering, where we shared our lives deeply without diminishing our previous relationships.

Inspired by Sister Martina, I have dedicated myself to being a spiritual mother to others. I strive to replicate the love, support, and guidance she provided me, helping other women navigate their spiritual journeys and life challenges. Whether through counseling, celebrating their successes, or simply being present, I aim to pass on the legacy of discipleship and spiritual mothering that Sister Martina embodied. This commitment to nurturing others in their faith and personal growth is a testament to the profound impact she had on my life.

A Clarion Call for Spiritual Mothers

Spiritual mothers—it's a gift to have one and a gift to be one. I want to make an appeal not just for you to find a spiritual mother, but for you to set your heart on being one. There is a generation of women who have not had who you are. Women need the testimony of how you made it, survived, and cried your way to the other side. There is a spiritual daughter waiting on you to rise up and help her see the beauty of how the gospel can save her soul and also transform how she walks, thinks, works, loves, serves, and fulfills her call. There is a woman waiting on you to break open the Bible and show her the way of Christ. There is a woman waiting on you to save her a seat at your family table and share a meal or give her a bed in your home.

There is a woman waiting on you to notice the gifts in her that others have ignored and teach her how to cook, garden, change a baby's diaper, and change her mind about a man she thought she loved. There is a woman waiting on you to teach her how to organize her home, ask for a raise at work, and start a ministry at church. There is a woman waiting on you to show her your success and your scars, your victories and your defeats, and invite her into the best and worst days of your life so she can watch you trust God. There is a woman waiting on you to teach her how to apply makeup as well as apply the Word to her situation, raise a teenager and raise her standards, and exercise her faith and her body.

Spiritual mothering is comprehensive and about not just Bible study but also Bible living. It's two people who have been saved by grace who are both following Jesus, but one person has been walking well a little longer than the other. And if you think you have to get your entire life together or be pain-free and wound-free before you can be a good spiritual mother to another, you should hear some of the stories of women who have laid their lives down for others despite their own suffering. Some of the best spiritual mothers have been victims of domestic violence and sexual abuse, survived divorce, and had their own diagnoses and disabilities. Some of the best spiritual mothers have stories of deconstructing and even walking away from the faith. Some of the best spiritual mothers are former lesbians or addicts or have even spent time in jail.

The application requirement to be a spiritual mother has no checkbox for perfection; rather, a woman must submit her life to a perfect God—a perfect parent who has called her to join his team of disciple makers and go make disciples. This is the call; this is the commission. It's not new, but I pray you sense this call anew in you. Where are the lionesses and mother bears who will rise up and protect, defend, teach, equip, and care for a generation of children who need more than what their own mothers could give?

I pray it's you. I pray you will say, "Here I am, God. Send me. I'm ready to help Christ be formed in them. I'm ready to stand in the gap and be an intercessor and initiator. I'm ready to help someone else grow. I'm ready to take someone shoe shopping. I will be a spiritual mother."

REFLECTION QUESTIONS

1. *What is your reaction to the idea that no one woman was supposed to provide all your maternal needs?*
2. *In what ways can you identify your need for a maternal corrective experience?*
3. *Can you identify people who have provided maternal corrective experiences for you?*
4. *Why is discipleship so important in the body of Christ, and how can discipleship aid in healing someone who has a mother wound?*
5. *Are you someone who will answer the call to spiritual motherhood? If you desire to either have or be a spiritual mother, what is one step you can take?*

PRAYER

Lord, thank you for the accessibility I have to a spiritual family as a Christian. Please provide me with women who can serve as instruments for a maternal corrective experience. Help me notice and be open to the women who are already willing and able in my life to disciple me, and may those relationships be glorifying to you. Give me a heart to not only want discipleship and spiritual mothering but also one day become a disciple maker and spiritual mother for someone else. Amen.

CHAPTER 9

PEACE IS WITHIN YOUR REACH

Peace I leave with you. My peace I give to you. I do not give to you as the world gives. Don't let your heart be troubled or fearful.

—JOHN 14:27

If you struggle to say no when necessary or find yourself constantly seeking approval, it may be difficult for you to discern when you are successfully speaking up for yourself, knowing and honoring your limits, and setting healthy boundaries. Particularly in Christian communities, people pleasers are celebrated as being altruistic, faithful servants, and nice while being encouraged—through mounting requests and expectations—to ignore their own needs, weaknesses, and exhaustion. People pleasers often engage in what author Ken Sande calls "peace-faking,"[1] where for the sake of appearing to have peace, we become experts at performing and stuffing negative emotions or conflict and falsely believing that sweeping problems under the rug is the mark of a true peacemaker.

---

1 Ken Sande, *The Peacemaker: A Biblical Guide to Resolving Personal Conflict* (Baker, 2004), 28.

Maybe you've wondered, *Is my disposition to make peace with my mother motivated by being a people pleaser (or peace-faker), or do I work against peace, instead becoming a peace-breaker in the name of "protecting my peace"?*[2] To resolve this potential confusion, I suggest letting Jesus's life be our model:

- Jesus did not secure our peace by faking peace. He confronted and called out our sin, confirmed the consequences for our sin, said that "there is no peace for the wicked" (Isaiah 48:22), and then provided the solution to our lack of peace by dying on the cross to create a means for peace between us and God.
- Jesus was not a people pleaser; he was a heavenly Father pleaser, which meant he sacrificed as his Father instructed him to (even to death), but he also said no to people, rested when he was tired, had limits, and pushed back when people wanted something from him that was not in line with his Father's will.
- Jesus also understood that peace was not always achievable even among family members when it came to allegiance to him. He made comments about peace that seemed paradoxical. He said, "I did not come to bring peace, but a sword" (Matthew 10:34), but before he ended his earthly ministry, he called his disciples to be peacemakers (see 5:9) and left them with the gift of peace (see John 14:27).

There is not a one-size-fits-all list I can offer, but it is a safe bet to always follow the way of Jesus. Let every yes, no, boundary, silence,

---

2 Sande, *Peacemaker*, 28. Sande wrote about three dispositions in conflict: peacemakers, peace-fakers, and peace-breakers.

speech, engagement, and retreat be prayerfully considered, biblically supported, and Holy Spirit scrutinized. That may simply mean praying and asking God for help and direction:

> *Lord, please show me what you want me to do in this situation with my mother. I know what I want to do, but I want you above all to be pleased with my decision. I don't want to shut down if you want me to show up. I don't want to engage if you want me to pull back for a season. I don't want a lesser version of peace if you want to give me a better version of it within myself or between my mother and me. Please teach me how to recognize when you've handed me a sword or a gift to be a peacemaker.*

Just simply praying demonstrates humility, dependency on God, a need for help, an unwillingness to be a slave to your feelings, and your faith in the power of prayer.

There is more to consider. For example, there are times when we are more focused on protecting our peace instead of keeping the peace or, better, working for peace even if that work is hard. I can't help but wonder if the avoidance, anxiety, anger, unforgiveness, pettiness, fatigue, or even confusion over what to do next in our relationships with our mothers has tempted us to come up with this cute phrase, "protecting my peace," to get us out of doing uncomfortable things that would lead to our growth and development and make us more like Christ.

This brings me to a hard question that you may not like, but hopefully you'll rejoin the discussion after throwing your book across the room or closing your device (smile). Are you ready? Here it is: Have you redefined peace according to the world's standards, and is the type of peace you are determined to protect a better or inferior version of the peace that God can give?

Have we, like the children of Israel, grown tired of waiting on the

Lord to help us in the wilderness of our mother wounds and decided to take our disappointments, desires, defeats, fear, anger, pain, and pride, melt them down, make them into a golden idol called "my peace," and worship it instead of God? Instead of a securing peace, we've just settled on self-preservation, which may have nurtured immaturity, passive-aggressiveness, avoidance, and fear.

Maybe the peace you need is related to the memories of the past and the pain that comes with your inability to restore a relationship with your mother, who is deceased. Or maybe you need peace for the pain of feeling unwanted or not belonging since you never knew your biological mother because you were given up for adoption. Perhaps you need a hopeful path and plan for peace in your current relationship with your mother, who is still living. Or maybe you need peace with a broken relationship that may never change on this side of heaven, but you also need peace to cling to hope, walk in faith, be Christlike, and rest in God's grace. Wherever you fall in your need for peace, you can have confidence that if you put your trust in the Lord, root yourself in God's definition of peace, emulate a biblical standard of peacemaking, and elevate your expectation by looking to Christ, peace is within your reach.

> Have you redefined peace according to the world's standards?

What the Bible Says About Peace

Peace is something everyone wants but far too few have. In fact, the Bible says a lot about it: "Various forms of the word *peace* are found 429 times in the King James Version of the Bible."[3] In English,

3 "What Does the Bible Say About Peace?," Got Questions, July 18, 2024, www.gotquestions.org/Bible-peace.html.

the word *peace* often projects passive pictures showing an absence of civil disturbance or hostilities, or a person free from internal and external strife.[4] However, the biblical concept of peace is grander than that.

There are three overarching types of peace described in Scripture:

- **Peace with God—Romans 5:1.** Peace with God is accomplished through humanity being reconciled to him through our faith in Christ. We receive peace with God as a work of grace that Christ has provided because of our faith in him.
- **Peace of God—Philippians 4:6–7.** The peace of God is an internal emotional state of tranquility, stability, and contentment despite life's pains, problems, and uncertainties. My father used to say, "The peace of God don't make no sense," because it is a calm and confident disposition that is present in the middle of life's storms. We have confidence and security in God, who can supply this mind-blowing peace.
- **Peace with Others—Romans 12:16, 18.** Peace isn't meant to be experienced between only us and God; it's meant to also flow into the relationships we have with others. Peace with others involves seeking to experience harmonious relationships with those around us, such as family, friends, co-workers, church members, and neighbors. It includes working to resolve inevitable conflicts; practicing forgiveness, empathy, respect, and understanding; and seeking to do all we can to be at peace.

---

4 Marty Boller, "4.1 In the Beginning: God's Blessing of Shalom," August 3, 2020, https://pastorboller.com/2020/08/03/4-1-in-the-beginning-gods-blessing-of-shalom.

Now that you have a reminder and refresher of how peace relates to us overall, let's discuss how the Bible gives us several important notes and instructions related to peace to help us better understand God's definition of it and guide our walk as Christians.

God Is a God of Peace

> God is not a God of disorder but of peace.
>
> —1 CORINTHIANS 14:33

God's nature is one of peace and not disorder or confusion. He is the God who commands chaos, not causes it. Where there is confusion and disorder, he wants to invade that space and bring peace. When Christians represent God, we should bring peace to chaos.

God Is the Lord of Peace

> May the Lord of peace himself give you peace always in every way. The Lord be with all of you.
>
> —2 THESSALONIANS 3:16

God is the source of true peace. We don't have to get it from somewhere or someone else; God gives it. But not only that, he is the "Lord of peace," meaning he is the ruler, operator, owner, controller, and CEO of peace. He has authority over it. That's a powerful and comforting truth. If the Lord supplies peace, he will take care of it. This peace that Paul prays for is perpetual (always) and for all circumstances and needs, such as peace for persecution, peace for strife, peace for our wounds from our mothers. We know this peace ultimately gets maintained through the presence of God.

Peace Is a Blessing from the Lord

The LORD gives his people strength;
the LORD blesses his people with peace.

—PSALM 29:11

Christians can be confident that God "blesses his people with peace." This is an exclusive peace reserved and dispensed for those who belong to him. The psalmist tells us this gift of peace from God is a blessing. Blessings in Scripture are a big deal. When the Lord blesses us with peace, it's as if he is giving us a superpower to be able to produce life with peace. In Genesis 3, before man and woman were expelled from the garden, she was given the name *Eve* (verse 20), which means "mother of all the living" or "life giver."[5] This is a core calling for women—to have the ability to give life (naturally and spiritually with making disciples). In both cases, the woman has the unique privilege in partnering with God to produce more disciples to represent him on the earth; one of her offspring (Jesus) would ultimately crush the serpent (see Genesis 3:15). In Psalm 29:11, a blessing of peace means we have the unique ability to partner with the God of peace as he rules the world and seeks to reconcile people to himself, but also in every area of life. If we have been blessed with a life-producing ability, then even where there is emptiness, desolation, infertility, and barrenness in our relationships with our mothers, we have the blessing of peace to create life.

The Peace Jesus Gives Is Different from the Peace the World Gives

Peace I leave with you. My peace I give to you. I do not give to you as the world gives. Don't let your heart be troubled or fearful.

—JOHN 14:27

---

5 Genesis 3:20, AMP.

Christians should know that before Jesus left us on earth, he promised to leave peace with us, but he makes a distinction that the type of peace he is leaving is countercultural and not the same type of peace the world gives. The encouragement to his people to not be troubled or fearful tells us something about the differences between Jesus's peace and the world's. The world's peace is fragile because it is dependent on circumstances; however, the peace that Jesus gives is a rest, stillness, steadiness, and confidence of heart that exists despite trouble. His peace flows during persecution, disappointment, confusion, sickness, marital problems, and relational discord with our mothers. It is peace that enables us to push through difficult circumstances, endure, and remain calm in the face of turmoil. We don't need to be troubled or fearful; we can trust in God no matter what is going on, and our propensity to fear and worry are replaced by peace. A song we used to sing at my church called "The World Didn't Give It to Me" had lyrics that make that point: "This joy I have . . . the world didn't give it to me and the world can't take it away."[6]

Peace Is the Fruit of the Spirit

> The fruit of the Spirit is love, joy, peace, patience, kindness, goodness, faithfulness, gentleness, and self-control. The law is not against such things. Now those who belong to Christ Jesus have crucified the flesh with its passions and desires. If we live by the Spirit, let us also keep in step with the Spirit.
>
> —GALATIANS 5:22–25

The fruit of the Spirit is not separate individual fruits to be acquired but instead represents aspects of one fruit that grows within a believer. These characteristics should be evident in a Christian's life when they

---

6 "The World Didn't Give It to Me (2025 Remastered)," track 11 on Shirley Caesar, *Gloryland Revisited (2025 Remastered),* Sonorous Records, 2025.

are being developed and sanctified by the Holy Spirit. We don't simply do these things on our own; rather, they are produced in us by the indwelling Holy Spirit as we submit to his leading and grow in relationship with Christ. When those things are evident, they reflect spiritual maturity and Christ being formed in you. Peace is the third fruit listed and represents the three core types of peace Christians are called to have: inner peace (tranquility) in our emotions, reconciliation with God, and living in harmony with others. Even amid difficulty and difficult people, when we develop this Christian characteristic of peace, our inner and external lives are characterized by it, but only if we make the decision to "keep in step with the Spirit" and cooperate with what the Spirit is trying to do in us and through us, which is to make us look like Christ.

Make Every Effort to Do What Leads to Peace

Let us pursue what promotes peace
and what builds up one another.

—ROMANS 14:19

Christians are to pursue what will encourage peace between people and work to build and uplift others, not bring others down. Though the path to peace may be difficult, a believer is supposed to be sensitive to others' emotional and spiritual states. Christians can do things to promote or advance peace, but we cannot force it; both parties have to work to create peace when there is contention.

Let the Peace of God Rule

Let the peace of Christ, to which you were also called
in one body, rule your hearts. And be thankful.

—COLOSSIANS 3:15

Christians have a duty to let the peace of God rule in their hearts, meaning we have the choice to either trust God and his promises or depend on ourselves and our solutions, thus rejecting his peace. Something will always rule our hearts: The devil wants to rule our hearts, our emotions want to rule our hearts, and sometimes others want to rule our hearts through control and manipulation. If we rehearse negative works, thoughts, and feelings about our mothers, those are what will fill us and rule us. The peace of Christ will rule our hearts when we surrender to him and fill them with his truth, obey his Word, and practice being thankful. Complaining and ungratefulness work to drive peace out, but thankfulness helps maintain peace in our hearts.

God Will Keep You in Perfect Peace

You keep him in perfect peace
whose mind is stayed on you,
because he trusts in you.
—ISAIAH 26:3 (ESV)

This beautiful verse assures us that there is a promise from God to be kept in an extraordinary state of "perfect peace," amplifying the promises of peace throughout Scripture. This promise is guaranteed to the child of God whose mind must be steadfast and firmly fixed on God: his truth, his promises, his character, his winning track record, and his Word. It is imperative to know that our minds aren't naturally fixed on God or on the Spirit; that is why we must make a point to put our minds there and keep them there. We do that by intentionally turning our attention from our problems and our frantic attempts to solve them to God's Word and talking with him (prayer).

Yes, we may have ruminating thoughts, and the issues with our mothers may tempt us to stay up all night and ponder the past, present, and future, but we must change the channel of our minds when those thoughts creep in, trying to rob us of life and peace. When we have those unsettling thoughts, we need to interrupt the regularly scheduled program and say, *Wait a minute; enough of this. I trust in God,* and change the channel. Trust in God is a prerequisite to having perfect peace, because what we trust in holds the remote control of the mind.

To Have Peace, Meditate on What Jesus Promised

> I have said these things to you, that in me
> you may have peace. In the world you will have tribulation.
> But take heart; I have overcome the world.
>
> —JOHN 16:33 (ESV)

As Christians, we are to find our peace in Christ. Even in difficult times, you can remember his words and promises and know that in the world, we often experience great pain, but the world has been overcome by him.

Pursue Peace with Everyone (Including Our Mothers)

> Pursue peace with everyone, and holiness—
> without it no one will see the Lord.
>
> —HEBREWS 12:14

In context, this verse follows one about working to improve something that is weak and watching where you walk to prevent something from getting worse. The goal is not to let something stay in a bad state but rather to address it and heal it (see verse 13). The concept of pursuing peace is directly connected to this instruction. Pursuing peace aids in healing before things are more fractured and difficult to repair. This verse also infers that we should pursue peace with everyone, even those whom it may be difficult to be at peace with. We are still called to try.

Seek Peace

All of you be like-minded and sympathetic, love one another, and be compassionate and humble, not paying back evil for evil or insult for insult but, on the contrary, giving a blessing, since you were called for this, so that you may inherit a blessing.

For the one who wants to love life
and to see good days,
let him keep his tongue from evil
and his lips from speaking deceit,
and let him turn away from evil
and do what is good.
Let him seek peace and pursue it,
because the eyes of the Lord are on the righteous
and his ears are open to their prayer.
But the face of the Lord is against
those who do what is evil.

—1 PETER 3:8–12

There is so much in these five verses that can be unpacked. Primarily, regarding peace, this passage again affirms the Christian moral obligation to seek peace and pursue it. Of important note is the context of this instruction. Peter is writing to Christians who are experiencing intense suffering that will only increase under Nero, their leader; they are losing their jobs, family support, and lives. Nero made it a capital offense to be a Christian, yet they are told not to give the same hate that they are receiving but instead to give a blessing. Additionally, they are told that this is the type of behavior that Christians are called to display and that will in return allow them to inherit a blessing. When it comes to our relationships with our mothers, we are called as Christians to not return the hate, to give a blessing, to do what is good, and to seek ways to maintain peace in hostile environments.

Do All You Can to Live at Peace with Everyone

If possible, as far as it depends on you,
live at peace with everyone.
—ROMANS 12:18

Let's take a deep dive into this verse, as it will help us achieve peace with our mothers. For people who can't envision peace being a reality between themselves and those with whom they have a breach in relationship, what would you guess is their most favorite word or phrase in this instruction from Paul? If you're anything like me, you probably guessed it's the word *if* or the phrase *if possible.*

I clearly remember someone quoting that scripture to me when they were offering me counsel and direction on dealing with someone who had harmed me. "Sarita, I know they hurt you and they aren't repentant and they don't have any evidence of a changed heart, but remember the Bible says, 'If possible, as far as it depends on you, live at peace with everyone.'"

I didn't let the last syllable escape their lips before I snapped back, "If! I-F possible." (I have a habit of spelling words when I want to emphasize them. I'll sometimes say, "I'm T-I-red," or "N-O way," or "It's H-O-T," and on that day, I wanted to make sure my kind friend, who was just trying to help me, did not miss observing the *if* in the text.) "Girl, it's not possible," I said.

My friends and family know to get quiet when I'm in that headspace, because they've witnessed enough times when they plant the Word—even if I'm trying not to let it take root in my heart—and Father God comes along and speaks to my wounded heart. That's exactly what happened, and in their wise silence, God came to see about me, and his voice took over: "But, daughter [my heart begins to melt when I sense him calling me his daughter], have you tried everything in your power to live at peace with this person?"

My mouth was shut, but my mind and ego raced to defend myself. *Yes, I've done everything I could do.*

Then I sensed a soft, fatherly question, dusting like a feather against my heart. "You've done everything to live at peace?"

I immediately broke into tears. I knew the truth, and God knew I knew the truth, but sometimes the truth hurts. The tears were about the pain, the offense, and his unwillingness to accept my answer. The tears were about his unwillingness to allow my solution though he allowed my suffering; they were also about how unfair it felt that I (the hurt person) had to think about how to live at peace with my offender. I wondered if God sent someone to talk to my offender, like he'd sent my friend to talk to me. I wondered if he was questioning my offender's choice to hurt me as much as he was questioning my choice to be utterly done with them and banish their memory.

My friend didn't talk over my tears, and neither did God. They both sat with me in silence, but only one of them knew my thoughts. I didn't need any more words, just space for my soul to wrestle with God's sovereignty. I needed space and time to let my heart catch up to my mind, which had been renewed by the Word of God. I needed a minute to give up the belief that maybe he would let the faithful be put to shame. I knew, but I just didn't like it in that moment.

We are called to not only know the truth but also live it, and that's hard. God's Word and ways are cool until they confront the parts of us that want to reserve lordship for ourselves. It's always easier to preach a message you don't have to live. It's always easier to give counsel that you yourself don't have to take. I knew exactly what that verse was saying, but I wanted to do what I wanted to do because somewhere in all my hurt, I realized I had to stick up for myself because God wasn't protecting me. I had already judged my offender as unworthy of my doing whatever was needed to make an attempt at peace. My offender did not deserve peace with me, even if I can think of a million ways to give it.

In moments like that, we struggle to make peace with the truth of the Word of God, which is why we struggle to make peace with someone else. Somehow in the moments when we are hurt, we are delusional enough to think that it is easier for God to live at peace with us than for us to live at peace with our offenders. I'm sharing this because I want to normalize the struggle but also point you to stability in God's Word. I am intentionally trying to get you to ask better questions of your soul, challenge your assumptions, and say yes to the narrow way. I want you to understand that your responsibility is to submit your will to God's direction, submit your actions in obedience to his Word, and rest in the outcome by leaving the results up to him.

You cannot force your mother to meet you on the road to peace, but you *are* responsible for showing up with a willingness to take the journey with her. You cannot force her to yield her heart to the Lord and obey his Word, but you can be sure that you are ready to obey. If your mother refuses peace, she refuses God, but you will have a clear conscience that you have done all you can to live in peace with her. The call is to peace, not perfection.

I want you to make peace with your mother wounds, make peace with the painful memories, make peace with what you can't control or change, and do everything you can to live at peace with your mother. I believe in a peace that the world can't give and the world can't take away. I believe in peace that isn't just a feeling or state of being but that tells the story of a person—the God-man Jesus, the Prince of Peace who brought *shalom* to a world in a dangerous conflict with God.

An Invitation to Investigate

Romans 12:18 is also imploring you to *investigate* if it is at all possible to live at peace with your mother. It's a prescription for living with difficult people wrapped in an invitation to search out the matter, explore the possibilities, and then decide. Have you ever wanted or had to do something difficult that after a cursory look at the situation or by judging it with only your emotions, it wouldn't seem possible to accomplish? Have you ever wanted to buy a house but didn't think you had the funds or the credit score? Have you ever wanted to go back to school but didn't think you had the money or time? Have you ever wanted to run a marathon, change careers, start a business, go on a mission trip, travel abroad, plan a conference, adopt a child, get a pet, record an album, or write a book and asked yourself, *Is it at all possible for me to do this?* Of course you have. We all have.

But let me tell you what I know is true: If you managed to do it, you had to take time to investigate and research all the possible ways you could get it done. You likely got counsel from others who had done what you wanted to do. You watched videos, read books and articles, and studied the matter. You did a cost-benefit analysis. You shared your dream with others to get their feedback, and if you are a wise Christian, you prayed. You took the desire, the dream, the "want to" or "need to" before the Lord and asked for his direction, help, and clarity. We've all heard the phrase "People do what they want to do," so I know you understand the concept of investigating how to get something done, but the problem is that living at peace with everyone, including your mother, may not be something you want to do, or the enemy has deceived you into thinking it's just too hard and not worth the work. However, here's what God is asking of us: "Care about peace because I care about peace, and then do everything you can to find a way to simply live in peace."

Embrace Your Identity as a Peacemaker

Finally, I want to discuss what it looks like to embrace your identity as a peacemaker. It starts with your having a relationship with Jesus, the Prince of Peace. When Isaiah refers to Christ as the "Prince of Peace" (Isaiah 9:6), he is alluding to Jesus's royalty, authority, and sonship and his mission to do the will of the Father to restore completeness and wholeness (*shalom*) to reverse the damage of sin that took place in the

Garden of Eden. The Prince of Peace came to change our relationship status with God from enemies to children and friends. When Jesus secured our peace with God, we were then filled and empowered to live at peace with others. Paul admonishes believers that we are now called to make every effort to emulate this mission: "I, the prisoner in the Lord, urge you to walk worthy of the calling you have received, with all humility and gentleness, with patience, bearing with one another in love, making every effort to keep the unity of the Spirit through the bond of peace" (Ephesians 4:1–3).

When Jesus secured our peace with God, we were then filled and empowered to live at peace with others.

We will not naturally be unified or easily live in peace with others; rather, we must work hard at it, and that's why we are called peacemakers. We must *make peace* because it does not occur naturally. In the Sermon on the Mount, Jesus says, "Blessed are the peacemakers, for they will be called sons of God" (Matthew 5:9), but still there are many misconceptions when people think of what it means to be a biblical peacemaker. Some think peacemakers are pacifists—that they want to avoid conflict or telling hard truths. Others think they want each party in the conflict to agree to disagree or that each party must be appeased and happy. Those are far from the characteristics of a peacemaker.

When Jesus says, "Blessed are the peacemakers," he is calling for active reconciliation. Don't miss that point. Everyone who is a Christian and aware of a breach between God and another person should be a peacemaker, even if not directly involved in the conflict.

I can only imagine that one of the frustrations you've had in trying to resolve conflict in your life, especially with your mother, is that you've felt alone in trying work toward peace. Sometimes family, friends, and church members conveniently mind their own business when you are at odds with your mother. They may share sidebar sympathy, but they are not personally rolling up their sleeves to get involved and help forge peace between the two of you. I want to say emphatically that while we must pray about each situation and our level of involvement, Christians are not called to mind their own business; in fact, we are called to see disunity with God and others as our business and help make peace. One writer points out that

> the word *make* in the term "peacemakers" comes from the Greek verb that means "to do" or "to make." . . . Someone has to drag the combatants to the table and give them a reason to put down their arms. Peace must be made. Peace never happens by chance.[7]

In the same way children grow up with their parents and take on many of their characteristics, we Christians are called to show off our special relationship with God by reflecting his peacemaking nature. Being a peacemaker is both an identity and a duty. But notice that a peacemaker isn't the same as a peacekeeper (someone who cares about things looking peaceful but, in fact, doesn't bring about real peace). We see a strong warning from God about this in Jeremiah 6:13–14: "From the least to the greatest of them, everyone is making profit dishonestly. From prophet to priest, everyone deals falsely. They have treated my people's brokenness superficially, claiming, 'Peace, peace,' when there is no peace." Is the relationship with your mother more about peacekeeping and not peacemaking? What might it look like to work on your relationship with your mother as a peacemaker? Can you envision yourself as a peacemaker to create a new and improved reality?

---

7 Rick Ezell, "Sermon on Matthew 5:9—What It Means to Be a Peacemaker," Lifeway, www.lifeway.com/en/articles/sermon-blessed-peacemakers-sons-god-matthew-5.

Resistance against you as a peacemaker isn't a sign that you are doing it wrong. In fact, persecution comes to peacemakers: You are misunderstood, disliked, mocked, and sometimes harmed. Despite the resistance that peacemakers receive (even from within), peacemaking is not *suggested* by the Prince of Peace; rather, it is a call to be like him.

If you have found Christ, you have found peace. And if you have found peace, you must embrace the duty and identity of a peacemaker.

REFLECTION QUESTIONS

1. *Is your relationship with your mother mostly a reflection of your being shaped by the world's views on peace or God's views? Explain.*

2. *Why is it crucial for a believer to see and embrace their identity as a peacemaker? What is the blessing Jesus promises for those who do?*

3. *How does this chapter help and challenge you in relation to how you see or interact with your mother?*

4. *What scriptures most stuck out to you in this chapter that can change your understanding of peace?*

5. *How will you respond to Jesus's invitation to investigate if it is possible to be at peace with your mother? What next steps will you take?*

PRAYER

Lord, please give me a heart for your view of peace. Help me where I have adopted worldly standards for peace that are not congruent with yours. Thank you that true peace is not achieved through peace-faking and that truth does not have to be sacrificed for peace. Where I am feeling challenged, speak into those tender and resistant places so that, above all, I would want to do your will. Thank you for pursuing peace with me and securing it through Christ, even when I didn't know I needed it and didn't deserve it. Amen.

CHAPTER 10

EMBRACE IT ALL

Faithful love and truth will join together;
righteousness and peace will embrace.

—PSALM 85:10

As we continue this journey of healing, I want to focus on additional aspects of our faith that will be a foundation for you on your journey of healing. Like I've already talked about, they are not always easy, but I believe you will be stronger in your faith and further along in your healing after embracing them. In this chapter, we will look at what it means to embrace suffering, humanity, and boundaries. Everyone's mother wounds look different, but my hope is that you will have some clarity as you continue to look at your next steps.

Embracing Suffering

No one wants to embrace suffering, but it is necessary for the Christian in order to live well and endure the hardness of life that will surely come. When I say "embrace suffering" as a means of embracing peace with your mother, I am not saying to "enjoy the suffering your mother may cause" or "give your mother opportunities to cause suffering" or "invite your mother to make you suffer," but rather to be prepared for the inevitable. Jesus told his disciples several things to prepare them for a difficult life as a Christian, including the call to take up their crosses,[1] be courageous even when they know suffering is coming,[2] endure,[3] and realize that the world will hate them because it hated Jesus first.[4]

One major obstacle for Christians who suffer is that despite the numerous warnings we see in Scripture, we are often shocked and confounded every time suffering happens. How much more shocking, then, is enduring suffering at the hands of your mother. Your mother is the one person you want or expect to love you the most. It is critical that you have a robust and theologically sound understanding and expectation of suffering to neutralize the surprise and normalize the hardships Christians face:

> Who then will harm you if you are devoted to what is good? But even if you should suffer for righteousness, you are blessed. Do not fear them or be intimidated, but in your hearts regard Christ the Lord as holy, ready at any time to give a defense to anyone who asks you for a reason for the hope that is in you. Yet do this with gentleness and reverence, keeping a clear conscience, so that when you are accused, those who disparage your good conduct in Christ will be put to shame. For it is better to suffer for doing good, if that should be God's will, than for doing evil. (1 Peter 3:13–17)

This message is spread throughout the Bible (see 2 Timothy 3:12–13; 1 Peter 4:12–16; 5:10). While it's clear from these verses that we should not be surprised that suffering comes and that when

1 See Matthew 16:24.
2 See John 16:33.
3 See Matthew 10:22.
4 See Luke 6:22–23; John 15:18–19.

we suffer well, God will strengthen and restore us, you may still be thinking, *I have an expectation to suffer for the faith, but not at the hands of my mother. They don't seem to be the same.* Here are two things I want you to know related to suffering and your mother:

1. Evil is present in the world, and your mother, even if she is a professing Christian, could be under the influence of the enemy, who is intent on stealing, killing, and destroying. Satan doesn't use only strangers to frustrate and harm us; he also uses even the members of our own families.
2. The enemy's common tactic in spiritual battle is distraction and discouragement. How distracting has it been to have a mother wound or a contentious relationship with your mother? How discouraging has it been to know that she is critical, harsh with her words, unsupportive, or emotionally or physically unavailable to you? How disheartening is it not to have a mother who is proud, present, protective, and peaceful? Do you see how, whether or not you share the gospel with others, just your being a Christian who's serious about your walk with the Lord and committed to representing him invites an attack from the enemy? What better weapon for him than your mother?

I would encourage you to increase your willingness to endure as God leads and is using you in your mother's life to see his grace and power at work. You don't know what fruit may be produced through your gentleness, patience, endurance, and commitment to peace. Try to remember what beautiful fruit was produced in your life when someone (a coach, family member, church leader, friend, or co-worker), at some point, was suffering with you.

We can sometimes neglect to remember someone who had to endure us in our unredeemed or spiritually immature state, and if you can't recall someone, God certainly had to endure us (see Numbers 14:18; 2 Peter 3:9). As you embrace suffering to accomplish peace on your mother's behalf (her peace with God and/or her peace with you), it is best to adopt the disposition of being long-suffering while still holding that you will not have to endure it forever.

The apostle Paul had an interesting mindset regarding his suffering. It was one of the goals he had for how he wanted to truly know Jesus, saying, "My goal is to know him and the power of his resurrection and the fellowship of his sufferings, being conformed to his death" (Philippians 3:10). That means Paul's singular ambition in life was to know Jesus experientially—not superficially through acquiring only head knowledge, but rather on the most intimate level he could. Paul understood what we must also understand: that knowing Jesus deeply will be accomplished only through embracing suffering.

You don't know what fruit may be produced through your gentleness, patience, endurance, and commitment to peace.

This isn't a dark, sadistic, self-injurious attitude Paul had. He wasn't excited to suffer and didn't search for suffering or view it as earning favor with God, and neither should you. Rather, it's an acceptance that when we do suffer, it is on-brand for us as Christians who've been called to partake in Christ's sufferings (see 1 Peter 4:13). A Christian worldview and healthy theology of suffering should anticipate that life will be at least peppered with suffering and, for some, filled with it. But despite suffering, we can rejoice, as suffering also works to our benefit and is redemptive:

- Embracing suffering can mature us and produce endurance in us.[5]

5 See James 1:2–4.

- Embracing suffering can refine and train us as Christians.[6]
- Embracing suffering can humble us so God can exalt us.[7]
- Embracing suffering can equip us to help others who deal with a mother wound.[8]
- Embracing suffering draws God's nearness and deliverance.[9]
- Embracing suffering can help us see the great glory that will be revealed in us.[10]
- Embracing suffering can help us see that afflictions are temporary and increase our hope for what is eternal.[11]
- Embracing suffering reminds us that God works all things "for the good of those who love [him]."[12]
- Embracing suffering proves the genuineness of our faith, resulting in God's glory.[13]
- Embracing suffering reminds us we are never alone; God comforts us, anoints us, and blesses us while our enemies watch.[14]

When it comes to our mothers, we would much rather be like Christ by demonstrating power like he did but not by modeling him in suffering. We want to be like him and perform a miracle and change our mother, lay hands on and heal her, speak a word of knowledge and prophetic truth to convict and transform her, but what if one of the

---

6 See Hebrews 12:7–11.
7 See Philippians 2:3–11.
8 See Hebrews 4:15.
9 See Psalm 34:18.
10 See Romans 8:18.
11 See 2 Corinthians 4:16–18.
12 See Romans 8:28.
13 See 1 Peter 1:6–7.
14 See Psalm 23:4–5.

greatest ways we can be like Christ and used by God is by increasing our willingness for the road to peace to be hard and accepting that at times we will suffer? God doesn't waste pain, as we see with his Son, Jesus. Jesus's suffering accomplished salvation, so remember, you have no idea what God will use your surrender to suffering to accomplish in the lives of others, including your mother.

One Romanian pastor put it this way: "Christ's cross was for the propitiation; ours is for propagation. Christ suffered to accomplish salvation; we suffer to spread salvation."[15] It's a hard truth, but if you study the formation of the early church, God always used suffering and persecution to spread the gospel and draw people to salvation. I am not suggesting that you tolerate violence or put your children at risk or ignore the number of ways you may need to have healthy boundaries and protect yourself from your mother; I'm simply saying that the road to peace with her may not be easy or without resistance, and your willingness to embrace the Christian's call to suffer may help the process. I also want to encourage you that whatever hardship you have endured and may endure because of your mother, the Lord knows, cares, and will take care of it and you. I pray that, like Paul, you have or will come to know the Lord intimately through any suffering you have experienced. When we share in his suffering, we also share in his glory.[16]

Embracing Humanity

Most Christians are familiar with Romans 3:23: "All have sinned and fall short of the glory of God." These words are a sobering reminder of our imperfection, the community of other imperfect people we are a

---

15 J. D. Greear, "What Is Lacking in Christ's Afflictions?," J. D. Greear Ministries, January 9, 2019, https://jdgreear.com/lacking-christs-afflictions/. See Colossians 1:24–25 regarding continuing the mission of the spread of the gospel and rejoicing in the suffering that accompanies and is used to spread it.

16 See Isaiah 30:20–22; Luke 22:28–30; Revelation 21:4.

part of, and the gaping distance between our flesh and a holy God. It should make us empathetic to the weak, humble us in the mirror, and make us grateful for Christ and gracious to others. However, when we are the victim of someone else's sin, our empathy, humility, and grace melt like cotton candy on the tongue. We convince ourselves we deserve mercy for us and justice for our offender. We see ourselves as not "that bad," believe we "would never do that," and unknowingly hold ourselves to a lower standard than we measure others by, even though we need a savior as much as they do.

One of the great healing ointments needed for any broken relationship is to embrace the other person as someone who has also been infected by sin. As with all diseases, sin debilitates us—and in some cases kills us—unless it is healed. Therefore, to embrace your mother as human means being willing to see her as flawed but deeply loved by God. We tend to operate in our faith from a very individualistic Western Christian mindset, and we forget that Christ died for the world, not just us, and the world includes our mothers. That doesn't take away from your pain or real hurt from her, nor does it invite you to make choices to put yourself in danger, but take some time to consider the following:

- Your mother has her own unique set of sin issues that the Lord is angry about but also trying to cleanse. *She's human.*
- If your mother is not saved, apart from Christ she will always struggle to show up for you and live and love well, but God wants to save her. *She's human.*
- Maybe your mother knows the Lord and is a believer but has not done the things to grow her faith. Maybe she is weak, defensive, and prideful and has a host of substitute saviors—such as drugs, sex, anger, money, and status—to give her a false sense that she is fine. And maybe she doesn't like it when you are around because you remind her she is not really fine. *She's human.*

- If your mother would just fully surrender to the Lord, she would be an amazing disciple in the kingdom because she is highly gifted and talented. But then this would also mean that the struggles you see are a part of the enemy's plan to keep her from flourishing. *She's human.*
- Your mom could be sad, angry, unfulfilled, and reeling from her own childhood trauma, which may have been the springboard for her addiction. *She's human.*
- Your mother may have low self-esteem, and her jealousy is rooted in wishing she could have lived the life you are living and been a better role model for you. *She's human.*
- Your mother may be embarrassed that she can't provide all your needs and is exhausted from trying to. *She's human.*
- Your mother may have an undiagnosed mental illness for which she refuses treatment to improve her life. *She's human.*
- Conflict may have been the language of her childhood home, where arguing was interpreted as passion and control was translated as love. Maybe she is just repeating patterns instead of creating new paths with you. *She's human.*
- Maybe your mother is a weak woman who never found her voice, her friends, her place, her passion, or her purpose. Maybe she's stuck and she's furious that you're free. *She's human.*
- Maybe your mother loves you, knows you need and deserve the very best, but is incapable of giving it to you. Maybe she is empty and untaught. Maybe for her whole life, she has been trying to be a mother she never had and she knows she is failing. *She's human.*
- Maybe your mother is a changed woman—committed to Christ, compassionate, kind, and settled—but she's late.

> Maybe this woman you see today didn't figure it out, go to therapy, or find the Lord when you needed her as a child. Maybe she's now magnificent, healed, repentant, and trying to rebuild with you, but her rap sheet is full of sins and mistakes that you had to pay for. *She's human.*

The list and possibilities could go on and on. Although you may know some things but not everything, what you do know is that she is human. The Bible says that your human mother is fallen, born in sin and shaped in iniquity (see Psalm 51:5), and even if she is saved now, she will still struggle at times in her flesh. When you are willing to embrace your mother's humanity, you can grab hold of everything that's made her *her.* You can embrace her history, her story, her fears, her tears, her joys, her mess, her brilliance, her weakness, her personality, her trauma, her crimes, her childhood, her parents, her relationships, her wins and defeats. You can let her be human, even though she is your mother, even if sometimes those things seem to be in opposition to one another.

I want us to imagine together the peace that could be escorted into your relationship with your mother if the red carpet of Jesus's blood was rolled out for the two of you to walk upon. And what if peace was greeted at the door by two imperfect people who knew but for the grace of God they would have been cut off by the Lord? Sobriety of one's own weakness makes us tender to the weaknesses of others. Where there is disbelief in your mother's faults, intolerance of her fragility, and hatred of her failures, there will be the erasure of her humanity. But she, like you, is human, and humans are immeasurably complex, deeply broken, weighed down by maladies, and overwhelmed by their own hypocrisy. Most people, on some level in the psyche, are like Paul: wanting to do good but struggling to do it, and not wanting to do bad but unable to stop themselves. We're wretched people who can be delivered from this body of death only by Christ the Lord (see Romans 7:15–25). Perhaps the dividing wall between you and your mother is the unwillingness to embrace her as not only imperfect but also that scandalous word, *human.* Perhaps your mother is difficult to embrace because you want to hold something more sophisticated, more elevated, more divine than human. For that embrace, you can reach for only Jesus; everyone else you will touch will just be dirt.

Embracing your mother's humanness is not an invitation to see and rewrite history through rose-colored lenses, dismiss the need for accountability, or excuse the work of repairing the relationship; rather, it's about seeing the both of you honestly and with sensitivity. Her humanness and your hurt can coexist. Embracing your humanness and hers brings about grace and patience.

Many times people aren't even on the same page with healing and desire for relationship, and that's okay. God knows our limitations (see Psalm 103:14), but sometimes we don't, and because of that we rush our offenders into awareness and change and we rush ourselves. The work that God is doing on us sometimes takes longer than we are comfortable with, but if our hearts are open to his process to grow us, repair us, strengthen us, mature us, stabilize us, heal us, and restore us, the results are worth it. Repair for human hearts and relationships is offered quickly as a solution, but in reality, change happens slowly. You cannot shout, "Fix it right now!" at human brokenness and pain, but patient love in the form of long-suffering, honesty, and purposeful strategies for healing, time, space, trust, and surrender to God's special gymnasium[17] for his beloved disciples will be the tender training we need in order to be worked on and prepared to work through anything.

---

17 The Greek word for *discipline* in Hebrews 12:3–13 is παιδεία (*paideia*), representing comprehensive training, instruction, and upbringing aimed at bringing someone to maturity through encompassing guidance and correction, not just punishment. It implies a fatherly process of teaching and shaping a child for responsible living, leading to growth and righteousness. See Michael Scott Robertson, "Discipline," *Lexham Theological Wordbook,* ed. Douglas Mangum et al., Lexham Bible Reference Series (Lexham Press, 2014).

Embracing Boundaries

Personal boundaries can be defined as the invisible lines that we draw for ourselves that define and communicate our personal limits and needs in relationships with others to protect our emotional, physical, mental, and spiritual well-being.[18] The call to set boundaries can be challenging and confusing. If you are a people pleaser, the idea of living with boundaries likely makes you anxious and concerned that a boundary could bring rejection and the loss of relationship. A boundary may be viewed as a threat to acceptance and will incur retribution from those who count on your being a "yes-person." However, there is another side to the boundary discussion. When you use the phrase "I'm protecting my peace," I want you to consider whether you're using it as a socially acceptable phrase that appears to exude strength and clarity but instead is an escape tactic to avoid doing the challenging inner and relational work that leads to true growth and peace. Some people have taken a good thing and used it for fear-based fortresses instead of neighborly fences. We've become more willing to build walls than to build bridges.

"A boundary is a 'dividing line.' In geography, a boundary is that which marks the end of one property or jurisdiction and the beginning of another."[19] In relationships with others, a boundary is a means of separating one person from another, affording each person to have their own identity, responsibilities, space, and privileges.[20] Author Nedra Glover Tawwab says, "Boundaries are expectations and needs that help you feel safe and comfortable in your relationships. Expectations in relationships help you stay mentally and emotionally well.

---

18 Sam Blum, "The Five Types of Personal Boundaries (and How to Set Them)," Lifehacker, July 23, 2021, https://lifehacker.com/the-five-types-of-personal-boundaries-and-how-to-set-t-1847349639.

19 "What Are Boundaries, and Are They Biblical?," Got Questions, January 4, 2022, www.gotquestions.org/boundaries-biblical.html.

20 "What Are Boundaries, and Are They Biblical?"

Learning when to say no and when to say yes is also an essential part of feeling comfortable when interacting with others."[21] Someone who has healthy boundaries knows they can share information without compromising who they are or what they value. Boundaries are good, and they are not a human idea. God is a God of boundaries, and we see him in Scripture using them to bring order to chaos in the creation of the world;[22] he used the boundaries of his law to bring order to the chaos of human depravity,[23] separate his people from the pagans,[24] guide behavior,[25] and protect communities.[26]

When God creates boundaries, he does not leave us empty, alone, or famished. Boundaries are limits but not total losses. We see this most clearly in Genesis 2:15–17, where we find the first boundary he set for his human creation:

> The LORD God took the man and put him in the garden of Eden to work it and keep it. And the LORD God commanded the man, saying, "You may surely eat of every tree of the garden, but of the tree of the knowledge of good and evil you shall not eat, for in the day that you eat of it you shall surely die." (ESV)

What most people tend to focus on regarding this boundary is the fact that God gave a command and a consequence, but what is often neglected in our understanding of his boundaries is the abundance that remained: "You may surely eat of every tree of the garden." There was just one tree the man and the woman needed to avoid, but all the other trees were for the taking. I wonder how the inclusion of abundance could influence how we respond when we set a boundary. In Scripture,

---

21 Nedra Glover Tawwab, *Set Boundaries, Find Peace* (Tarcher, 2021).

22 See Genesis 1:4–10; Psalm 104:9; Proverbs 8:29–30.

23 See Exodus 20:1–17.

24 See 2 Corinthians 6:14.

25 See Romans 13:1–4; Galatians 5:22–23.

26 See Acts 17:26.

we see boundaries and abundance, not boundaries and barrenness. When it comes to this idea of investigating ways to live at peace with your mother, I want you to consider, *What's left? Is there any evidence of abundance amid a necessary boundary, or are all my boundaries resulting in barrenness?*

Is it possible to have both boundaries and abundance? If so, what could they practically look like with your mother? The following chart gives suggestions for practical ways that boundaries and abundance can coexist. I created it to help you get the conversation going with yourself, a therapist, or a trusted friend or church leader.

Is it possible to have both boundaries and abundance?

ISSUE	BOUNDARY	ABUNDANCE
Time	For now, we can't live together. For now, I am not comfortable with meeting at my home or her home.	We can make plans to spend time together and visit each other at our homes. I am willing to meet my mother at a neutral location.
Children	For now, I don't feel comfortable with my children spending the night at my mother's house or her babysitting them alone. For now, I am not comfortable with my mother contacting my children on their private phones or via email.	I am willing to let my mother spend time with my children and enjoy them if I am present. I am willing to allow my mother to speak to my children on the house phone or if she calls my phone to talk to them. I am willing for my mother to attend my children's sporting events, recitals, and other activities and sit with our family.

ISSUE	BOUNDARY	ABUNDANCE
Communication About Our Problems	For now, I am not ready for a conversation with my mother to talk about our relationship.	I am willing to talk with my mother in person or on a videoconference with a therapist.
Communication in General	For now, I am not comfortable with talking with her for a long time on the phone.	I am willing to text my mother. I am willing to have a brief conversation on the phone with my mother in which I check in, ask how she is doing, and share some general updates about my life. I am willing to talk to her on the phone or in person and even discuss challenges between us, but if profanity is used or name-calling or screaming begins, I am not willing to continue talking to her under those circumstances.
Family/Life Memory Keeping	For now, we aren't making many new memories just one-on-one.	I am willing to share pictures of my family with her. I am willing to take pictures with my mother or allow her to take pictures with her grandchildren. I am willing to show up for something she invites me to, such as attending church or a family event with her.

ISSUE	BOUNDARY	ABUNDANCE
Celebrations	For now, I am not willing to spend in-person holidays with my mother. OR For now, I don't want to spend *every* holiday with my mother.	I am willing to call my mother on holidays. I am willing to talk to my mother about what holidays we are both comfortable spending together, even if it's not all of them. I am willing to attend birthday parties where she'll also be and invite her to graduations. I am willing to acknowledge and celebrate my mother in some way on Mother's Day.
Support	For now, I am not comfortable receiving money from my mother and don't want to be locked into the responsibility of paying her bills.	I am willing to give gifts to and receive them from my mother. I am willing to give financial support to my mother if she has a need, and I am willing to find ways to be a blessing to her without her asking.
Vulnerability	For now, I am not comfortable asking her for advice or sharing my problems in real time.	I am willing to share my decisions and life updates with her. I am willing to pray for and with my mother.
Care	For now, I cannot physically care for my mother's health needs.	I am willing to pay for a nurse or aid, and I commit to spending time with my mother and talking to her at least weekly.
Mom's Relationships	For now, I am not willing to be around my mother's boyfriend/husband.	I am willing to spend time with my mother as long as her boyfriend/husband is not there.

Perhaps these suggestions seem too stringent and unnecessary in regards to where you and your mother are. These suggestions may feel like a lot of uncomfortable stretching that you aren't ready for. The goal is to demonstrate that boundaries aren't bad (in fact, they are healthy) and don't have to result in barrenness. Notice that I intentionally started all the boundary statements with "For now" because as you heal and if the relationship with your mother improves, some of the boundaries may not be necessary any longer. It also offers hope for growth and deeper levels of intimacy over time. It would be good for you to consider your relationship with your mother and think about what boundaries you believe are necessary "for now" but also what abundance can exist. Here is a healthy reminder about how to think through boundaries:

> The way to know which boundaries are godly [or sinful] is to examine the motive. Are you protecting yourself or someone weaker from potential harm . . . ? If so, then you are setting healthy and needful boundaries. However, if you are maintaining distance simply because you desire to exclude someone, that is sinful.[27]

One of my favorite psalms is number 16. In verse 6, the psalmist declares, "The boundary lines have fallen for me in pleasant places; surely I have a delightful inheritance" (NIV). Boundaries are God's idea and design, and that fact is supported by Scripture, practiced by Jesus,[28] and should be experienced as beneficial, not burdensome or barren. "Instead of fostering hostility in our relationships, boundaries encour-

---

27 "What Are Boundaries, and Are They Biblical?"

28 See Matthew 12:46–50; 14:13, 23; 26:18, 20; Mark 10:32; Luke 5:15–16; 23:8–9; John 11:6.

age honesty. Rather than being restrictive rules,[29] they serve as guiding tools that bring us back to the freedom God desires for us."[30]

WHEN PEACE IS IMPOSSIBLE, EMBRACE THE SWORD

We've discussed what you can embrace to pursue peace, but what do you do if resistance to your attempts at peace are so toxic that peace feels impossible? When should you "embrace the sword," and what does that even mean? Let's take a moment to read Matthew 10:34–39:

> Don't assume that I came to bring peace on the earth. I did not come to bring peace, but a sword. For I came to turn
>
> a man against his father,
> a daughter against her mother,
> a daughter-in-law against her mother-in-law;
> and a man's enemies will be
> the members of his household.
>
> The one who loves a father or mother more than me is not worthy of me; the one who loves a son or daughter more than me is not worthy of me. And whoever doesn't take up his cross and follow me is not worthy of me. Anyone who finds his life

---

29 Those with rigid boundaries often avoid intimacy and close relationships, are unlikely to ask for help, have few close relationships, are overly protective of personal information, may seem detached from even romantic partners, and keep others at a distance to avoid rejection. Those with porous boundaries overshare personal information, have difficulty saying no, get over involved in others' problems, are dependent on the opinions of others, accept abuse and disrespect, and fear rejection if they don't comply; see Cultivative Counseling, "What Are Healthy Boundaries and How to Practice Them," March 2, 2023, https://cultivativecounseling.com/2023/03/02/what-are-healthy-boundaries-and-how-to-practice-them.

30 Julie Brown, "Redefining Boundaries," Grace, August 13, 2024, https://discovergrace.com/redefining-boundaries/.

will lose it, and anyone who loses his life because of me will find it.

If you don't understand what Jesus is saying in that passage, you may be tempted to distrust him and the Bible. You may be thinking, *Didn't he just say that he brought peace to the earth as the Prince of Peace, but now he's talking about bringing a sword and turning members of one's family against one another?* But there is a simple and straightforward explanation. Jesus is talking to his disciples, letting them know that the gospel message is going to be offensive to many and will bring resistance. He is saying there will be a clear separation and division regarding his identity and ministry and that it sometimes will bring conflict and division with the people closest to us if they reject him.

As Christians, we should have our primary allegiance to Christ and follow his example in taking up our crosses daily. This isn't an excuse for us to turn into angry sword swingers with mean spirits and unnecessarily cutting words. People should stumble over the cross, not over us. How might we apply this to difficult relationships with others, including our mothers?

Sometimes the sword creates a division on orthodoxy, and other times it creates a division on orthopraxy. This doesn't mean pursuing peace or doing all you can to live at peace is no longer the goal, but there may come a time when, based on your mother's rejection of the faith or rejection of the command on how to live it out, there will be a dividing line that will dramatically impede fellowship. Your mother may not want you because you want Christ. Your mother may hate you because you love and live for Christ. Your mother may reject you because your presence, changed character, Christlike love, forgiveness, peace, witness, and worship may bring conviction and correction and she wants no part of it.

When you live in the light, it burns the eyes of those living in darkness. How can you recognize if the sword of truth is bringing a necessary separation, whether long-term or seasonal? Here are some ways to think about it:

- If her desire is for you to have a greater allegiance to her than to God, it may be time to embrace the sword.
- If her disdain for Christ creates unmitigated hostility toward you, it may be time to embrace the sword.
- If you are tempted to preserve her happiness with you rather than lose everything, even her affection, for the sake of Christ, it may be time to embrace the sword.
- If she wants you to prove your love and loyalty to her by following her into sin, it may be time to embrace the sword.
- If her emotional and spiritual unhealth puts you or your child in danger, embrace the sword.

Sometimes there will be a division based on our faith or our practice of our faith that we will have to endure and navigate. But God is not wanting us to misuse the Matthew 10 passage to quickly justify shunning someone. The sword isn't about cutting someone off or out of your life as much as it is about a clear line being drawn in the sand as a follower of Christ and providing a warning that the Christian must be prepared to lose everything and everyone for the sake of Christ (see Philippians 3:7–8).

NO CONTACT

Kristina Scharp, director of the Family Communication and Relationships Lab at Rutgers University and Michigan State University, defines estrangement as "an 'intentional distancing' between at least two family members 'because of a negative relationship—or the perception of one.'"[31] A 2019 study by Karl Pillemer reports that "twenty-seven per cent of Americans are currently estranged from a relative."[32] A concept that used to be taboo is gaining traction with online communities and support groups developing their own language and terms to describe variations of estrangement such as low contact, very low contact, and no contact. Advocates of the choice to be estranged argue that society feels comfortable telling people to leave a toxic relationship with a partner but often lacks the same conviction when it comes to a toxic family member, especially a parent. What causes adult children to become estranged from a parent is as varied as one could imagine, from abuse to disagreement in lifestyle choices and values. In his book *Rules of Estrangement,* Joshua Coleman names several things that often cause children to cut their parents out of their lives: the parents' divorce; a difficult in-law relationship; the child's mental illness or addiction; advice from the child's therapist;[33] feeling too close to the parent; disagreement about choices, values, and lifestyles; and a general societal shift of loyalty to the family unit being replaced by the pursuit of individual fulfillment.[34] Other adult children say their reasons for going no contact are rooted in self-preservation when all forms of boundary setting have failed, there is no progress in attempts to reconcile, and from their perspective the relationship has become too toxic to safely manage. Here's what estrangement statistics reveal:

---

31 Kristina Scharp, quoted in Anna Russell, "Why So Many People Are Going 'No Contact' with Their Parents," *The New Yorker,* August 30, 2024, www.newyorker.com/culture/annals-of-inquiry/why-so-many-people-are-going-no-contact-with-their-parents.

32 Russell, "Why So Many People Are Going 'No Contact.'"

33 Sometimes in therapy, the therapist makes faulty or exaggerated attributions of causality between a parent's past behavior and the child's present state of mind. Sometimes therapists recommend estrangement as a worthwhile intervention to address the child's feelings about the parent.

34 Joshua Coleman, *Rules of Estrangement: Why Adult Children Cut Ties and How to Heal the Conflict* (Harmony, 2021), 30–33.

- "Among adult children who go no contact, 80% cite emotional abuse, manipulation, or ongoing boundary violations as the main reasons.
- 70% of adult children who go no contact report feelings of guilt or sadness, even if they believe it was the right decision for their well-being."[35]

Psychotherapist Matthias J. Barker beautifully describes and reframes the difficult decision to go no contact with a parent:

> I know you might feel guilty for pushing away your parents, but we have to be honest here: Sometimes it's not that you're pushing them away; it's that they're declining your invitation to step into a healthy relationship.[36]

Instead of critiquing children who go no contact as being selfish, ungrateful, entitled, and ungodly, maybe an empathetic reframe is that some people's choice to go no contact from their mother may be the result of the mother's choice to decline the adult child's invitation for contact that's rooted in safety, mutual respect, and health. Pain and struggles in relationships are normal. We will never live in a fallen world and have pain-free interactions with people. Therefore, access to your life should demand not perfection but rather safety and the willingness of your mother to demonstrate that her life *and* yours are valuable and worthy of fundamental human dignity.

Take, for instance, the basic principle of healthy communication. Some mothers may think, *You are my child, so I can talk to you any way I*

---

35 "When Adult Children Go 'Low Contact' or 'No Contact' with Their Parents: A Guide to Understanding and Coping," Insight and Action Therapy, October 31, 2024, www.insightandactiontherapy.com/post/when-adult-children-go-low-contact-or-no-contact-with-their-parents-a-guide-to-understanding-an.

36 Matthias J. Barker, (@matthiasjbarker), Instagram video, October 7, 2025, www.instagram.com/reel/DPg7huBkc9a/?igsh=Zjk4YzNhYWRicG56.

please, but Scripture teaches, "With [the tongue] we bless our Lord and Father, and with it we curse people who are made in the likeness of God. . . . My brothers, these things ought not to be so" (James 3:9–10, ESV). Jesus ultimately sets the standard of how all image bearers should be treated, and if your mother is in outright violation of that, God's Word is rejected and you don't have to lower a requirement of basic human dignity that he won't change.

> Love the Lord your God with all your heart and with all your soul and with all your mind. This is the great and first commandment. And a second is like it: You shall love your neighbor as yourself. (Matthew 22:37–39, ESV)

This passage shapes how we are to treat all image bearers but also how we as image bearers ought to be treated. It is not selfish, entitled, ungrateful, or dramatic to require the dignity due to those made in the image of God. Perhaps the reframe needed for some is, *I do want a relationship with my mother, but a relationship without addiction and exploitation. I want a relationship without being cussed out, slapped, ridiculed, threatened, or disrespected in front of my children.* Perhaps you are inviting your mother into a type of relationship that she refuses to participate in.

Many Christians wonder whether going no contact is unbiblical. Let me say unequivocally that it is not unbiblical to suspend contact with someone who endangers your life or your family's, refuses to honor healthy boundaries, and dishonors God by acting evil toward you. While I am not advocating no contact as a first line of action for every relational tension, nor do I believe that some situations are too far gone for God's healing and reconciliation, I do feel this discussion deserves nuance and wisdom when navigating these difficult situations.

Here is a list of questions to consider when prayerfully discerning if your mother's behavior and disposition toward you make contact unattainable for a period:

- *Has my mother physically attacked me or threatened me with a weapon?*
- *Is my mother verbally abusive (cursing, name-calling, belittling, mocking, insulting), and does she make no effort to correct her conduct and speech and refuse to apologize and change?*
- *Does my mother scare my children?*
- *Does my mother refuse to let me speak, talk over me, or yell anytime we try to communicate?*
- *Is my mother hateful and disrespectful toward my spouse?*
- *Does my mother want a relationship with me only to use me?*
- *Does my mother refuse accountability for the ways she's injured me and, in turn, blame, mock, or trivialize my concerns?*
- *Does my mother refuse to acknowledge that I was sexually, physically, or emotionally abused by someone she protected or believed over me?*
- *Does my mother demand that I keep secrets and protect abusers?*
- *Is my mother currently married to, in a relationship with, or living with someone who abused me?*
- *Is my mother an active drug or alcohol user who refuses to get treatment?*
- *Is the turmoil with my mother putting my psychological or physical well-being at risk (depression, anxiety, suicidal ideation, self-harming behavior, inability to function and take care of daily life responsibilities from the stress)? Do I have hair loss, physical sickness, or some other physical condition that is caused by or exaggerated by my interactions with my mother?*
- *Am I becoming more vulnerable to unhealthy coping strategies like drinking, drugs, and overspending?*

- *Does my mother threaten to harm herself if I don't comply with her wishes?*
- *Am I in such a fragile emotional state and enmeshed relationship with my mother that I am unable to differentiate myself and make decisions beyond her control?*
- *Have I discussed with a mental health practitioner, family systems therapist, spiritual support counselor, spouse, or other healthy family member my considering going no contact with my mother? Have I received helpful, balanced counsel and support?*

Although some people may misuse the option of no contact as retaliation and punishment or avoidance of doing the work of repairing relationships, sometimes the no-contact status is appropriate for getting well, healing, and being in a better position to engage in the future. I pray that most people reading this are not in a situation where division and perpetual no contact is the only option, but sometimes despite your best efforts to pursue peace and be a peacemaker, your mother's choices will make relationship with her impossible. The goal for the Christian is to have a heart open for peace and use the sword appropriately. You would not spread peanut butter and jelly on bread with a samurai sword, and you would not opt to defend yourself against an attacker with a butter knife.

It is heartbreaking to imagine that the one person we are most desperate to experience love from can't or won't give it. It is crushing to have lived our childhoods and maybe even our adult lives constantly striving and working to receive love from our mothers. It's gut-wrenching to add up all the years we've spent walking on eggshells, minimizing insults, and absorbing maltreatment.

It is more than exhausting; it's just downright sad. It's the reality that all the dysfunctional behavior learned from trying to survive your mother's dysfunction puts you at risk of repeating those relational patterns with others in the future. Another question you may ask is, *Can I ever stop trying so hard, succumbing to unhealthy tactics to strong-arm love from my mother?*

One of the most profound quotes I've heard that expresses that painful reality was in response to this question: "What do you consider to be the definitive symptom of childhood trauma?" The speaker responded, "The definitive symptom of childhood trauma is about trying to get a difficult person to be good to us."[37] The impact of trauma can mask itself as the biblical behavior of embracing peace, when really all your efforts are motivated by trying to get your mother to embrace you. So many people are trying to get their mom to love them, but that is not the goal of being a peacemaker. A peacemaker's motivation is not self-driven or self-serving; it's not about being nice and accommodating with the real goal of ending the hunger and pain of our longing soul; it is about God's glory and bringing unity. If we are driven by anything but the ministry of reconciliation first to Christ and then to one another, the sword must be embraced so we can recalibrate our priorities and be established in our mission and ministry as disciples of Jesus, not just the children of our mothers.

If division comes between you and your mother by hostile rejection of the faith or ungodly practice, hopefully it lasts for only a season. In Scripture, we see temporary separations, such as Paul and Barnabas, who had a dispute over John Mark but later are believed to have reconciled,[38] or at least Paul affirmed his respect for Barnabas and John Mark by positively mentioning them in his letters (see Acts 13:13;

---

37 Agate Murasko (@peaceful.mamabear), Instagram video, August 16, 2025, www.instagram.com/reel/DNbBceYNkpk/?igsh=dTQzNHA3ZnZtOXBi. Recorded from the Dr. Ramani Network of Dr. Ramani Durvasula (@doctorramani).

38 Darryl Dash, "When Christians Disagree," The Gospel Coalition Canada, February 16, 2022, https://ca.thegospelcoalition.org/columns/straight-paths/when-christians-disagree.

15:37–39; 1 Corinthians 9:6; 2 Timothy 4:11).[39] We also see permanent separations, like King Saul and David, because David not only went no contact but also literally ran for his life because the king was jealous and wanted to kill him (see 1 Samuel 21–23).

We also see a permanent separation between Jesus and Judas, who were separated and unreconciled by Judas's death (see Matthew 27:3–8; Acts 1:18–19). God used "cherubim and the flaming, whirling sword" to block Adam and Eve from regaining access to the Garden of Eden and the tree of life after they sinned (Genesis 3:24). The use of the sword was an act of mercy so they wouldn't stay in their sinful state eternally by eating from the tree of life. God used the sword to keep Adam and Eve out, but he also promised that there was a way back into paradise to have eternal fellowship with him through his Son, Jesus. God denied access, designed the repair plan, and set the terms for reconciliation and fellowship in the future. What a beautiful picture of hope in the face of the sword!

Conversely, although God desires all would be saved, everyone won't be reconciled back into relationship with him. In the end, God himself, the perfect parent, will go permanently no contact with those who violate his boundaries, those who refuse to acknowledge their sin and repent, and those who refuse to become his children by embracing peace and having access to eternal life through his Son. Even God embraces the sword.

I pray that you and your mother will receive the embrace of the

39 We don't know why John Mark deserted Paul, or who was even right in the matter concerning Paul and Barnabas, but "we do know, however, that Paul didn't want to take John Mark with him again. Things got so heated that Paul and Barnabas experienced a 'sharp disagreement' and separation, leading to two teams (Paul and Silas on one, Barnabas and John Mark on the other) instead of one. We're never told which one was right. We do know that the conflict resulted in two teams instead of one, and that Paul later reconciled with both Barnabas and John Mark, mentioning them both positively in his letters (1 Corinthians 9:6; 2 Timothy 4:11)"; Dash, "When Christians Disagree."

Peacemaker, embrace him back, and then one day be able to embrace each other. The impact of the sword doesn't have to be a permanent status for you and your mother, but it may be in the best interests of everyone for a season.

As Christians, we always put our hope in Christ, the one who can redeem and mend any brokenness. Our responsibilities are to have the proper heart posture that welcomes our mothers if they repent and to offer them the forgiveness God offered us. Ending no contact doesn't mean everything is fine, but transitioning out of no-contact status can stem from a unique call from God to move toward our mothers and try again with support or—if there is sufficient acknowledgment of harm, an apology, observable change, and a commitment from our mothers—to do the work of repair. Our hope and confidence rests on knowing that even when we are divided, the Peacemaker is always at work in all our lives (see Isaiah 58:12; Joel 2:25–26).

REFLECTION QUESTIONS

1. *Which call to embrace was most helpful for you? Why?*

3. *What is your reaction to the counsel to embrace suffering? What might that look like in a relationship with your mother, and what shouldn't it look like?*

3. *How can embracing your mother's and your humanity help you move forward toward healing and peace with each other?*

4. *How does the counsel on embracing the sword convict or encourage you? Are you using a samurai sword and butter knife appropriately?*

5. *What hope do you see in God's embrace of the sword and his promise and plan for restoration of relationship?*

PRAYER

Lord, where my heart and hands are closed, help me willingly open them so I can embrace everything you've called me to embrace. Thank you for never prying my hands open but always patiently waiting on me to surrender to your will. Reading these words in this chapter is a grace to me, and I receive it. Lead me and guide me in the life of a peacemaker who has been wounded; I can't do it on my own. May my life reflect that I have been forever changed because you embraced me first. Amen.

CHAPTER 11

HONOR YOUR MOTHER

THE TENSION AND THE TRUTH

Honour thy father and thy mother: that thy days may be long upon the land which the LORD thy God giveth thee.

—EXODUS 20:12 (KJV)

The Tension

I admit that when the Lord gave me the title of this book, *Honor Thy Mother*, initially it seemed like a contradiction. It felt oxymoronic to introduce a book aimed at helping wounded adult children that had a title that was an unmistakable and ancient command to honor the very person who hurt them. It wasn't that I was conflicted on the issue of honor being a righteous command from God, but I thought of the people who have been hurt by their mothers and how hard it would be to hear any talk about honoring their offenders. Maybe that was a little of my own projection, but then it hit me: That's the message of the gospel wrapped up in the tension of having to give something good to someone who hasn't earned it.

Isn't that a picture of grace working through the law? I want to challenge you for a moment to question the belief that your mother deserves honor only if she earns it or has a track record of living honorably consistently. I want to invite you to be curious regarding what God had in mind when he gave his people this command to govern their lives and shape the family and world. Pondering these things may have hit your spiritual gut in a nauseating way, but stay with me.

I realize this is the section of the book where you could take a dive if you aren't firmly rooted in God's truth. Even if you are a professing Christian, you may be tempted to believe that your pain is being minimized or ignored or that you are being asked to continually subject yourself to maltreatment. You may be turned off by the notion that God is calling the offended to do the heavy lifting in the relationship. If you aren't a Christian or are very new to the faith, this is the section of the book where you could assume that all the validation, support, naming of pain, and talk of healing is now going out of the window in exchange for dangerous religious dogma about obeying a God who does not care about your suffering.

Let me unequivocally say to you, none of that is true. In fact, everything that has been shared up to this point has been preparing us to dive deeper into the beauty of God's commandments, the power of honor, and the blessings that flow from obedience to him, our perfect parent. I hope you are excited to discover his heart on his command to honor parents and that you will receive the wisdom and strength needed to live this out in your daily life. You will learn of the blessings that come your way when you obey the fifth commandment.

You may wrestle with the what and why (*What does this command mean and why did God include it?*), you may wrestle with the how (*I understand and accept the truth and goodness of this command, but how do I practically do it?*), or you may struggle with all three. It is my prayer that at the conclusion of this chapter, those questions will be answered in a way that's faithful to Scripture, gives you some practical steps to implement, and reveals the love and care of God and his good plan for your life and your mother's. I think you will be humbled and empowered, and likely you will be pleasantly surprised that what he intends with what this command requires from you isn't as impossible as it may feel. The Bible assures us, "This is the love of God, that we keep his commandments. And his commandments are not burdensome. For everyone who has been born of God overcomes the world. And this is the victory that has overcome the world—our faith" (1 John 5:3–4, ESV).

The Truth

THE TRUTH ABOUT HONOR

Honor is a biblical term that refers to the respect, worth, dignity, esteem, high regard, and reverence given to God, individuals, and principles. The specific word *honor* appears at least 150 times in the English Bible. The term is derived from the Hebrew word *kabod* and the Greek word *timē,* both of which convey a sense of weightiness, value, severity, or importance. The root conveys the idea of physical heaviness (see 2 Samuel 14:26; Job 6:3). Honoring something or someone "carries the nuance of weighing [someone] down with honor or respect and it means to treat someone with the respect and deference that his or her position deserves."[1] Honor is a multidimensional idea in Scripture and encompasses the respect due to God;[2] authorities, leaders, and elders;[3] spouses;[4] the elderly;[5] the wise;[6] the physical body;[7] people in general;[8] and, of course, parents.[9]

---

1 Mark Rooker, *The Ten Commandments: Ethics for the Twenty-First Century,* New American Commentary Studies in Bible and Theology, ed. Ray Clendenen (Broadman and Holman, 2010), 107–8.

2 See 1 Samuel 2:30; Proverbs 3:9; 14:31; Malachi 1:6; John 5:23; Revelation 4:9–11.

3 See Philippians 2:29–30; 1 Thessalonians 5:12–13; 1 Timothy 5:17; Hebrews 13:17.

4 See Hebrews 13:4; 1 Peter 3:7.

5 See Leviticus 19:32; 1 Peter 5:5.

6 See Proverbs 3:35.

7 See 1 Corinthians 12:23–24; 1 Thessalonians 4:3–5.

8 See Romans 12:10; 13:7; 1 Peter 2:17.

9 See Exodus 20:12; 21:17; Deuteronomy 5:16; Matthew 15:1–9; 19:19; Mark 7:10; Ephesians 6:2–3; Colossians 3:20.

God is serious about honor, and something you may have noticed is that one's personal integrity and righteousness are related in Scripture to honor. As Proverbs 21:21 states, "The one who pursues righteousness and faithful love will find life, righteousness, and honor." When you have a life of integrity it brings honor from both God and from others: "A gracious woman gains honor" (11:16). However, that is often why children with mother wounds—who view their mother to have lived dishonorably, particularly in relationship with them—struggle to understand how to honor to her. You may wonder, *If my mother hasn't been gracious, shouldn't she be denied honor?* But it is important to note that honor, when used as a verb (to give honor), is a command and virtue "integral to the moral and social fabric of biblical teaching."[10]

Believers are encouraged to cultivate a culture of honor in their personal lives, families, churches, and communities. "Honor is not merely an external act but a reflection of the heart's posture towards God and His creation."[11] There are cases in Scripture where the command is given for honor to be bestowed and for people to be esteemed without the condition of human appraisal of deservedness (see 1 Samuel 24:1–8; Romans 13:1, 7). God values the positions he's established for family, church, and societal order, and he wants those ordained positions honored. That means you may be called to honor the individual in the position even if you struggle to like the person. Embracing this truth is universally helpful not just in your relationship with your mother but for all levels of authority God sanctions in the world and the church, whether it means rising in a courtroom for a judge, respecting your boss, or honoring religious leaders, even those we disagree with. We honor God when we respect the offices and positions he honors and has established to maintain order and peace and reflect his kingdom values, even when people poorly steward those positions.

---

10 "Honor," BibleHub, https://biblehub.com/topical/h/honor.htm.

11 "Honor."

Honoring people in positions of authority doesn't mean blind or total obedience, but we will discuss that more later.

THE TRUTH ABOUT THE FIFTH COMMANDMENT

In her book *Mother Hunger,* licensed professional counselor Kelly McDaniel stated, "Although Judeo-Christian theology calls us to 'honor thy father and mother,' sometimes it is impossible—and indeed unwise—to 'honor thy mother.'"[12] While I understand the harmful behaviors and dishonorable lives many of your mothers have lived, I do not believe that it is impossible or unwise to honor our mothers, because McDaniel's view doesn't encompass what honor is in God's view.

Why would someone believe that it would be impossible or unwise to honor one's mother? I believe it is because they have a misunderstanding or misapplication of this commandment. In McDaniel's example, the implied point is that to honor a parent requires obedience in every situation and overriding your own convictions about what is right or wrong for you to do. But does God mean for us to equate honor with absolute obedience to parents? He doesn't, and that is why it is imperative to have a biblical comprehension of what honor is and is not, of God's heart behind this command, and of the power and wisdom available to us to keep it, despite the character and behavior of the mothers we have. When you have this foundation and understanding, you are able to move forward and honor your mother in a way that is healthy and safe and honors God's command.

The parental law is important and transitional as the law moves from obligations to God to obligations to fellow neighbors in society. According to author Kevin DeYoung, "'Honor your father and mother'

---

12 Kelly McDaniel, *Mother Hunger: How Adult Daughters Can Understand and Heal from Lost Nurturance, Protection, and Guidance* (Hay House, 2021), 94.

is the foundation upon which love for our neighbor is built."[13] Now let's dive deeper into the beauty, seriousness, and uniqueness of the fifth commandment. It is also the only commandment given with a promise.

Honor "reflects the order and harmony intended by God, promoting a society where respect, love, and righteousness prevail. The call to honor God and others is a reflection of the believer's transformation and commitment to living according to God's will."[14] Our relationships with our parents or parental figures are the first and most important ones. They shape and inform all other relationships. From our relationships with our parents, we learn what it means to have someone in authority over us, listen to others, do things we sometimes don't want to do, and show respect and honor. Can we accept that it is difficult to listen to anyone when you don't feel loved by them? It is difficult but perhaps not impossible. What if, over the course of time, wounded children learn to have relationship with a perfect God, listen to him, unlearn some things they "heard" at home, and through that relationship change the trajectory of how they relate to others? As adult children, we learn the purpose and art of honoring our human parents, regardless of who they are or who they have been.

THE TRUTH ABOUT WHAT HONOR IS NOT

Before I discuss God's heart and command to honor, I want to acknowledge that you may have had an abusive, strained, or toxic relationship with your mother, and therefore it is important to say what honor is not.

Honor is not motivated by guilt. The Bible teaches that fulfilling the duty to honor and please God flows from a heart of love, thankful-

---

13 Kevin DeYoung, *The Ten Commandments: What They Mean, Why They Matter, and Why We Should Obey Them* (Crossway, 2018), 80.

14 "Honor."

ness, and a renewed mind in Christ rather than compulsory or shame-driven works (see Hebrews 10:22). God doesn't want his children to draw near to him with a guilty conscience; he frees us from guilt and allows us to have sincere devotion.

If your mother has thrown out a distorted "Big Joker card" ("You aren't being a good Christian or a good child because you are supposed to honor me—the Bible says so"), that's a demand she cannot make and a guilt trip she cannot hang on you. Honoring one's parent must be motivated by love for God and an internal compulsion to obey him by fulfilling that sacred duty. If you do any works in the name of honoring your mother in which you think more about what she demands and not what God commands, that is not healthy, love-driven honor. Doing things for the sole purpose of appeasing your mother, rooted in feeling guilty, may appear to work for a moment, but it is not sustainable, will build resentment, and will distance you from the Lord.

God uses godly sorrow to bring us to genuine repentance. Godly sorrow can be life-giving, not life-condemning. Godly sorrow when we miss the mark produces godly grief, not mommy-projected guilt. Telling children what the Bible tells them to do, while simultaneously ignoring what the Bible requires a parent to do, is hypocritical, prideful, and unloving. Healthy relationships with our mothers and the ease of honor would more likely happen if everyone, including our mothers, obeyed what Jesus taught in Matthew 7:3–5:

> Why do you look at the splinter in your brother's eye but don't notice the beam of wood in your own eye? Or how can you say to your brother, "Let me take the splinter out of your eye," and look, there's a beam of wood in your own eye? Hypocrite! First take the beam of wood out of your eye, and then you will see clearly to take the splinter out of your brother's eye.

We don't honor God to seek his love and approval; we honor him because we already have it. Conversely, you don't honor your mother to seek her love and approval; you honor her out of love for God and a desire to obey him.

Honor is not obedience. The fifth commandment is not "*Obey* your father and mother"; rather, it is "*Honor* your father and mother." However, the Bible unquestionably places great emphasis on children obeying their parents as a form of honor, and we see this come into play when they are in the home and not yet adults (see Ephesians 6:1–3; Colossians 3:20). Most, if not all of us, can understand the value of obeying parents and its subsequent impact on how children will obey their teachers, church leaders, and other adult neighbors. One of the first things people tend to say if they experience a disobedient child who is not their own is, "He doesn't have any home training." But you may be wondering, *Are there any limits or an expiration date for unquestionably obeying my parents? I'm a grown adult; does God still want me to do everything my mother tells me to do?* You are right to ask those questions.

As you look deeper at the context and language used in the passages on obeying one's parents, there is a subtle switch in the honor language when referring to adult children. When speaking about adult children honoring their parents, the language focuses more on honor taking the form of respect and care (provision), thus meaning that obedience is a specific form of honor for young children. That isn't a license for an adult child to cop an attitude with their parents, saying something like, "I'm grown, so I won't be doing anything you ask me to do," because God cares about us honoring them and that would be a heart posture that does not show love or respect for one's parents. But there are four exceptions to obedience to parents that I want you to know about:

1. **Adult Versus Child.** If you are no longer under your parents' roof and you are a self-sustaining adult, you are not

required to obey your parents to the degree you were required to as a child. The task of parents is to raise their children to become independent adults able to function outside their authority, whether as single adults or married. But in cases where adult children continue to live at home with their parents, they should humbly do things that their parents might ask of them, such as chores, contributing to the household expenses, and respecting their space. Doing those things are pleasing to the Lord.

2. **Manipulation and Control.** As an adult, you are free to make adult decisions that don't always align with your mother's wishes. If you have spent years being controlled, dismissed, or invalidated by her, or struggled with needing approval from her, it is important to know that God is not requiring you to obey your mother, especially when obedience has been used as a tactic of manipulation and control. That may be a common experience for those parents who assert a biblical precedent to demand obedience. It is important to differentiate honor from obedience so that you aren't burdened by guilt. It is healthy and wise to see that ultimate obedience is owed to God.

3. **Sin.** If your mother requests that you sin in any way, you are not obligated to obey her. In Colossians 3:20, Paul instructs children to obey their parents "in everything," but that statement is clarified in Ephesians 6:1 with the statement "in the Lord." Paul is emphasizing that children should obey their parents if what the parents ask is not contradicting the teachings of the Lord. The biblical principle that applies is Acts 5:29, "We must obey God rather than people [even mothers and fathers]," because our primary responsibility of obedience is to God, not our parents.

4. **Abuse.** Theologian Tim Challies states that if your parents' demand for obedience becomes abusive, that is an acceptable time for disobedience.[15] Your parents cannot demand that you consent to and obey their demand to treat you unrighteously with abusive speech, violence, or sexual exploitation. Any desire of parents to engage in any form of abuse does not have to be obeyed.

Since obedience will naturally end as a child grows, and since obedience can sometimes be sinful, God does not command that we obey our parents, but he does command that we honor them.

Honor is not relationship. Some mothers have acted so wickedly that their children must break free from her. "Victims of child abuse are likely to struggle with the 5th commandment. In such a situation, disturbed parental behavior has to be resisted."[16] God does not require children who were abused by their unrepentant parents to maintain relationship with them as adults. Relationship after abuse or any offense can happen only through the parents' true repentance and asking and offering forgiveness that moves toward reconciliation. Forgiveness and reconciliation are not the same thing. By God's grace, injured children will be able to get to a place of forgiveness (canceling the sin debt as if it never happened), but reconciliation (the reconnecting of lives for relationship) takes time, work, and agreement between both parties:

> In such cases, honoring God may mean honestly facing the trauma, leaving vengeance in his hands, and acknowledging before God that he made no mistakes in choosing the parents. It means letting go of bitterness, trusting God through the

15 Tim Challies, *The Commandment We Forgot*, Cruciform Quick (Challies, 2017), 20.

16 David L. Baker, *The Decalogue: Living as the People of God* (InterVarsity, 2017), 96.

pain, and dwelling deeply on the display of his compassion on the cross.[17]

Honor is not agreement. Honoring our parents does not mean we must agree with them about everything they believe, say, or do. For example, if your mother has racist attitudes, cheats on her taxes, uses drugs, has profane speech, or only sees herself as a victim, you can still honor her without having to agree with her sinful or unhealthy thoughts and actions, even if she becomes angry with you and works against peace. Our first obligation is agreement with God: "Agree with God, and be at peace" (Job 22:21, ESV).

Honor is not enabling. Honoring your mother doesn't mean you have to enable her sinful or unhealthy behavior. You do not have to cover up or conceal her sin, and if you were abused, you do not dishonor your mother by seeking to have her prosecuted for sexually or physically abusing you or another child. Enabling can also expand beyond sinful things to unwise things. You do not have to buy her packs of cigarettes, especially if she has cancer or other medical conditions that cigarettes worsen or it goes against your conscience (see Acts 24:16; Romans 14:23; 1 John 3:21).

Honoring your mother does not require you to pretend bad things didn't happen in your family or that your mother has a flawless reputation. In fact, that would be a different sin: lying. One way a misunderstanding of honor can reveal itself is the pressure to engage in image control for your mother. You are not your mother's public relations agent. Many people grew up in homes where truth telling was frowned upon and considered "airing the family's dirty laundry." Every detail of your life and your mother's actions doesn't have to be for public consumption, as that wouldn't be wise, but you should have people

---

17 Challies, *Commandment We Forgot,* 44–45.

you can tell the truth to without doing the hard work of pretending. While you don't have to go out of your way to disparage your mother, you also don't have to lie. For instance, there is a difference between the following statements:

> "My mother is the worst mother on the planet." (DISPARAGING)
>
> "My mother was always kind and apologized easily for her mistakes." (PRETENDING)
>
> "My experience with my mother was filled with moments when she showed care and concern, but I also experienced painful moments where she acted insensitively toward me." (TRUTHFUL)
>
> "I hate my mother. She's dead to me." (DISPARAGING)
>
> "My mother was always good to me, and any problems we ever had were because I'm really sensitive." (PRETENDING)
>
> "I have a really challenging relationship with my mother that has caused distance, but I pray for a time when we can heal and be restored in God's way. It will be hard and take time, but I put my hope in him and believe anything is possible." (TRUTHFUL)

Pretending imprisons us, but truth frees us. Secret keeping is almost always harmful because secrets keep us sick, but in my opinion, pretending is worse than secret keeping because not only is there a suppression of truth, but there is also the manufacturing of more glorious-appearing lies. God can handle the dark and messy parts of his children's lives, and he wants to empower us to do the same. He never sanitized the Bible; he told us the raw truth about the patriarchs and matriarchs of the faith.[18] I love that he told us the truth, and his plan of salvation was not so fragile that he could not overcome and save the most broken of people. You can honor your mother without lying for her.

A refusal to pretend involves navigating the necessary but delicate balance of grace and truth. It is not about exposing your mother's faults to anyone who will listen; rather, being full of grace and truth means you are first willing to humbly expose the relationship and experience of your mother to Jesus, who's the one who can do something about the pain of the past, transform the most hardened of hearts, and give you wisdom and direction on how to communicate about it. The more truthful you are with Jesus, the less pressure you'll feel to pretend with people.

Honor is not a feeling. God calls us to treat our parents with honor, not make sure they feel honored. That is an important distinction. He is clear that honor is what we are called do to, but even when you do it, your mother may not agree that she is being honored if she wants you to do something beyond the scope of honor. The point is that you may be making great efforts to honor your mother and she might say, "I don't feel honored," if she doesn't understand biblical honor or is disappointed or angry that the scope of biblical honor falls short of her expectations of you, especially if what she wants is for you to obey, affirm, overlook, accept, worship, or submit to her will. With that said, remember that honor is the bare minimum; in time, your relationship with your mother could improve to the place where not only is honoring her easy for you to do but you both enjoy experiencing other parent-child interaction and joy that flow from a healthy relationship.

18 Some examples include Moses (murderer), David (adulterer and murderer), Rahab (prostitute), the woman at the well (had many husbands), Sarai (suggested sexually exploiting her servant to get a baby), Abram (agreed to Sarai's suggestion and was a liar), Rebekah (showed favoritism to one child and deceived her husband), Peter (denied Jesus), and many more we could name.

THE TRUTH ABOUT WHAT HONORING YOUR MOTHER LOOKS LIKE

I am compelled to reiterate this: Depending on where you are on your healing journey, it may be months or even years before you can physically or emotionally feel safe enough to engage in some of the suggested behavior we'll discuss in this section. But I want to say sensitively and carefully, but also as clearly as possible, that there is no exception clause in the fifth commandment to *honor* your parents. When thinking about the thousands of people who have suffered because of their parents, I had hoped there was an exception to the rule. Before you allow your frustrated or angry emotions to run away with you, remember what we have learned about what honor is not.

Honor still has certain characteristics and expectations from God, despite the parent's character. Each display of honor may look different, and I am in no way providing an exhaustive list, but the goal is to obey God by finding ways to honor our mothers. I understand that each reader has a varying degree of vulnerability. You might be in a much safer position than others to more easily begin or improve upon your duty of honor and the work of rebuilding and repairing your relationship with your mother; on the other hand, you might still be deeply grieving and suffering from pain from your mother's abuse or other forms of evil behavior that may require you to severely limit proximity. In that case, the idea of being called to honor feels impossible and unfair.

On a human and emotional level, I get it, but I am responsible for doing my best to share what the Bible teaches and convey God's heart in these difficult circumstances. What I know for sure is that he loves you (see Psalm 36:5, ESV), is near even if he feels far (see Deuteronomy 31:8), and will deliver you from your affliction (see Psalm 34:18–19, ESV). God is angry because of any harm done to you and assures you that you need not attempt to seek vengeance for yourself, because vengeance belongs to the Lord and he will repay (see Romans 12:19).

I know that if God tells us to do something, such as honor our parents, he has already factored in their flaws and our frailty, fear, and fatigue. He never intends for us to live as righteous disciples without the supernatural power we need in order to do his will. Honor is hard, honoring those who've lived dishonorably is harder, but "nothing will be impossible with God" (Luke 1:37).

In addition to what I am offering as a way forward, I want to encourage you to seek the Lord and other wise counsel about how you can practically honor your mother even with the unique set of circumstances and trauma you may face. I also want to affirm that there is a difference between parental failure and parental abuse:

> In such cases where behaviors and abuse make it difficult or impossible for the children to be close to their parents, it is the parents' abusive behavior that has placed the limits on the relationship, not the child's failure to obey the [fifth] commandment. . . .
>
> An abusive parent contaminates everything God intends parenting to accomplish.[19]

I am reiterating the sensitivity around abuse not to give a loophole for honor but rather to not forget what we learned about what honor isn't. Holding both what honor is and what it is not is critical so children who have suffered abuse (referring to extreme behavior, whether verbal or physical, that caused harm) don't misunderstand God's heart, protection of the most vulnerable, and his intent in the fifth commandment and, in turn, subject themselves unsafely to their mothers. I like how one writer put it: "'Honor thy parent' doesn't mean destroy thyself."[20]

---

19 Cecil Maranville, "How to Honor a Parent Who Isn't Honorable," Life, Hope and Truth, December 8, 2025, https://lifehopeandtruth.com/life/blog/how-to-honor-a-parent-who-isnt-honorable/.

20 Katia Beeden, "'Honor Thy Parent' Doesn't Mean Destroy Thyself: Choosing No-Contact Without Guilt," Medium, November 29, 2025, https://medium.com/

Conversely, another important point is for those of us not dealing with extreme abuse from our mothers but rather parent failure. (Both abuse and failure are wrong and must be addressed.) In our trauma-obsessed cancel culture, God is calling many of us to humbly scrutinize our attitudes and behavior toward our mothers' failures where we feel entitled to withhold honor and refuse being open and available to repair, forgive, reconcile, and maybe even repent to our mothers for shared responsibility in the brokenness. Abused children might feel pressure to do too much too soon, and non-abused children may be applying an unnecessarily restrictive and hopeless disposition toward their mothers because they have experienced offense and feel pain.

Despite the limits some face for relational contact, it is important to think through the boundaries and abundance of how can honor look. Honoring one's parents can take many forms, but what we find in Scripture are three broad categories that honor should reflect in adult children: love and respect, care, and gratitude.

Love and Respect

The fifth commandment broadens the connotation of *honor* to mean we are to respect our parents (see Leviticus 19:3). The Hebrew word *yirah* means "fear" or "awe," is conceptually related to honor, and is frequently used to express one's response to God (see Deuteronomy 10:12). As the relationship between Israel and God is often expressed in filial terms, the verbs *honoring* and *fearing* are used to express proper attitudes toward both God and parents.[21] The parental law within the Ten Commandments affirms that honoring one's parents is related to one's spiritual commitment to God and therefore

---

@katiabeeden/honor-thy-parent-doesnt-mean-destroy-thyself-choosing-no-contact-without-guilt-8d06617215b1.

21 See Leviticus 24:10–16; Numbers 15:30; Deuteronomy 21:18–21; 27:16; 1 Kings 21:12–14.

presupposes the spiritual dignity of parents. Mark Rooker, a professor of the Old Testament, gave a jaw-dropping explanation of why we should honor our parents by respecting them:

> Parents should be viewed as representatives of God. The occurrence of the term *fear* in Leviticus 19:3 as a response to parents is a remarkable statement about the unparalleled relationship between parent and child. This shows that "fear" (respect) has a religious foundation; it does not convey merely a noble respect for parents since fear normally expresses one's relationship to God. Scripture makes reverence to parents comparable to reverence for God. . . . [The] association of God with parents establishes again the esteemed position parents have in the world. It also stresses the truth that God is honored or dishonored by man's [or woman's] relationship with his parents. If the fifth commandment is classified with the first section of the Decalogue, which focuses on God, we see once more the special value that is assigned to parental authority. The root *kbd* is used in the fifth commandment with reference to parents; it's never used in association with priests or prophets. Thus, we find in this commandment that the relationship between child and parent is of paramount importance. . . . It is easier to obey than to honor. An individual may hate but still obey, whereas one cannot both hate and honor simultaneously.[22]

The last sentence from that quote also speaks to the importance of motive as we honor our parents. Bible teacher Jen Wilkin notes that all the Ten Commandments relate to honor because they all relate to heavenly submission, earthly submission, and mutual submission—in that order. She advises we connect Rooker's idea to the New Testa-

---

22 Rooker, *Ten Commandments,* 107.

ment's Greatest Commandment, which we are told sums up the law (see Mark 12:30–31). She suggests reading the Greatest Commandment (below) and filling in the blanks with the word that belongs there (based on Mark 12:30–31, ESV), then reading it a second time and replacing that word with *honor.*

> You shall _____ the Lord your God with all your heart and with all your soul and with all your mind and with all your strength. . . . You shall _____ your neighbor as yourself.

According to Wilkin, "Honor is an [expansion and] expression of rightly ordered love. When we love as we should, we honor the object of our love as we should."[23] I've been asked this question more times than I can count: "Would you rather be loved or respected?" That always feels like an impossible question to answer if your heart as a leader is to lead in a way that honors God. But now I understand why that question is so off-putting to me and so many other Christian leaders: Motive matters. Is it really love if there is no respect, and is there real respect without love? God wants us to honor him by loving and respecting him, and he wants us to honor our parents by loving and respecting them.

The following are ways that honor can be given to your mother in the form of love and respect:

- **Speak respectfully to her and about her.** You don't have to make up untrue and disingenuous platitudes about your mother, but you can say what is true and good. Where she has earned a compliment or a word of thanks, don't withhold it. But as the old adage says, if you don't have anything good to say, don't say anything. We can find ways to

23 Jen Wilkin, *Ten Words to Live By: Delighting in and Doing What God Commands* (Crossway, 2021), 77.

disagree without using abusive language, cursing, or screaming. Even when our mothers may not give us the same courtesy, we don't have to become who they are. God forbids the dishonoring of a parent. It is important to note that covering shame (see Genesis 9:20–27) and not disrespecting your mother are not the same as covering up sins or pretending bad things didn't happen. It begins and ends with your heart posture, motivation, and how and with whom to share truth. Do you tell the truth in a way to bring healing and get help, or do you tell the truth in a way in which your intent is to mock, bring shame, and expose out of anger or disregard for your mother's humanity?

- **Keep your commitments and word.** If you promised to do something for your mother or if you said you would show up, barring an exigent circumstance, respect her by following through. A young woman once told me she was convicted because she used to feel no remorse if she canceled plans with her mother. She said, "My mom never kept her word, so in some ways I was showing her how awful it felt to be let down." This woman later realized she wasn't operating with integrity and it was unkind and unbiblical to repay evil with evil. She said she apologized to her mother for her behavior while also sharing with her how hurt she was in the past when her mom had let her down. They ended up having a positive conversation that led to her mother apologizing for how she had hurt her.
- **Acknowledge and celebrate her birthday and other special occasions.** Acknowledging your mother's special days is a simple way to show love and respect. You can send a card, call, leave a voicemail message, or show up if it is safe to do so. Attend her retirement celebration, support some special work she may be involved in at church or in

the community, remember her marriage anniversary, and find ways to acknowledge or show support on grief days, such as the death of her parent, spouse, children, or siblings. Sometimes we think we are losing when we give to someone, especially a parent who didn't give to us the way we wanted, but that is what Jesus did. It is always going to be hard to show respect and love for someone who wasn't there for you the way you hoped or needed, but Jesus loved us while we were sinners and rejected him. He didn't just move toward us when he was unwelcome; he came and loved us despite us. Finding ways to do that for your mother would be emulating Christ's example of unconditional love.

- **Listen to her.** It may be difficult to talk to your mother at times, but increasing your willingness to listen can be an opportunity to show her respect and love. Most people want to be known, heard, and understood. Take time to ask her nonthreatening questions like "What most makes you happy?" "When was the last time you had a big belly laugh?" "What dreams do you still have for yourself?" and "What do you wish I understood about you that you don't think I understand?" Invite her to share her heart and humanity and even perspective and gripes with you. It demonstrates that her life has value and she has a story, opinion, history, worth sharing. As frustrating as it may be, refuse to challenge, correct, or dismiss her. Your silence doesn't mean you agree, lose, or have nothing to say (even if she believes that). You can honor her by telling her, "Mom, we may not always agree, but today I just want to listen to you." This is an exercise in love and respect, and love is not self-seeking. Model it for her, and divorce yourself from the expectation to have it reciprocated.

Listening also has the potential benefit of informing, maybe even enlightening our long-held interpretations of our mothers' behavior. For instance, here's a story from one of my clients:

"My mom never let me do anything. I couldn't do sleepovers, she micromanaged my life, she asked a million questions every time I wanted to do something, and she criticized all my choices as foolish, unwise, and what she deemed unnecessary risks. She even called me 'fast' when I just wanted to date a nice guy. She was the personification of a worrywart, and as I got older it caused great conflict, as I was determined to get out from under her control. All my life, I believed that my mother's behavior (denying me fun, being jealous of my opportunities) was a lack of trust and respect for me. But her prison-warden behavior was actually rooted in her own childhood sexual abuse by a family member. She parented out of fear and probably some anger (her word was always *concern*), but she tried to protect me the only way she knew how. My mother's only vision of protection was to create a prison. I still felt like I'd lost out on a lot (special events, out-of-the-country travel opportunities, parties), and even as an adult, I received harsh criticism from her as I raised my own daughter. But I began to understand her behavior, and that softened my heart even though it couldn't change my hard experience."

The story she had rehearsed for years was true but incomplete. I am not promising that your willingness to listen to your mother as an act of honor will yield a powerful and happy ending, but you can never lose if you obey God and do all you can to show love and respect, even when it feels impossible. Wouldn't it be beautiful if both of you could overcome the painful emotions and have powerful empathy that can transform hearts and relationships?

- **Pick your battles wisely.** I am using the word *battles* loosely because I don't like characterizing difficult conversations as battles, but my point is that you can show love and respect to your mother by using wisdom on what to address and what to leave alone. Sometimes we overcorrect for years of emotional stuffing and silence by adopting the mantra "If I'm upset, I'm going to be honest and say everything on my mind all the time." The Bible wouldn't agree with that position, as Proverbs 29:11 says, "A fool gives full vent to his spirit, but a wise man quietly holds it back" (ESV). Sometimes we can dishonor our mother by not exercising discretion. When my husband's or my parents have said or done something offensive, he and I discuss if it is worth bringing up or not. He always says, "If you can't overlook it, don't." Meaning, if it is so bothersome that you can't move on or be in fellowship without it being a sticking point, then we should wisely approach our parent to share how they hurt us. However, if we can forgive it and overlook it without communicating the offense to them, we should. According to Proverbs 19:11, "A person's insight gives him patience, and his virtue is to overlook an offense."
- **Pray for her.** When we have been injured by our mothers, we often pray to God *about* them, but we may not pray *for* them. There are very few acts that demonstrate love and respect that can top speaking on behalf of someone to God in prayer. It is hard to pray for someone you hate, and it is hard to hate someone you pray for. Praying for your mother means asking for God's blessings over her, for his power to be manifested in her life, for her life to reflect his

perfect will, for her health to be well, her heart to be clean, her mind to be healed, and her own heaviness to be lifted. Praying that way means asking God to intervene for her, not against her. The Bible gives us clear direction and the why beyond praying for those it is hard to pray for (see Matthew 5:43–46).

- **Forgive her.** Christians are called to forgive anyone who shows genuine repentance (see Matthew 18:21–22; Luke 17:3–4; Ephesians 4:32). You may wonder how you can truly know if your mother's repentance is genuine. The short answer is that you can't truly know what is in her heart, but repentance should have signs of changed behavior and changed attitude over time; even then, she could fail you again. At the core is having the heart of forgiveness, even in the absence of an apology. That's hard, but it is the example Christ set for us.

  Forgiveness can sometimes be discussed in such complex ways that we miss the simple truths God wants us to grab hold of. Forgiveness is a command, much like honor, that flows from a heart posture that says, *I am giving up my right to collect the debt my offender owes me—a debt I usually attempt to resolve through some form of punishment like bitterness, resentment, revenge, gossip, or ghosting.* Forgiveness says, *I cancel the debt, even if it may take a long time for there to be reconciliation of the relationship.* The struggle to forgive is real. Here are some common misconceptions and fears people have about forgiving:

  » *Forgiving will look like what they did was no big deal.*

  » *Forgiveness will make me look weak.*

  » *They don't even think they did anything wrong.*

  » *Forgiveness should be earned.*

» *Forgiveness means I must act like everything is okay between us.*

There are so many other misconceptions and fears. Which ones come up for you when you think about forgiving your mother? Here are ten steps you can begin to take to move toward forgiving your mother:

1. Spend some time alone with the Lord by reading scriptures on forgiveness and praying. Among the passages, consider how Jesus encouraged his disciples to pray a transactional prayer about forgiveness: "Father, forgive me as I forgive others" (see Matthew 6:12–15).
2. Cry out to God in lament and be honest about the struggle you are having to forgive and the pain of even having to forgive your mother for some of the things she's done.
3. Spend time in praise and worship of God. Thank him for Jesus and the forgiveness you have received from him. Think about the things Jesus had to endure to secure your right to be forgiven.
4. Thank God for your mother, even though she has harmed you. Agree with him that he didn't make a mistake and that his plan for your life is good and he has a good purpose for allowing your mother to be your mother.
5. Lean into the truth that forgiveness is humanly impossible, not a natural behavior, which is why it takes supernatural power. Agree with God that the power needed to forgive your mother comes only from Christ. Take a moment and listen to the song "Give Me a Clean Heart," by Fred Hammond,[24] and call out to God

24 "Give Me a Clean Heart," track 3 on Fred Hammond and Radical for Christ, *Purpose by Design,* Zomba Recording, 2000.

for a "strength exchange." Trade his power for your weakness.

6. Make a list of the offenses you need to forgive your mother for.
7. When you are ready, in prayer to God, surrender. Give up your right to punish your mother for her offenses. Over the list of offenses, write, "I choose to give up my right to punish my mother. I release her from this debt. I forgive my mother." Write out Ephesians 4:31–32.
8. Process with church leaders, friends, and other healthy, godly people who will help you walk through the forgiveness journey. Find helpful resources on forgiveness and offense to read.[25]
9. Normalize the process of forgiveness. One of the things that shocks people who "forgive" is the recurring angry or sad emotions that come up. It is important to know that we likely have to forgive our mothers multiple times, not just for new offenses but also for old ones that we already forgave. For instance, when the memories and emotions resurface, when we are tempted to punish her, simply say, *I choose again to forgive her.* Normalize that when you obey God and forgive, you are

---

25 Some resources on forgiveness are Yana Jenay Conner, *Living Beyond Offense: Doing the Hard Work of Forgiveness God's Way* (Harvest House, 2025); Leslie Leyland Fields and Jill Hubbard, *Forgiving Our Fathers and Mothers: Finding Freedom from Hurt and Hate* (Oasis Audio, 2013); Alexandra Hoover, *You Can Let Go: Make Peace with Your Past, Break Free from Offense, and Move Forward with God* (Christian Audio, 2026); Timothy Keller, *Forgive: Why Should I and How Can I?* (Penguin, 2023); R. T. Kendall, *Total Forgiveness: When Everything in You Wants to Hold a Grudge, Point a Finger, and Remember the Pain—God Wants You to Lay It All Aside* (Charisma House, 2007); and Charles Stanley, *The Gift of Forgiveness: Put the Past Behind You and Give* (Zondervan, 2002).

not lowering his standard for what a healthy, safe, and loving relationship is supposed to look like. Affirm his standard for reconciliation!

10. Affirm that forgiveness is one of the highest ways you can identify with Christ, and meditate on what it means to be conformed into his image. See your act of forgiveness as sanctifying and making you look more like Jesus. What a beautiful gift.

Care

Especially in the Western world, there are people who believe "Honor your father and mother" mostly relates to children obeying their parents. According to Jewish tradition, the focus of the fifth commandment is more about caring for aged parents who are past their productive years and no longer can work.[26] The uniqueness of this focus highlights that the fifth commandment is more specifically addressing older children. In Israel and throughout the East, to honor parents includes practical support and care. In the Old Testament, there are several examples of caring for parents (see Genesis 45:9–11; 47:12; Ruth; 1 Samuel 22:3–4).

In the New Testament, Jesus criticizes people who offer to God what they should have used to support their parents (see Matthew 15:1–9; Mark 7:9–13). Jesus also provides for the care of his mother before he dies (see John 19:25–27) and restores the widow's only son to life, ensuring she would have someone to support her (see Luke 7:12–15).[27] In the Pastoral Epistles, we see God's instructions to honor widows by providing for their needs (see Acts 6:1; 1 Timothy 5:3–8). In our current day, care of your mother can mean making

26 Rooker, *Ten Commandments,* 108.

27 Baker, *Decalogue,* 93.

sure her physical needs are met and that she has proper medical care, shelter, food, clothing, and safety.

It is important to consider our cultural presuppositions when making decisions about the care of our mothers:

> A North American adult can say, "My parents live in a retirement home," and people will think the family has done something good and noble. The parents are glad they saved diligently and can afford to be in a nice retirement community. . . . But if an Indian adult [or African adult] says, "My parents live in a retirement home," their Indian [or African] peers will be horrified and think the family has done something woefully shameful. . . . One culture's honor is another culture's shame.[28]

The goal is to ensure that our decisions around care of parents are guided more by biblical expectations than cultural norms, but we also should be careful to demonstrate honor so that it is "appropriate to our culture and meaningful to our parents while still remaining faithful to Scripture."[29] Those explanations may seem contradictory, but the point is that some cultures may place too many demands on children that go beyond what the Bible would affirm as the only means of care (for example, that you must move your parent into your home). Other parents may not want to burden their adult children with having to care for them with such things as home-cooked, nutritious meals or setting up a meal service and instead resign themselves to eating only frozen meals. Those adult children may have to work more diligently and creatively against their parents' opposition to make sure their parents are healthy and cared for.

The following are a few practical ways you can provide care for

---

28 Challies, *Commandment We Forgot*, 26.

29 Challies, *Commandment We Forgot*, 27.

your parents if it is necessary and your parents are no longer able to care for themselves:

- Make sure their basic needs are met (food, clothing, shelter).
- Help them with their financial affairs and end-of-life wishes and decisions.
- Ensure they have appropriate health care and can get to their appointments.
- Make sure they live in a safe environment and have adequate security.
- Support them with help, aids, and necessities for personal hygiene.
- Get them appropriate medical alarm devices for if they fall, medical equipment such as a walker or wheelchair, and over-the-counter medicines or humidifiers to increase comfort.
- Teach them how to navigate the complexities of technology. Many care-related needs require parents to work through online banking and fill out electronic forms.
- Welcome them into your home to live when they are unable to safely live on their own.
- If there are circumstances that involve financial assistance, use wisdom, discernment, and counsel of others to help you navigate. If you are married, both you and your spouse should be involved and in agreement about how financial help is given.

When children are younger and weaker, they require parents to care for them, and when parents are older and weaker, they require children to care for them. This seems like a logical and fair expectation unless you are a child who received no or very little care when you were young, weak, and dependent on your parents. The only salve for that aching soul is to know that God saw what your mother didn't do to care for you, and she was wrong. He has always provided and cared for you when she abdicated her responsibility to do so. The truth of a mother's failure to care does not excuse a child from the call to offer care.

Gratitude

Having and showing gratitude is one of the best ways we can honor our parents. Mothers who have struggled in their parenting can still be honored for what they managed to do to the best of their ability. Many of us know that our mothers have not had easy lives; some have had very traumatic childhoods themselves. Some have worked multiple jobs to feed, clothe, and educate us and provide a roof over our heads. Some may not have had the emotional capacity to nurture us the way we wanted and deserved but did their very best to give what they likely never received. So, all in all, there must be *something* your mother did that you can be grateful for. Here are some practical ways you can show gratitude to her:

- Thank her for what is true of her work, sacrifice, efforts, and care—not just in the past, but also presently.
- Listen to and follow any sound advice your mother gives and tell her you've done so.
- Write her a letter or send a card of thanks.
- Ask how you can help her.
- Show affection (hugs, kisses, holding hands).
- Remember what was good and enjoy pleasant memories of experiences your mother created for you (vacations, dance

or music class, fun outings). Celebrating what was real doesn't mean you are pretending about what wasn't. The more you are honest about what needs repairing, the less you will feel unable to touch the good.

- Esteem her privately and publicly. Pastor and author Tim Challies said that parents need to see themselves in you,[30] and not just physical genetic traits. It means a lot to parents to know they had some positive impact on your life. You can show gratitude by saying things like "I got my fashion sense from you," or "You gave me my love for books and writing." Wherever you can do it honestly, show gratitude by giving your mother credit and appreciation for the good things she deposited in you or exposed you to that made your life better. Rarely is anyone all bad, and I believe that most mothers, barring serious demonic oppression or thought disorder, hope they have done something good for their children, despite all the ways they may have failed.

Although your mother may not have done much for you to be grateful for, one thing we all can have gratitude for is that our mothers gave us life. Even if your life hasn't been easy, you are here, you have gifts and talents, and people love you. God loves you the most! He has kept you, brought you further than your mother could, and gave you a wonderful inheritance and purpose from the foundation of the world. You would not know the beauty of Christ if your mother had not birthed you into the world. The Bible shares narratives of the human experience of despairing life, but God's response to his people is always concern, care, comfort, and hope in Jesus (see 1 Kings 19:1–8; 2 Corinthians 1:8–10; 1 Timothy 4:10). The Bible also tells us that we were created and known

30 Challies, *Commandment We Forgot*, 31.

by God in our mothers' wombs (see Psalm 139:13–16). At the very least, we can be grateful for our mothers having brought us into the world so we could live out God's preordained plans for our lives.

I want to encourage you to make a list of what you can truthfully be grateful for about your mother. Just admitting those things may unlock a freedom, peace, and new perspective about your mother that has been imprisoned by pain and has prevented your giving her honor in the form of gratitude. As we grow, heal, and mature as Christians, we can increase our capacity to hold the truth constant that we can groan but also have gratitude. Say that out loud: "I can groan and also have gratitude. Amen."

THE TRUTH ABOUT WHY WE SHOULD HONOR OUR MOTHERS

Our mothers are created in the image of God. Like us, our mothers are image bearers of the triune God (see Genesis 1:26–27). That is not a small identity marker; rather, it signals an innate worth and dignity not earned but instead bestowed by God. The Hebrew word for *image* refers to a statue or copy of the original, meaning God made your mother to reflect something unique about himself. Humans are the only segment of creation given the distinction of imaging God, verifying just how much he loves the people he created and the wonderful purposes he intends for us. If you can't find anything good about your mother, at the very least she deserves honor for the wonderful part of her that only God sees, loves, and intends to express through her life.

God commands that we honor our mothers. We must honor our mothers because God said so. Nothing trumps God's command, and any argument or lofty opinion that would attempt to raise itself above his knowledge is a stronghold that must be taken captive in order to obey Christ (see 2 Corinthians 10:4–5). The apostle Paul is quoting this Old Testament command to honor our parents, signaling that God intends for this law to be upheld and practiced among Christians today. We have gathered enough biblical evidence in both the Old and

New Testaments to support that this is a command from God, and we also know that in honoring our mothers, we honor him, too. Honoring our mothers is an act of obedience to him that ensures blessings.

There are blessings and consequences for honoring our mothers. God placed the motivation for honoring parents within the fifth commandment when he stated that it should be done "so that you may have a long life in the land that the LORD your God is giving you" (Exodus 20:12). He is unequivocally stating that children who honor their parents are rewarded with good and long lives.[31] The promise is not only *quantity* of time but also *quality* of time.[32] The Ten Commandments were given by God to his people to set the order of how he wanted them to live. Since we know that not all good and God-fearing people have long lives, it's important to remember that these blessings and consequences should be viewed as a general implementation and overflow of obeying God's commands rather than an absolute guarantee:

> God was not saying, "Honor your parents and I guarantee you will live to see at least eighty birthdays" [nor] "If you have a short life, it is proof you have dishonored your parents." Rather, [. . . God is] saying those who honor their parents generally experience a better life than those who do not. . . . Because those who honor their parents are doing things God's way.[33]

A plain reading of this command does not ask you to honor your mother because she has earned it; the motivation, at the root, to honor your mother should be your love for God, your commitment to obey him, and the peace in knowing that he has reserved blessings for your

---

31 See Exodus 23:26; Deuteronomy 4:40; 5:33; 6:2; 11:9; 1 Kings 3:13–14; Psalm 41:1–3; 91:16; Proverbs 10:27; Ephesians 6:2–3.

32 Rooker, *Ten Commandments,* 110.

33 Challies, *Commandment We Forgot,* 13.

life because you are willing to do what he says. Where your mother may have made life challenging for you, God promises that if you honor her, he will bless you. A blessing from him for a long fruitful life because of your obedience is greater than the satisfaction you think you will have in denying your mother honor. God's blessings are more powerful and enduring than your mother's woundings.

God, above all, deserves honor, and there are significant consequences for dishonoring him. The Bible is clear that there are also grave consequences for dishonoring or withholding honor where he commands it, particularly involving one's parents (see Proverbs 20:20; 30:17). As God gave the law that would govern the nation of Israel, he included penalties for those who would boldly and unrepentantly violate the fifth commandment. What may be surprising is that God takes the honor of parents so seriously that the penalty for dishonoring them was the same for murder and other heinous crimes. Those consequences are found in more detail throughout the Bible's civil laws and in the Wisdom Literature:

> The motivation, at the root, to honor your mother should be your love for God [and] your commitment to obey him.

- "Whoever curses his father or mother—his lamp will go out in deep darkness" (Proverbs 20:20).
- "The eye that mocks a father and scorns to obey a mother will be picked out by the ravens of the valley and eaten by the vultures" (Proverbs 30:17, ESV).
- "Whoever strikes his father or his mother must be put to death. . . . Whoever curses his father or his mother must be put to death" (Exodus 21:15, 17).
- "The one who plunders his father and evicts his mother is a disgraceful and shameful son" (Proverbs 19:26).

- "If a man has a stubborn and rebellious son who does not obey his father or mother and doesn't listen to them even after they discipline him, his father and mother are to take hold of him and bring him to the elders of his city, to the gate of his hometown. They will say to the elders of his city, 'This son of ours is stubborn and rebellious; he doesn't obey us. He's a glutton and a drunkard.' Then all the men of his city will stone him to death. You must purge the evil from you, and all Israel will hear and be afraid" (Deuteronomy 21:18–21).

As you think about your interactions with your mother, how do you react to those scriptures? Had you ever considered how serious God takes the dishonoring of a parent? Take a moment to recall if you have dishonored your mother in any of those ways. What do you think is an appropriate next step to take? Pray, process, confess, repent, apologize, cry, or share what you've discovered with someone? If nothing else, talk to God about what you read and are feeling.

Though the language of the Wisdom Literature in the previous list of poetic scriptures is colorful and metaphoric and the language of the civil laws is sharp and dire, what is clear is that God demands that children honor their parents. Though we no longer are under the civil laws of his nation, his blessings continue to extend to us. If he still reserves blessings for those children who honor, he also hasn't changed his position about dishonor. "The general rule remains: If we live in God's ways, we receive God's favor, and if we defy God's ways, we forfeit God's favor."[34] If we honor our parents, we can expect the favor and blessings of God; if we dishonor them, we can expect that life will not go well for us.

As I mentioned earlier, this commandment is the only one with a

34 Challies, *Commandment We Forgot,* 16.

promise. When asked why, seminary professor Dr. Donald Sunukjian said, "One possible answer is that when we honor our parents, the natural outworking of that action has a physiological benefit. . . . If you obey God by finding ways to honor your mother, you will have a fruitful life that can be characterized by stability and peacefulness, resulting in longevity."[35] Another potential result is that you will have a blessed life that is full and flourishing regardless of the years God has appointed for you to live.

Something to consider, especially for those who have good reason to struggle with honoring a dishonorable mother, is that perhaps the good life is also the result of a life marked by deeper intimacy with God. In order to obey him when things are deeply challenging, it requires you to be a person who has surrendered to his will, soaked in his Word, been steadied in prayer, and been comforted by the Great Comforter. The enemy of our soul wants us to be deceived into believing we will lose more than we will gain if we honor our mothers, but God often uses the most painful parts of our lives as classrooms for growing our faith and intimacy.

Submit, Pray, and Entrust

Living the Christian life often feels as though God is constantly calling us to do impossible things. The truth is, as followers of Christ, we are called to that. When we vow to pick up our crosses and follow him, we set off on journeys of self-denial for the sake of the spread of the gospel, the magnification of Jesus, and the commitment to kingdom mission. All my children, natural and spiritual, and all those under my leadership and teaching have repeatedly heard me say, "The majority of the Christian life is doing the opposite of how we feel." We are called to be what Peter calls us in his first epistle, "a peculiar people"

---

35 Donald Sunukjian, quoted in Jan Frank, *Honoring Dishonorable Parents: Helping Heal and Restore Family Relationships* (Grace Chapel, 2014), 108.

(2:9, KJV), meaning we don't follow our hearts; we lead them (by the truth of Scripture). And we don't follow the proclivities and thinking of culture; we follow Christ. Christians are called to be different. We are not like the world, and the world is not like us (see John 17:14).

Most Christians know that and gladly accept it, but knowing and accepting don't relieve us of the challenge of the call. Being different is difficult. God calls us to do things that to the world (and many times to our own emotions) don't make any sense. Because we live in a fallen world, honoring will never be easy, but it is a picture of grace and mercy at work through us to others as we have had grace and mercy given to us by God. Grace means receiving something positive we don't deserve, and mercy means not receiving something negative we do deserve. Both grace and mercy are unfair, but they are a beautiful picture of God's love.

> The majority of the Christian life is doing the opposite of how we feel.

I pray you've gained understanding and clarity and even corrected some faulty assumptions about honor. I want you to see God more clearly and understand his heart to want a healthy, ordered, and right relationship with you as the springboard for you to have healthy, ordered, and right relationships with others.

You didn't choose your mother, but God did, and he wanted her (and your father) to be his representative of him in your home. If you're reading this book, probably you or someone you care about had a mother who didn't do that well. In fact, no one will ever fully be able to represent God perfectly, because he is free of human weakness and sin, and we are not. He loves us and will never call us to do something he won't give us the wisdom and power to do. He also sent his own Son, Christ, to model for us what it looks like to honor our parents, and for Jesus, honor required him to give his life so we could have eternal life.

Honoring your mother is an opportunity to display the beautiful outworking of the gospel. The gospel is a message about not just salvation but also transformation. God rescues us to change us so we can look more like Christ. When honoring your mother, you will get the gift of showing the world, those closest to you, or maybe just your mother the glory of grace and mercy at work. When you give her grace, you offer her something she doesn't deserve on her own and cannot earn (honor), and when you offer her mercy, you withhold punishment from her that she does deserve. That's exactly what Jesus did for us: treat us with mercy, thereby freeing us to do the same for others.

I want to end by encouraging you to, as you move forward—facing the tension of honoring your mother, understanding God's heart, and learning to embrace living out honoring your mother in practical ways—be like Jesus and honor your earthly parents as he did; submit your will to the Father; pray for strength, endurance, and help; and entrust yourself to the one who judges justly.

REFLECTION QUESTIONS

1. *This chapter was subtitled "The Tension and the Truth." As you reflect on the tension you had about the commandment to "honor your father and mother," what truth did you learn that was the most helpful?*

2. *Which of the "Honor is not" statements was important for you to learn? Why?*

3. *Reflect on what you can do to honor your mother through love and respect, care, and gratitude. Which of the three categories is most challenging for you right now?*

4. *How would you answer the question "Why should I honor my mother?"*

5. *How are you helped in honoring her by having the mindset "Do things God's way and leave the results to God"?*

6. *How did God speak to you most through this book? Consider journaling your thoughts and talking with trusted people about the experience of reading this book.*

7. *After reading this book, what are the next steps you plan on taking to help you grieve, heal, make peace with your mother wounds, and begin to honor your mother?*

8. *If your mother is no longer living or you never knew her, how has this book helped you or given you a way forward in life?*

PRAYER

Lord, I trust and believe in the goodness of your truth, wisdom, and guidance. Please help me honor the way you call us to honor our parents. I trust you with my hurt, my pain, but am choosing to fully believe in your promises, strength, and goodness.

What a journey this has been. Hopefully you stayed the course with an open heart and mind. I am praying that the Lord will honor your efforts and give you the faith and strength you need as you continue to grieve, heal, and make peace with your mother wound and your mother. Blessings to your becoming a cycle breaker and peacemaker for the glory and honor of Jesus Christ!

ACKNOWLEDGMENTS

I give honor first to my Lord and Savior Jesus Christ and the providential way he burdened my heart to write this book. I keep a list of book ideas in the notes section of my phone, and *Honor Thy Mother* was not on that list. It was an unexpected call from God at an unexpected time in my life, but I'm so glad I answered yes. Two years prior to that, a pastor I had never met prophesied over my life that I was "a carrier of *shalom* and a mender of breaches." He told me God would use me to mend brokenness on the earth. Though I didn't fully understand that word at the time and only related it to my counseling work, over the next couple of years, the truth of that calling began to unfold in both beautiful and painful ways. I suffered the loss of my mother. I was hit by a breach of trust and broken relationships from unexpected sources. I witnessed the restoration of broken hearts and crushed spirits. I welcomed the beauty God gave for ashes through the birth of my granddaughter, Amira. In so many ways, this book is my surrender and joyful acceptance of my duty to bring *shalom* to chaos and help others mend their personal and relational brokenness, even as I've worked and prayed to mend my own. Thank you, Jesus, for being the Prince of Peace, the ultimate carrier of *shalom* and the mender of all the breaches and brokenness in the world.

To my loving husband Mark, thank you for your unwavering love and support. Your faithful, steady, wise, and humble leadership sets the tone for our family and always makes room for me to be all that the Lord has called me to be in every area of life. No one gets me like you do, and I couldn't have written this book without your prayers, investment, and push. Thank you for loving me through this process by patiently listening to my ideas, reading chapters over and over, setting up writing retreats so I could get away to work and rest, and comforting my heart when writing this book brought up so much grief for me. I admire, respect, and love you. Mark, you are my favorite pastor, pilot, and person in the whole wide world. I love you.

To my children, Malachi, Sophia, Olivia, and Gabriella. I love you all so much. You are answered prayers and the pride and joy of my life! Thank you for celebrating each step of the journey, making me laugh, giving me suggestions, and telling me, "Mom, this book is going to help so many people." You are all such smart, creative, honorable children. I love catching you reading your Bible or ear-hustling on your sibling conversations about the Lord. I am so proud of each of you, and being your mother is one of my greatest honors. Writing this book as a mother was humbling and at times convicting. Though I strive to be a godly mother, I know I am not perfect, and I pray that I will live my life in a way that makes it easy for you to honor me.

Daddy, I am blessed to be your daughter. You make me want to be a better Christian. Your spiritual stamina and generosity are inspiring. Thank you for setting the example of Christ's love in our home. Thank you for loving me well and loving my mother well. These last two years have been difficult after losing Mommy, but we've gotten through it together with the help of the Lord. Sometimes, with tears in our eyes, we just hold hands and hold space for one another—no words are needed, we know. I will always be there for you, Daddy. And can you believe it? I wrote another book! I know you always say you dream of seeing me on "Whoopi's show," "talking to Oprah," or being "a guest on the Arsenio Hall Show," and maybe this—or at least two-thirds of it (smile)—will one day happen. You've told me, as only a dad would,

"This book needs to go all over the world—send it to Tyler Perry and Obama," and I know you say it with absolute sincerity. I love you for that!

To my Epiphany Fellowship family—pastors, pastors' wives, staff, leaders, and covenant community members—I'm grateful for your love and support. It's been a joy and sanctifying to serve the local church. I can't say enough about the women of Epiphany—you all hold a special place in my heart; I think of you often and even talked with many of you as I wrote this book. Thank you for sharing your stories about your own mothers and trusting me with your pain and testimonies of healing.

To my spiritual daughters near and far—I love you; thank you for loving me, too, and giving me the honor of being a spiritual mother (and, for some, a spiritual grandmother). May the Lord continue to use our relationship for his glory. I will always love each of you.

To my agent, Jevon Bolden of Embolden Media Group, thank you for everything. I remember our car ride in Florida when I first mentioned my idea for *Honor Thy Mother* and you immediately responded with an excited "Yes—ohhh, that's good." Your support, wisdom, and willingness to go above and beyond always emboldens me as an author (see what I did there?). It's a blessing to have you on my side. In my Tina Turner voice: "You're simply the best!"

To my WaterBrook team at Penguin Random House. Thank you for supporting the vision of *Honor Thy Mother*. Thank you for your prayers and all your hard work to create this book and expand its reach. I always enjoy our team meetings and appreciate each one of you: Campbell, Johanna, Ginia, Shauna, Beverly, Jessica, Cara, Sadie, Karissa, Richard, Julia, Kim. And a special thanks to my wonderful editor, Jamie Lapeyrolerie; I'm grateful for your commitment to making this book the best it could be. I've grown as a writer because of you.

To my many friends, family members, and sisters in Christ who have supported me through prayers, sharing stories, reading chapters, and offering feedback, I greatly appreciate each of you. Other than with my husband, I talked about this book the most with Dannet Mitchell, Nicole Bowens, and Sarah Lowney. Thank you for sitting with me, listening to me, and reading what God was stirring in my heart, and for offering so much love and support, even, at times, through tears.

Special thanks to Sarah Lowney for being a faithful executive assistant, co-laborer in ministry, and spiritual daughter. You and Asher are a part of the Lyons family. I could not do the work God has called me to do without you. Thank you for holding up my arms, praying over me, caring for me when I've been sick on the road—giving so much to ensure I can do what God has called me to do with excellence. May we always serve God faithfully, love his church, laugh wildly, and have tons of fun while finding rest and strength for the journey!

To my mother-in-love, Mary Louise Lyons. Thank you, Mom, for raising an amazing son. Mark would not be the man he is without your guidance, love, spiritual nurturance, and prayers throughout the years. You and Dad did a great job, and I'm the beneficiary of your faithfulness. Thank you for accepting me and loving me as your daughter. I will always love our family and strive to be a virtuous wife to your son. I honor you.

In loving memory of my mother. It's unbelievable to me that she is not here, especially for this book. I didn't think I could write *Honor Thy Mother* as my heart was aching so much for her. But God! Strangely, the grief I carried these last two years has become fuel for my empathy, my desire to be exponentially sensitive to God's voice, my commitment to help others heal from their mother wounds. I carried a different type of pain, but God used it all. My mother was and is deserving of honor—as all mothers are. So much of who I am has been shaped by her care, wisdom, presence, and walk with God. I was well loved, and I'm so thankful for my mother. Until I can no longer stand and I take my last breath, I will always rise and call Etta Mae King Taylor, blessed.

ABOUT THE AUTHOR

DR. SARITA T. LYONS is a bestselling author, women's leader, Bible teacher, ministry consultant, and psychotherapist. She is on staff with Epiphany Fellowship Church in Philadelphia, Pennsylvania, as the Director of Discipleship and Women's Ministry. For nearly thirty years, Dr. Lyons has worked and advocated at the intersection of mental health, justice, and faith. She is a highly sought-after speaker for conferences, churches, retreats, corporate organizations, and educational institutions around the country. She is married to Pastor Mark Lyons, and together, they have four children and one grandchild.

ABOUT THE TYPE

This book was set in Caslon, a typeface first designed in 1722 by William Caslon (1692–1766). Its widespread use by most English printers in the early eighteenth century soon supplanted the Dutch typefaces that had formerly prevailed. The roman is considered a "workhorse" typeface due to its pleasant, open appearance, while the italic is exceedingly decorative.